IRRESOLUTE PRINCES

Kremlin Decision Making
in Middle East Crises, 1967–1973

Fred Wehling

MACMILLAN

First published by
MACMILLAN PRESS LTD
Houndmills, Basingstoke, Hampshire RG21 6XS
and London
Companies and representatives
throughout the world

ISBN 0-333-73115-8

A catalogue record for this book is available
from the British Library

10 9 8 7 6 5 4 3 2 1
06 05 04 03 02 01 99 98 97

Internal design and typesetting by Letra Libre

Printed in the United States of America by
Haddon Craftsmen
Bloomsburg, PA

To the memory of my father
Robert Wehling

A prince is further esteemed when he is a true friend or a true enemy, when, that is, he declares himself without reserve in favor of someone or against another. . . . Irresolute princes, to avoid present dangers, usually follow the way of neutrality and are mostly ruined by it.

—Niccolò Machiavelli
The Prince

Contents

List of Tables

Acknowledgments

I would first like to thank all the makers and analysts of Soviet and Russian policy toward the Middle East and other regions whom I consulted while researching and writing this book. I am grateful to Yuriy Abramov, Yuriy Anchabadze, Vadim I. Batyuk, Grigory L. Bondarevsky, Vladimir Chagall, Vagan A. Gevorgian, Vladimir A. Isaev, Said K. Kamilev, Nikolai P. Medvedev, Andranik Migranyan, Vitaliy V. Naumkin, Aziz Niyazi, Aleksandr Pikaev, Andrei Shumikhin, and Vladimir Zantaria for their invaluable advice and insights.

I would also like to express my gratitude for the financial assistance of the RAND, no. UCLA Center for Soviet Studies, the Carnegie Corporation of New York, the University of California Institute on Global Conflict and Cooperation (IGCC), and the International Research and Exchanges Board (IREX), all of whom contributed generously to support the research for this book.

Next, portions of Chapter Three are based on material originally presented in my article "The Dilemma of Superpower: Soviet Decision Making in the Six-Day War, 1967" from *Conflict Management in the Middle East,* edited by Steven Spiegel, copyright 1992 by Westview Press, reprinted by permission of Westview Press. Likewise, a section of Chapter Seven is based on material in "Pitfalls on the Silk Road: Moscow's Dilemmas in Central Asia and the Caucasus," *Orient* 6 (November–December 1996).

Finally, my heartfelt thanks go out to Sharyl Cross, James Goldgeier, John Hatch, Arnold Horelick, David Lake, Deborah Welch Larson, Jennifer Pournelle, Lawrence Robertson, Steven L. Spiegel, Jeannette VanWinkle, Karen Wolny, and several anonymous reviewers for their comments on various drafts and pieces of this book. The road to this point has been long and hard, and I'm grateful to everyone who encouraged me to make the trip and helped me along the way.

Fred Wehling
Albuquerque, July 1997

Introduction

*There comes a time in the life cycle of a nation when no decision that can be made
is the right one, and no action that can be taken is intelligent.*

—Joseph Heller
Picture This

As the Soviet Union's influence in world affairs increased in the
1960s and 1970s, and especially as its role in the developing world
expanded, Soviet leaders were frequently forced to balance their expanding commitments to regional allies against the need to avoid a dangerous confrontation with the United States. They thereby found
themselves caught in a classic foreign policy dilemma, created by an inherent contradiction between regional and global interests. This dilemma became especially acute when Soviet and American allies in the region
approached and went over the brink of war, which they did three times between 1967 and 1973, forcing the Politburo to choose between preserving
U.S.-Soviet détente and supporting their "Arab brethren." While any group
of decision makers might be expected to balk at or even agonize over such
a difficult choice, the pre-glasnost consensus of analyses of Soviet behavior
during these three crises has been that Soviet leaders did not find the decision particularly difficult, that they followed the same predetermined script
each time, sacrificing their regional objectives in favor of their global goals,
and that the threats they issued during each crisis were empty face-saving
gestures.

This book argues that this consensus is wrong. Considering the dilemma
from Moscow's perspective, using new evidence, and applying a new analytical approach, we find that Soviet decision makers basically acted as we might
expect any group of politicians to act. They delayed making a decision as long
as possible, tried to shift responsibility for their situation onto somebody else,
and finally acted forcefully to pursue *both* of the contradictory objectives. In
so doing, they failed to achieve either, as this pattern of procrastination

followed by coercion ultimately destroyed the USSR's credibility with its regional allies and undermined détente with the United States.

This behavior may seem surprising, puzzling, or self-defeating, but it is entirely predictable and not very different from what we might expect of any group of decision makers in similar circumstances. In analyzing how and why the Politburo acted during these Middle East conflicts, we can learn much about how other decision makers act in similar crisis situations. For this reason, this book is not just about a small group of now-deceased communists, but about how leaders dealt with a recurring foreign policy dilemma that existed long before the Cold War and will continue long after its end.

This dilemma, the need to manage contradictory goals, is referred to in the language of decision science as *value conflict.* A number of studies in cognitive psychology, management science, and international relations find that decision makers sometimes find means of resolving conflict between values, but often attempt to cope with value conflict by denying its existence or blaming others for contradictions between their own objectives. Drawing upon this research, this book will present a framework for analysis of the effect of value conflict on decision making and employ this framework to examine Soviet behavior during crises and wars in the Middle East in the Brezhnev era.

The first two chapters concentrate on theoretical issues. Chapter One outlines the models most commonly used to explain Soviet decision making in crises and presents the case for complementing these perspectives with an approach centered on value conflict. Drawing upon previous studies of the effects of cognitive dissonance and contradictory goals on decision making in a variety of contexts, Chapter Two will derive hypotheses on the relationship between situational factors and the means that decision makers are likely to choose to deal with conflicts between their objectives. Two crucial factors that weigh upon leaders in crisis situations, time pressure and autonomous risk, will serve as independent variables, and efforts will be made to assess their value from the Soviet perspective. Because the specific goal of this study is to explain Soviet actions in regional crises, the likelihood that Soviet decision makers will opt for a strategy of coercion rather than accommodation will be used as the dependent variable, and a framework for testing hypotheses on the influence of situational variables on risk-taking in conflicts where decision makers face contradictions between objectives will be outlined. To illustrate the advantages of this analytical perspective, conventional conceptions of Soviet crisis decision making that model regional crises as games of "chicken" (in which the USSR followed a predetermined strategy of acting tough early on, but "swerving" at the point of highest tension) will be offered as alternative explanations.

Chapters Three, Four, and Five will then test the analytical framework developed in Chapter Two in three cases of regional crisis. Each chapter considers an instance of eruption of the Arab-Israeli conflict into violent confrontation, and each will examine Soviet communications and actions in the period of escalation toward war as well as Soviet behavior during the wars. Utilizing new evidence that has become available since the collapse of the USSR, each of these empirical chapters will summarize Soviet regional and global objectives at the time of the crisis and point out the contradictions between Soviet goals in preparation for study of how these contradictions affected the choice of coercive or accommodative strategies. The third chapter details the Six-Day War of 1967, when Soviet leaders' failure to resolve conflicts between regional and global objectives contributed to their allies' shattering defeat. Chapter Four outlines the events of the protracted War of Attrition, 1969–1970, when a comparatively low level of time pressure allowed the Politburo to attempt to control the risks of Soviet military intervention. Chapter Five examines Soviet decision making before and during the October War of 1973, when Soviet leaders had foreknowledge of their allies' intentions but could not foresee the precarious situation created by the reversal of their initial success.

In each case, it will be shown how Soviet decision makers tended to accept the conflicts between their goals and rely on accommodation when time pressure and autonomous risk were low, but tended to take risks in support of a coercive strategy in an attempt to ignore the inherent contradictions in their objectives when time pressure and autonomous risk were high. This pattern of changes in the balance between coercion and accommodation in Soviet strategy is exactly opposite to that predicted by conventional empirical models of Soviet decision making. Overall, the case studies will show that Soviet behavior in regional crises cannot easily be explained by traditional empirical or game-theoretic models without the additional insight provided by analysis of the effects of value conflict.

The book's sixth chapter summarizes the findings of the three case studies and assesses the usefulness of the value conflict approach in comparison to traditional formulations. The majority of the evidence from these conflicts indicates that the USSR's leadership did not have a predetermined strategy either to support or sell out their allies. Rather, they exerted great efforts to avoid choosing between their regional and global objectives, efforts that often led to major setbacks for their own policies and disasters for their allies. The chapter thus shows how a new perspective on the dilemma faced by Soviet leaders in the Middle East challenges the claim that the USSR followed a deliberate strategy of "no war, no peace" in the Arab-Israeli conflict. Finally, Chapter Seven discusses the implications of the study's findings, showing how value conflict analysis can contribute to our understanding of deterrence and crisis management, particularly in the fracture zones of Central Asia and the Caucasus, which are likely to become a new arc of crisis in the early years of the twenty-first century.

Before embarking on an examination of Soviet actions in the deadly quarrels from which this study derives its evidence, the author would like to clarify the reasons why this book employs an approach grounded in cognitive psychology. The objective of developing an analytical perspective that focuses on value conflict is not to treat decision makers as information-processing units whose actions may be predicted by psychological theory. Nor is it intended to argue that complex psychological processes underlie every decision, as the value conflict perspective essentially points out that people who cannot pursue one goal without sacrificing another will naturally tend to avoid making a decision between the two for as long as they are able. Instead, this book is intended to advance our understanding of the role of the human element in decisions where all-too-human leaders are forced to act under the dehumanizing pressures of confrontation and crisis. While domestic politics frequently resembles a soap opera, foreign policy often takes on the outline of a heroic tragedy. Therefore, this book seeks to explain why leaders often play Hamlet on the global stage, unable to make up their minds in a crisis, desperately trying to delay a difficult decision, and finally opting for a violent solution.

ONE

Understanding Crisis Decision Making

The easiest period in a crisis situation is actually the battle itself. The most diffi-cult is the period of indecision—whether to fight or run away. And the most dan-gerous period is the aftermath. It is then, with all his resources spent and his guard down, that an individual must watch out for dulled reactions and faulty judgment.

—Richard Nixon
Six Crises

How did conflicts between the USSR's regional and global interests affect Politburo decisions in Middle East crises? The objectives of this chapter is to define the terms of this question and to suggest a means for answering it. With this in mind, this chapter begins with a defi-nition of its subject, Soviet crisis decision making. Following this definition, it proceeds to outline three traditional approaches to studying this phenom-enon, which respectively characterize it as rational calculation, as a compe-tition in risk-taking conducted according to an operational code, and as a struggle between political factions. Finally, it shows how complementing these analytical perspectives by considering Soviet crisis decision making as an attempt to cope with conflict between values or goals can provide addi-tional insight into crucial Soviet actions during Middle East conflicts.

Definitions

The expression "Soviet crisis decision making" has three components, and the central one in every sense is "crisis." This book will use the definition of a crisis developed by the International Crisis Behavior (ICB) project, which includes three necessary and sufficient conditions deriving from a change in a nation's internal or external environment: *threat to basic values, sharp increase in the probability of military conflict,* and *finite response time.*[1] These conditions are perceptions held by decision makers at the highest level of national leadership. The ICB definition of a crisis allows for the consideration of intrawar crises, in which case the second condition is replaced by a high probability of a deterioration in the military situation.

As the crises that will be examined here originated as regional conflicts rather than direct superpower confrontations, it must be considered whether the possibility of allied forces rather than a nation's own forces becoming involved in military conflict is sufficient to meet the first condition of the definition. There are two reasons why the potential for combat involving allied forces meets this criterion in the Middle Eastern conflicts considered in this study. First, fighting between Israeli and Arab forces had great potential to directly impact the interests at risk for both nations. While the region was and remains much more important politically and economically to the West than to Moscow, the Soviet interests at risk in the conflicts were important enough to constitute a threat to decision makers' basic values. Second, each of the three crises studied here involved the implicit or explicit threat of Soviet military intervention, and the USSR did intervene in 1970 with forces that engaged in combat. It is therefore reasonable to conclude that the military conflict that loomed and eventually broke out in all three cases was sufficient to meet the conditions set forth in the ICB definition of a crisis.

Decision making will be defined as the process of choice of a course of action, including the search for and processing of information, formulation and evaluation of options, and the selection and implementation of one or more of those options. This study is most concerned with a specific type of decision making, namely that which was conducted by the Soviet Politburo during situations that fit the definition of a crisis given above. There is widespread agreement that both "crisis decision making" and "Soviet decision making" can be expected to have unique features.[2] There is equally widespread disagreement, however, over which analytical perspective is most useful for examining Soviet crisis decisions.

Contending Models of Soviet Crisis Decisions

Research into Soviet crisis decision making tends to use one of three conceptions or models of decision making as a starting point. This section will not attempt to provide a comprehensive list of studies of Soviet crisis decisions, but will outline the rational actor, operational code, and Kremlin politics conceptions of Soviet decision making and give examples of the application of each of these perspectives to the analysis of decisions in crises.

The *rational-actor* model of decision making is the conception most often used to analyze not only Soviet crisis decision making but decision making in general. The defining characteristic of this conception, which is sufficiently pervasive to command the status of a paradigm, is the central assumption that decision makers attempt to maximize some value or values and, given the constraints on the decision making process, will choose courses of action that promise the maximum expected utility toward those values. As John Steinbruner points out, this assumption is tautological in the absence of independent means of establishing expected utility values.[3] In other words, the rational actor perspective assumes that the course of action chosen by decision makers is the one that offered the highest expected utility according to their calculations.

In his seminal work on crisis decision making, Graham Allison concludes that because this method of analysis proceeds from the effect (the decision) to the assumed cause (rational calculation), the rational-actor conception is not a model of decision making but rather an inference pattern for decision analysis.[4] A central assumption of rationality underlies major theoretical treatises on decision making in international conflicts and crises, including the works of Thomas Schelling, Glenn Snyder and Paul Diesing, and Robert Powell, all of whom employ game theory to analyze international conflicts.[5]

In a thoroughgoing analysis of great-power behavior in crises, Snyder and Diesing conclude that the winner of a confrontation is likely to be determined not by successful manipulation of risks, but by the relative *bargaining power* of the contenders. They define bargaining power as political power expressed bilaterally (each opponent having some degree of power over the other) and measured by the relative capacity to achieve gains and avoid losses. They divide the sources of bargaining power in international crises into three categories: relative *military strength*, the *interests* engaged in the conflict and perceptions of the legitimacy of those interests, and perceptions of *resolve*.[6] The main objectives of bargaining tactics, according to Snyder and Diesing, are first to ascertain the relative levels of bargaining power and then to increase one's own bargaining power and reduce that of the adversary.

Game theory is not the only means through which the assumption of rationality can serve as a basis for analysis of crisis decisions. Eric Herring, for example, employs a comparative case study method to explain how perceptions of both risk and opportunity affect decision making.[7] A wide range of studies of Soviet actions in crises similarly use the rational actor perspective as an implicit or explicit starting point.[8] Recently, rational-choice models have begun to incorporate findings derived from prospect theory, which contends that decision makers often value loss avoidance higher than the possibility of gain.[9]

Despite, or perhaps because of, the rational-actor model's long tenure of dominance over the analysis of international politics, and over deterrence in particular, the plausibility of the assumption of rationality in crisis situations, when decision makers are often subject to overpowering levels of psychological stress, has been challenged with increasing frequency.[10] Some specific contentions advanced in these critiques of the rational model will be examined in upcoming sections that develop this study's analytical framework. Although its proponents have given some ground, the rule of rationality has so far withstood these challenges well, and the continued viability of the rational-actor approach for the analysis of decisions sets it up as the standard against which all other analytical perspectives should be judged.

One such alternative approach is based on the concept of the *operational code*. Alexander George describes an operational code as a set of general beliefs, including rules of conduct and norms of behavior, that are shared and internalized by a group of decision makers. These beliefs are not considered to be rigid, mechanistic rules for cognition, decision, or action, but are presented as unexpressed but nonetheless highly influential guidelines for the decision-making process.[11] The concept of the operational code as a tool for political analysis owes its existence to Nathan Leites, who conducted extensive studies of Bolshevik and Soviet writings to identify the belief systems of Soviet leaders.[12]

Hannes Adomeit's analysis of Soviet behavior in the Berlin Crises of 1948 and 1961 exemplifies the operational-code approach. He adopts Schelling's position that crisis bargaining is essentially a competition in risk-taking and contends that Politburo decisions to accept or avoid risks were guided by a set of empirically derived operational principles, which he constructs on the foundations laid by Leites and George.[13] While he does not construct an operational code as such, Richard K. Herrmann uses a similar set of empirical generalizations systematically to account for the effects of the belief systems of Soviet leaders on foreign policy decisions.[14] James Goldgeier looks at how the political belief systems of Soviet leaders, formed during crucial domestic struggles, influenced Soviet decisions during the 1973 October War and other crises.[15] Other recent studies focus on the change in Soviet leaders' belief systems represented, and accelerated, by the rise of Mikhail Gorbachev to primacy in the Kremlin.[16]

Critics argue that works utilizing the operational code fail to draw clear linkages between theory and case studies.[17] These criticisms point out the conflict between deductive and inductive reasoning that once pervaded the field of Soviet studies, setting proponents of empirical models against partisans of formal theory. More generally, empirical models of crisis decision making may also suffer from a dearth of relevant cases from which observations may be drawn. All analyses of crisis decisions, however, are constrained by the limited number of cases, regardless of the analytical perspectives they adopt. As analysts have little choice but to look where the data is, international relations theorists will probably reanalyze the outbreak of World War I until the outbreak of World War III.

The third major analytical perspective on Soviet crisis decision making differs from the first two in that it does not consider the leadership of the USSR to be a unitary actor. The *Kremlin politics* approach considers Soviet decision making during the period covered by this study as a process of conflict between factions of the Communist Party of the Soviet Union (CPSU). These factions are often considered to have been organized along institutional lines, introducing into the analysis an element of competition between organizational interests as well as the political ambitions of Politburo members.[18] The Soviet military establishment receives special attention in most analyses of decisions which focus on internal politics, as not only was the military a powerful interest group during the Brezhnev era, but military leaders enjoyed a monopoly on strategic information.

It is far from clear, however, that institutional disputes over foreign policy in the USSR were always strongly connected to the struggle for power and position within the CPSU hierarchy. While few analysts would maintain that there was no struggle for power in the Kremlin, many contend that this struggle has no significant effect on consequential foreign-policy decisions because the Soviet elite tends to unify against external threats to Soviet security and other vital interests.[19] The collapse of Communist power has allowed analysts access to a limited amount of data that can shed light on the linkages between CPSU factional conflict and crisis decisions, some of which will be referred to in the empirical chapters of this book.[20] But considering that written records of Politburo meetings are not known to exist, the release of documents relating to crisis decisions has been highly selective, and much material remains highly classified. The primacy of Soviet security interests over Communist Party politics will remain an arguable (and much argued) conclusion.[21]

Studies of the effect of Soviet domestic politics on foreign policy decisions do not always adopt the traditional Kremlinology approach. For example, Philip Stewart, Margaret and Charles Hermann, and Richard Anderson propose models of Soviet decision making based on the types of roles that leaders involved in factional conflicts may play in the decision process and apply this framework to an analysis of Soviet policy toward Egypt in the period leading up to the October War of 1973.[22]

Each of the three approaches outlined in this section have survived with remarkably little modification and have been widely used by Western analysts for over thirty years. Scholars have debated their merits for decades. Why then has a dominant paradigm for analyzing Soviet crisis decision making not emerged? One reason is that the process for making national-security decisions in the Communist-controlled USSR was so closed to outside observation that no school of thought could produce enough evidence that would unequivocally support it over its rivals. But disagreements continue to rage over the most appropriate perspective for analysis of crisis decisions made by the leadership of any and all nations, including the United States, where the decision-making process is arguably the most transparent. Therefore, even if a wealth of new data on Soviet decision making is eventually released, it seems unlikely that one perspective will become dominant. The overarching dilemma for the study of crisis decision making, best expressed by John F. Kennedy, still remains: "The essence of ultimate decision remains impenetrable to the observer—often, indeed, to the decider himself."[23]

The result of this unresolved rivalry between analytical perspectives is that anyone intending to study crisis decisions is immediately confronted with the difficult task of determining which approach to adopt. One solution to the problem of contending perspectives may be found by returning to the question the analyst is most interested in answering. If the objective is to explain the *outcome* of a decision process, the student of decision making has a hard row to hoe, as any consequential decision will be influenced by so many factors that an analysis from any frame of reference cannot help but be incomplete. This may partly explain why studies that are most concerned with the dependent variable (and thus ask, "Why did the Soviets decide to do X?") tend to adopt a rational-actor approach and attempt to infer the causes for a given effect. On the other hand, efforts that focus on examining the effects of an independent factor (asking, "What was the effect, if any, of X on the Soviet decision to do Y?") are better served by starting from a frame of reference designed to test a hypothesized relationship between an influence on the decision process and its result. The Kremlin politics perspective, for example, would clearly be the best approach for studying the impact of factional disputes on Soviet foreign policy decisions. However, such an approach would be limited in its ability to assess the impact of internal politics relative to other factors.

Many of these "other factors" come into play during crises, when both the assumption of rationality and the relevance of domestic politics become questionable. This book is primarily concerned with the effects of one specific factor, the conflict between Soviet regional and global interests, on Soviet crisis decision making. A number of studies explore the effects of analogous conflicts on decisions made by political leaders. The next section presents a brief survey of both studies of how value conflict influences the process of decision and of criticism of these attempts to apply a value-conflict perspective to political analysis.

Value Conflict and Crisis Decisions

Value conflict may be defined as opposition between two or more interests or desired goals that necessitates a trade-off between them. Such conflicts are quite common in foreign policy. For example, before the 1978 Camp David accords, America's central dilemma in the Arab-Israeli conflict was the need to protect Israel while simultaneously ensuring a continued ample supply of Arab oil. American decision makers, accepting the necessity for a trade-off between these goals, chose to support Israel during the Yom Kippur War in 1973, and the American economy suffered serious consequences in the form of an oil embargo.[24] Conflicts between regional and global interests have historically led nations with global ambitions into many similar dilemmas, which were often resolved by taking assertive or aggressive measures in the hope of avoiding losses. British imperial expansion in Asia and Africa in the nineteenth century, some of which was driven by the need to defend India, offers a classic example.[25]

In the 1960s and 1970s, Soviet and American interests conflicted in the Middle East, as they did in many regions. In all these regions, each superpower acted to defend its interests against threats and challenges from the other. The intense antagonism and strategic volatility of Middle East conflicts, and the vulnerability of both powers' regional allies, made the defense of regional interests frequently necessary and always dangerous Both powers also attempted to exploit regional conflicts and resolve them on favorable terms to gain advantages in their global political competition. At the same time, both sought to avoid the escalation of a regional conflict into a nuclear confrontation, and both realized the benefits of lower tensions during the era of détente.[26]

For both Moscow and Washington, therefore, regional interests often conflicted with global interests, and choices between the two had to be made or avoided. As we might expect from politicians with conflicting goals, avoidance of such a choice was usually the preferred option. In day-to-day policymaking, the Politburo avoided this choice through procrastination, while in crises, it sought to avoid it by coercion. Value-conflict analysis shows that although specific features of Soviet decision making shaped the way in which Moscow tried to balance its regional and global interests, neither the problems the Politburo faced nor the solutions it attempted were uniquely Soviet.

Psychological theories of cognitive consistency and dissonance hypothesize that when people are confronted with a value conflict, they frequently turn to a variety of coping mechanisms to ameliorate or deny the opposing nature of the two values and the necessity of choosing between them.[27] The results of such denials can be disastrous options that offer the illusory prospect of having one's cake and eating it too are often dangerous temptations when quick decisions are required.

Robert Jervis outlines several ways in which avoidance of value conflict can result in spectacularly bad foreign-policy decisions.[28] One of these is "belief system overkill," whereby a person comes to believe that if a policy contributes to one value, it is likely to contribute to others as well. This can allow interests to be seen as coinciding with morality when in fact the two are opposed. Another method is adopting the belief that a favored strategy is dominant (i.e., is the best option no matter what the opponent does). Advocates of either firmness or concession may see their policies as offering the only alternative to war or surrender, while employing spurious logic to keep this view consistent.[29]

Irving Janis and Leon Mann, in their general model of decision making under pressure, use the term *defensive avoidance* to describe the denial of the need to choose between values.[30] They theorize that in a situation of challenge or opportunity where values are in conflict, decision makers will tend to react with defensive avoidance if three conditions apply: there are serious risks if policy does not change; there are serious risks if policy *does* change; there is no hope that an option that will resolve the value conflict will become available. If these primary conditions exist, the most probable form of defensive avoidance, out of three possibilities, will be determined by two subsidiary conditions. If risks are not serious if the decision is postponed (in other words, if time pressure is not great), the decision maker is most likely to adopt a strategy of procrastination. If there is significant time pressure, however, the decision maker will ask if responsibility for the decision can be turned over to someone else. If it can be, either the decision itself or the responsibility for the consequences of the choice adopted will be shifted. If shifting responsibility does not appear possible, Janis and Mann argue that decision makers will accept the least objectionable option and tend to *bolster* it by magnifying its benefits and ignoring its risks.[31] Evidence from empirical studies supports their conclusion as well as similar hypotheses derived from cognitive-dissonance theory on this type of postdecisional reinforcement.[32]

Of course, decision makers do not always resort to psychological coping mechanisms. Even under crisis conditions, decision makers sometimes demonstrate the ability to make trade-offs between values or to devise courses of action that actually enable simultaneous pursuit of conflicting goals. Recognizing this, Alexander George identifies the primary ways in which crises affect decisions and decision makers and outlines the means available to leaders for coping with value conflict.[33] He finds that leaders may deal with value conflict analytically (i.e., by rational calculation), or they may resort to defensive psychological means, or they may combine both approaches. Decision makers may deal with value conflict analytically in two ways. First, they may *resolve* a conflict by finding a creative solution that does not compromise any of the conflicting values. The classic example of such a creative resolution is the Berlin Airlift, which allowed the United States and its allies to supply the population and maintain their political position in that beleaguered city without greatly increasing the risks of military conflict with Soviet forces. Alternatively, decision makers may *accept* the existence of a value conflict and choose one of the opposing values over the other. George terms this *value integration.*[34] He notes, however, that what appears to be a brilliant resolution of a value conflict may actually be a comforting illusion and that value trade-offs may also be made ineptly.

Richard Ned Lebow draws upon the work of Jervis, George, and Janis and Mann in an exploration of the effects of psychological factors on decision making in a number of international crises, but his conclusions on the ability of decision makers to overcome cognitive biases are pessimistic. He notes that the prescriptions for improving decisions based on cognitive theories are often paradoxical, as they recommend that the pervasive psychological factors they identify be guarded against to make decision making more closely resemble the rational-actor model, and he questions whether this is possible. Lebow further concludes that unless leaders can meet three preconditions for effective decision making (legitimate central authority, consensus on fundamental values, and freedom from domestic pressures and constraints), the decision procedures prescribed by crisis-management theories are probably not feasible.[35]

Not all studies of the effects of value conflict or cognitive bias offer such a gloomy forecast. One study by Jack Snyder argues that when some of the options available for resolving a crisis involve trade-offs between values, decision makers are likely to deny the necessity of a choice between objectives. As a result, leaders may tend to adopt strategies designed to force an adversary to concede both values and to play down or ignore the risks of these strategies of compellence.[36] He recognizes, however, that decision makers sometimes accept the necessity of choosing between opposing goals and are then able to successfully integrate conflicting values.

For this reason, Snyder concludes in a later study that in order for research that focuses on the psychological effects of value conflicts to be useful for explaining crisis decisions, the analytical frameworks employed must be able to determine when these effects are most likely to influence decisions and, conversely, when rational calculation is likely to carry the day.[37] Apropos of this, other scholars have noted that the effects of stress on individuals and groups is not linear. It is generally recognized that the ability of decision makers to process information and evaluate options often increases with stress until some threshold level is reached, after that it begins to decline. This curvilinear relationship between stress and quality of the decision process is referred to as the "inverted 'U' phenomenon."[38] In other words, under normal circumstances, a moderate amount of stress can serve to concentrate decision makers' minds and facilitate making a rational trade-off between conflicting objectives.

Circumstances in crises, however, are by definition not normal. Studies of the cognitive effects of value conflict on decision making suggest two factors that can hamper decision makers' ability to arrive at a compromise between conflicting goals. The first of these factors is *time pressure*. Janis and Mann find that time pressure reduces the probability of value integration. They conclude that if decision makers feel that they do not have enough time for a thorough search for alternative courses of action, they will tend to attempt to cope with value conflict by adopting the first option that appears to offer the possibility to minimally satisfy both goals at the same time. Janis and Mann term this reaction to time pressure *hypervigilance*.[39]

Janis and Mann's and George's theoretical discussions of decision making in crises thus suggest that time pressure could be expected to impel decision makers towards a self-defeating attempt to avoid setbacks on two conflicting goals by trying to pursue both at the same time. Evidence from experimental studies generally supports their conclusions.[40]

Autonomous risk is another factor that could lead decision makers to a suboptimal resolution of value conflict or to deny that a conflict exists. Glenn Snyder and Paul Diesing define autonomous risk as the danger that the parties doing the bargaining will lose control of events.[41] They identify three possible sources of loss of control in a crisis. The first is the "logic of war," the notion that once violent conflict breaks out, it will escalate to the fullest extent possible due to some internal dynamic. A second possible source of autonomous risk is the effect of violent conflict on popular passions or leaders' own emotions, which could lead to feelings based on irrational or emotional impulses that decision makers have no choice but to respond to in kind. In other words, violence may cause decision makers to lose control of events basically because they lose control of themselves.

The third source of autonomous risk, loss of control over subordinates or local actors, is the most significant in regional crises because superpower decision makers usually have little or no control over allied military forces. In the Middle East crises of the 1960s and 1970s, neither Soviet nor American decision makers had any significant degree of direct control over their allies' military units, and their influence over allied governments could not often be relied upon. While the Politburo often found it impossible to restrain its allies, it frequently attempted to convince the United States to put restraining pressure on Israel. This tactic was especially successful in the final stages of the Yom Kippur War, although the Politburo's chosen method itself (hinting at the possibility of unilateral Soviet intervention to guarantee a ceasefire) entailed substantial risks.[42]

The inability to control allies and subordinates is a manifestation of the common tendency of decision makers in crises to perceive their own ability to control events as decreasing, while the opponent's control over the situation is increasing.[43] The archetypal victim of autonomous risk, Kaiser Wilhelm II, illustrates this perception in his lament, shortly before the outbreak of World War I, that while he could not restrain his Austrian allies, Britain could easily hold back France and Russia but refused to do so:

> [Foreign Secretary] Grey knows perfectly well, that if he were to say one serious sharp and warning word at Paris and Petersburg, and were to warn them to remain neutral, both would become quiet at once. But he takes care not to speak the word, and threatens us instead! . . . England *alone* bears the responsibility for peace and war, and not we any longer.[44]

Ole Holsti observes that Kaiser Wilhelm's perception in August 1914 that he had "no choice" but to order a general mobilization led to a policy that attempted to compel Germany's adversaries to back down.[45] Many other analysts also find that when leaders shift responsibility for their decisions onto others, they tend to adopt strategies of compellence that do not require value trade-offs. Jack Snyder concurs that when decision makers shift the responsibility for the consequences of their own actions onto the adversary, they are more likely to adopt compellent strategies in an attempt to force concessions on two conflicting values.[46] Overall, the various cognitive theories of decision making point to the same conclusion: When factors that decision makers believe are beyond their control threaten losses on two conflicting values, they are likely to feel that no satisfactory compromise between them is possible and that they are therefore not responsible for finding one.

It seems reasonable, then, to suspect that time pressure and autonomous risk, by heightening uncertainty and facilitating shifts of responsibility, decrease the likelihood of value integration and increase the probability that even risk-averse decision makers will attempt to avoid value trade-offs by compelling their opponents to concede on both conflicting goals. Before we can determine how these theoretical relationships affect actual crisis decisions, however, we must consider how specific features of the decision unit and decision process under study may intensify or ameliorate the effects of value conflict.

Characteristics of Soviet Decision Making

Analysts continue to debate how the structure of the Soviet government and governing elite in the Brezhnev era affected crisis decisions. Some authors maintain that while differences of opinion existed within the Politburo on the value of the USSR's Middle Eastern allies, shared concern for strategic interests dominated the making of Soviet policy toward the region.[47] Others contend that Soviet politicians and interest groups expressed their policy preferences on Middle Eastern questions and that decisions on these issues were made primarily by forming and maintaining coalitions.[48] During the Soviet period, scholars blamed the lack of progress in the application of decision theory to the study of Soviet decision making on the dearth of data available on Politburo decisions.[49] The volume of data available in the post-Soviet era is still not great, and more data has not led to more agreement, as disagreements over the effects of some characteristics of Politburo decision making often stem from the model selected to guide the analysis.

Moreover, as discussed above, decision making during crises can be powerfully influenced by factors that do not usually apply to everyday foreign policymaking, such as a short time horizon, threat to basic values, and high probability of escalation of violence. These factors may make consultation with constituencies, development of new options, and formation of coalitions that constitute the bulk of normal policymaking difficult or impossible. For this reason, analysts cannot automatically assume that the process of taking decisions on Soviet Middle East *policy* was identical to what was carried out during a Middle East *crisis*. In particular, studies of factional conflicts over periods of months or years may not be the most reliable basis upon which to build a framework for analyzing decisions that must be made in days or hours.

Nevertheless, a number of empirical studies suggest two characteristic features of decision making in the Brezhnev era that could reduce the likelihood of value integration in crises. The first of these is the small number and the insularity of participants in decisions taken at the level of the Politburo or the Defense Council. The Politburo had a maximum of 16 voting members during the period from April 1967 to October 1973.[50] The Defense Council was an even smaller body whose exact composition and function during the Brezhnev era still remains unclear, though Brezhnev, USSR President Podgorniy, Prime Minister Kosygin, and Defense Minister Marshal Grechko are generally considered to have been members during the period of this study.[51]

The small size of the bodies charged with making crucial decisions may increase the likelihood of the tendencies toward shared illusions of unanimity, moral superiority, and invulnerability that Janis describes as *group-*

think.[52] The operation of this decision pathology within the Politburo or the Defense Council can hardly be regarded as a certainty, as other small decision units have demonstrated an ability to function in crises without succumbing to it. Janis himself holds up the ExComm that Kennedy assembled during the Cuban Missile Crisis as the classic case of small-group decision making that did not exhibit many of the symptoms of groupthink

Another feature of Soviet decision making that can be expected to have a major impact on the operation of cognitive factors is the role of the military. Until the last few years of Soviet power, the military establishment was the sole supplier of military-technical and strategic advice to the Politburo. Many analysts suggest that because of this monopoly on strategic information, the General Staff was likely to play a greater role in crisis decision making than it did in routine policy formulation.[53] The availability of a restricted number of channels of information may facilitate the filtering out of dissonant information, reinforcing postdecisional bolstering.

The KGB and the Foreign Ministry certainly provided intelligence to Soviet decision makers, but their expertise and institutional roles in analyzing the risks and opportunities present in ongoing military conflicts and military options under consideration is open to question. One advantage of the analytical framework developed in this study is that it may offer a means for determining when options favored by the military are likely to appear more or less attractive to decision makers. For example, military options that claim to be able to effect a "quick fix" to a conflict between regional and global interests could be expected to look especially appealing when leaders are hypervigilant. In any event, the small size of the decision unit and reliance on a limited number of channels of information may well have increased the probability that Soviet decision makers, acting under conditions of high time pressure and autonomous risk, would adopt a risky course of action after a suboptimal search for other options.

Overall, limitation of participation in crucial decisions to a small group and heavy reliance on the General Staff as a channel and filter of information were likely to have decreased the probability of value integration in crisis situations. In addition to emphasizing these two distinguishing features of Soviet decision making, some empirical studies attempt to characterize the manner in which Soviet leaders perceived and reacted to autonomous risk in the Brezhnev era. These studies tend to agree on three main points. First, Soviet leaders were highly sensitive to the possibility of loss of control over events and forces. Douglas Hart contends that Soviet decision makers viewed the possibility of loss of control as the major source of crisis instability.[54] Interestingly, Hart observes that Soviet leaders regarded the possibility of loss of control as highly context-dependent. In other words, the Politburo tended to perceive that the probability of losing control of events was a function of the specific features of the conflict or crisis situation, including the character of the governments and forces involved. Hart notes that his view contrasts with the prevailing Western view of instability and uncontrolled escalation, that tends to regard instability as an inherent property of actions or technology that is independent of the features of any particular conflict.

Second, and apropos of Soviet views of the sources of instability, Soviet leaders tended to set great store on political signals of risk and intentions. Stephen Meyer concludes that Soviet crisis decision making was very sensitive to the prevailing Soviet-American political climate during the crises to which it was a party.[55] He speculates that Soviet decisions to take military action in a crisis might well depend ultimately on political signals of risk. This view again differs from the mainstream of Western strategic thought, which tends to regard military activities as the most reliable indicators of the risk of escalation.

This focus on political signals should not be construed to mean that Soviet leaders would have been likely to ignore or discount obvious preparations for an attack on the basis of political signals alone. It does imply, however, that Soviet perceptions of the riskiness of limited military activities, such as low-level alerts, would have been heavily dependent on the political context surrounding them. Preparations that might be thought of as prudent by a Western strategist might have appeared provocative to Soviet leaders if they were made during a period of sharp superpower antagonism. Conversely, the Politburo might have been prone to underestimating the provocativeness to Western observers of readiness measures taken during a prevailing atmosphere of détente or cooperation. Such disparities in perception could result in misinterpretation of military moves intended as signals during crises.[56]

Third, Soviet military thought at the lower, military-technical level of doctrine (as distinguished from the higher, "sociopolitical" level) had historically emphasized preemption. While a comprehensive survey of Soviet military doctrine would be out of place here, a number of surveys of Soviet military-technical doctrinal writings of the period from 1964 to 1977 concur that in a nuclear crisis where a massive attack on the USSR appeared likely, Soviet military leaders might well have displayed greater predisposition toward a preemptive strike than their American counterparts would in a similar situation.[57] While likely Soviet behavior in regional, nonnuclear crises could certainly not be directly extrapolated from Soviet writings on strategic nuclear doctrine, it is reasonable to wonder whether Soviet strategists might not have had a relatively low threshold of preemption in other conflicts.

Preemption is also by no means a uniquely Soviet propensity, and at times (particularly during the Khrushchev era) Soviet emphasis on preemption was arguably a logical response to U.S. nuclear doctrine and force posture rather than a product of institutional preferences. Nevertheless, Soviet military-technical writings indicate that preemption was deeply ingrained in Soviet military thought, and when this observation is considered in the light of the military monopoly on military-strategic advice, it is not unreasonable to speculate that Soviet crisis decision making might be affected by an institutional bias toward preemption.

What is the likely net effect of these distinctive features of crisis decision making in the Brezhnev Politburo? Some characteristics, such as the marked fear of loss of control and the tendency to limit risks, might be expected to cancel out others, such as the possibility of bias toward preemption, leaving no clear basis to determine whether the structure of Soviet decision making facilitated or frustrated value integration. The fact that the effects of crisis-induced stress on individuals and groups are not linear, however, suggests an answer. Soviet decision makers might have had a higher threshold for the effects of cognitive or motivated biases, but once that threshold was crossed, the impact of these biases might have been more pronounced. The demonstrated tendencies of Soviet leaders toward risk-aversion may have impelled them to react with caution to low or moderate levels of uncertainty caused by autonomous risk, which may have encouraged acceptance of the losses to one or both goals inherent in making value trade-offs. Decision makers who are predisposed toward limiting risks could also be expected to place a higher value on avoiding a confrontation that carries the risk of disaster and so be more inclined to select options that reduce the likelihood of escalating a conflict, especially when losses could be limited by the use of face-saving gestures.

When uncertainty-producing autonomous risk was very high and was coupled with intense time pressure, however, the structure of Soviet decision making in the Brezhnev era may have facilitated avoidance of value conflict. The small number of decision makers and limited, narrow channels of information involved in the decision making process could have lead to very poor searches for alternatives; early resorts to shifting of responsibility or other forms of defensive avoidance; acceptance of higher risks in an effort to make the opponent concede on conflicting objectives (possibly by taking preemptive action); and, more selective processing of information in bolstering the chosen course of action.

Janis and Mann identify conditions that make a decision unit susceptible to groupthink.[58] One of these conditions, insulation of the group, may have applied to the Brezhnev Politburo at all times to a greater or lesser degree, as its members traditionally had little concern for or reliable means of assessing public opinion and were dependent on the military establishment for strategic intelligence. Another enabling condition of groupthink, high stress with slim prospects of finding a better solution to the problem at hand, could easily have been created by the combination of time pressure and autonomous risk in crisis situations. In such situations, the Politburo's insularity and need to present a public image of unanimity could have made it more vulnerable to premature cognitive closure, compared to an analogous group of leaders in a more democratic political system.

In the Arab-Israeli conflicts of 1967–1973, the Politburo was faced with two trade-offs: a strategic choice between regional and global goals and a tactical choice between coercion and accommodation. Neither of these choices was easy, and in a crisis situation any group of leaders might well be tempted to opt for a deceptively easy solution to the tactical problem that also purports to alleviate the need to make an unpalatable strategic decision. The next chapter will examine how and when we can expect decision makers to succumb to this temptation in a regional crisis.

TWO

Value Conflict and Crisis Decisions

Some people are very decisive when it comes to avoiding decisions.

—Brendan Francis

In the Arab-Israeli conflicts of 1967, 1969–1970, and 1973, the USSR acted more coercively than most models of crisis bargaining would predict, considering the prevailing balance of interests and bargaining power. At critical points in these wars and their antecedent crises, the Politburo took actions that heightened the intensity of regional conflict, significantly increased the probability of escalation, and raised tensions at both the regional and global levels. Moreover, these actions were taken while the crises were still ongoing, when important Soviet interests and the vital interests of their regional allies were directly at risk.

Conventional analyses of Soviet actions in Middle East crises cannot account for this pattern of behavior. Regardless of whether they use empirical methodology or formal models of bargaining, most analyses contend that the Soviet Union followed a predetermined strategy of risk avoidance. Focusing on the USSR's inferior bargaining position, they conclude that Moscow's dominant strategy in Middle East conflicts was to withhold strong support for regional allies until the Arab states met with disaster. The USSR would then step in after the crisis had passed to protect its clients from destruction or total humiliation. Following this well-scripted course, Soviet decision makers might have made some coercive moves that did not involve substantial risks, but would have had to follow a primarily accommodative course until the crisis was resolved. After the peak of the crisis had passed, empty threats and other similarly fatuous coercive moves would have served as face-saving gestures and allowed Soviet leaders to claim credit for protecting their regional allies while maintaining them in a state of subordination and dependency.[1]

The Politburo's risky behavior and repeated overreliance on coercion in these crises challenges conventional explanations of great-power behavior in regional conflicts. To understand why Soviet leaders deviated from their normal risk-averse behavior at critical junctures in Middle East conflicts, we must reexamine the events from the Soviet perspective, using an approach that focuses on the fundamental contradictions between Moscow's global and regional objectives. This chapter therefore presents an analytical framework designed to examine how value conflict affects decisions, shows how the framework may be used to explain Soviet actions in Middle East crises, and outlines how it may be tested against conventional models of decision making. As crises always require leaders to choose between conflicting goals, and refusing to make such choices frequently leads to disaster, the approach developed here may enhance our understanding of crisis management and risk-taking in many international conflicts.

The Soviet Dilemma in the Middle East, 1967–1973

Table 1 on page 23 diagrams the dilemma that Soviet leaders faced many times in the Middle East between 1964 and 1979. The figure describes a Middle East crisis where armed conflict between U.S. and Soviet allies is occurring or imminent, but no Soviet or American forces are directly engaged. In such situations, the main Soviet global objective (development and preservation of détente) clashed with Moscow's primary regional goal (expansion of Soviet influence).

In a Middle East crisis, the balance of interests would have favored the United States, and the United States possessed greater bargaining power overall. The risks of a major confrontation, and the probable damage to U.S.-Soviet relations even without such a confrontation, would thus have outweighed the potential gains in the global arena. For the illustrative purposes of Table 1, because the USSR's value structure favored avoidance of a Soviet-American confrontation, pursuit of the USSR's global goal meant avoiding escalation of the regional conflict into a major global clash, while concession of this goal would have been to risk heightened U.S.-Soviet tensions and abandonment of détente.[2]

In any regional conflict, the Soviet regional objective of expanding Moscow's influence in the region must also have been either pursued or compromised. The context of the Arab-Israeli conflict would have made this choice fairly straightforward. Soviet decision makers may have chosen to either support their regional allies against Israel or withhold support and increase

Table 1   Soviet Options in a Middle East Crisis

Regional Goal	Global Goal	
	Concede	Pursue
Concede	*Option One:* USSR champions Arab cause publicly and at the UN, but extends only limited material or military support.	*Option Two:* USSR abandons allies or offers only rhetorical support.
	Probable Outcome: Possible diplomatic conflict with U.S., but little chance of serious confrontation. Good prospects for cooperation with U.S. to contain regional conflict. High chance of alienating Arab allies.	*Probable Outcome:* No chance of confrontation with U.S. U.S.-Soviet relations improve. Serious U.S. breach with regional allies. Major loss of influence in Middle East likely.
Pursue	*Option Three:* USSR supports Arab states with major military aid and possible military intervention.	*Option Four:* USSR sends significant military aid and signals with military forces, but stresses cooperation. Suggests joint intervention to contain conflict.
	Probable Outcome: Confrontation with U.S. certain, possible military conflict. Alliance with Arab states secure. Soviet role in Middle East forcibly	*Probable Outcome:* Diplomatic conflict with U.S. certain; may become major confrontation. Friction with Arab allies over insufficient support likely.

friction between the USSR and its Arab allies. The necessity to make choices simultaneously along the regional and global dimensions of the crisis created a situation where four general courses of action were possible. Of course, the actual range of options available to Soviet leaders was broader and the choices between pursuing and conceding goals were not that stark, but this representation of Soviet options illustrates the need for Soviet decision makers to wrestle with the conflict between two opposing goals.

Each of the four cells in the table contains a description of Soviet actions and a projection of the likely outcome. The actions outlined in each cell suggest measures the USSR could have taken to implement the chosen option.

These general courses of action have been abstracted from actual Soviet behavior at various points in the crises considered in this study or from reconstructions of Soviet options in previous case studies. The likely outcome presents an estimate of the probable gains and losses to Soviet interests. The actual outcome of the crisis, and the resulting impact on Soviet regional and global interests, would of course have been determined by a number of factors outside the Politburo's control. Soviet decision makers would have incomplete information on factors such as American intentions, actions of other parties to the conflict, and the results of military operations, and would therefore have to rely on assessments analogous to the estimated outcomes listed in each cell.

Each option in Table 1, therefore, describes an option for dealing with the conflict between Soviet regional and global objectives and the likely results of selecting that option. In two of these options, one goal is sacrificed in favor of the other. In Option Two, in the upper right cell, Soviet decision makers sacrifice regional interests to avoid a U.S.-Soviet confrontation, ensuring that conflict with the United States will be avoided but entailing a high risk of a complete breach with regional allies. Not all Western analysts would consider this outcome to be a disaster for Soviet Middle East policy, however. Alvin Rubinstein suggests that the Politburo expected eventually to increase its influence over its defeated and alienated allies after the Six-Day War, especially in Egypt, where the defeat was expected to lead to socialist-inspired reforms.[3] Henry Kissinger quotes an ungrammatical but revealing 1970 memorandum from Richard Nixon that indicates that the president shared this view:

> We have been gloating over Soviet "defeats" in the Middle East since '67—&
> State et al said the June war was a defeat for Soviet. It was *not*. They became
> the Arabs' friend and the U.S. their enemy. Long range this is what served
> their interest.[4] [emphasis in the original]

Snyder and Diesing likewise contend that the optimal Soviet strategy in that conflict was to allow its allies to be defeated and step in at the end of the war to protect them from complete humiliation.[5] While these arguments are plausible, it is likely that even the most Machiavellian Soviet leaders could not be certain of maintaining influence over their allies after abandoning them in their hour of need.

Conversely, in Option Three in the lower left cell, a confrontation with the United States is almost certain, but alliances with friendly regional powers are strengthened, with the allies possibly made more dependent on Soviet support. This option holds out the possibility of greatly expanding the USSR's role in the Middle East, if only temporarily. The USSR's choice of this course of action, however, would guarantee a forceful American response and entail a high probability that Soviet and American forces would come into direct conflict sooner or later. The risks inherent in a major U.S.-Soviet confrontation therefore would have made this an extremely unpalatable option for the Politburo.

In Option One in the upper left cell, Soviet decision makers attempt to minimize risks by making compromises on both goals. The USSR extends some aid to its regional allies and supports their cause publicly, especially in the United Nations, and opposes efforts by the United States to end the conflict on American terms. This situation entails risks of increased friction with Soviet regional allies and of diplomatic conflict with the United States, but the chance of a major U.S.-Soviet confrontation is minimized. Soviet allies could be placated with support for face-saving gestures in the short run and replacement of lost military hardware in the long term. This option, concession of both goals for the time being, would be the most likely to appeal to risk-averse decision makers.

In Option Four in the lower right cell, on the other hand, the Politburo refuses to compromise on either regional or global goals and attempts to pursue both. Soviet actions in this situation cannot fail to be self-contradictory. Substantial military aid to Soviet allies or threats to intervene with Soviet forces risk a serious confrontation with the United States, while limitation of support to its allies in order to avoid antagonizing the United States risks alienating the Arab governments aligned with or leaning toward Moscow. Additionally, the United States and the Soviet regional allies are likely to feel deceived or betrayed. This option thereby runs a significant risk of damage to both regional and global interests. Such an outcome might be ironic, but analogous situations occur frequently in politics, when an intermediate level of effort toward opposing goals is inadequate to satisfy the supporters of either objective but sufficient to anger the opponents of each.

Each option outlined in the figure corresponds to a means of dealing with the value conflict faced by Soviet decision makers. In choosing either Option Two or Option Three, where one value is sacrificed in favor of the other, Soviet leaders would have made a clear trade-off between opposing goals. In George's formulation, these options describe situations where Soviet decision makers accept the conflict between their values and decide to strongly pursue the goal they determine to be more important.[6] As each of these options entails a substantial loss to either global or regional Soviet interests, neither option represents a compromise between regional and global goals, but rather a sacrifice of one set of goals for the other. The greater bargaining strength of the United States and the risk of disaster inherent in a serious U.S.-Soviet confrontation make it appear quite unlikely that Soviet leaders would retreat on global goals in favor of regional interests. The reverse, while more probable, still entails losses to regional interests that could be difficult to accept.

Option One, making moderate concessions on both goals, represents a value trade-off made by settling for partial satisfaction of both objectives. While an all-out effort would not be made in pursuit of either goal, making limited concessions on both objectives would offer a significant probability of realizing gains while minimizing losses to both regional and global interests. Decision makers would recognize limitations on resources and endeavor to work within the constraints they impose, while attempting to steer clear of policies that work at cross-purposes. This option, like Options Two and Three, represents an acceptance of the conflict between Soviet goals. Acknowledging constraints on resources and scaling back expectations on both objectives also would afford the best chance for resolving the value conflict via a creative solution that would allow pursuit of both.[7] In terms of Janis and Mann's model of decision making, Options One through Three represent successful value integration and careful search for and appraisal of options, or in their terminology, vigilant information processing.[8]

Option Four, on the other hand, represents a refusal to compromise. Standing firm in an attempt to pursue both opposing goals simultaneously reduces the likelihood of gains on both objectives and raises the risks of losses to Soviet interests and of escalation of the conflict. Additionally, efforts to pursue both goals simultaneously are likely to contradict and frustrate each other. In this option, the USSR would be working at cross-purposes with itself. This corresponds to George's description of coping with value conflict by avoiding it and blaming it on outside forces.[9]

Such a course of action is not necessarily a prescription for disaster, as events could still turn out in the Soviet Union's favor, but it severely limits the possibility of limiting and controlling risks. Leaders who enjoyed an advantage in bargaining power great enough to offer some prospect of forcing concessions from the opponent, whose critical risk (the maximum acceptable risk of war) was quite high, or who were risk-seeking rather than risk-averse might find this option attractive. In conflicts where the USSR's bargaining power is inferior to that of its adversaries, however, Option Four is clearly a suboptimal resolution of the conflict between global and regional objectives. Why then would Soviet decision makers ever choose such an option?

If they had time to think about it and believed that better options were available to them, they probably wouldn't. Under conditions favorable to vigilant information processing (in other words, when the assumption of rationality is most plausible), Soviet leaders would probably arrive at some form of compromise between their conflicting goals. In crises, however, the short time available to make decisions and the inherent uncertainties and risk of loss of control can seriously degrade decision makers' ability to strike an optimum balance between conflicting objectives. A crisis in the Middle East adds an additional layer of risk and uncertainty, because it is all too easy for allies or local actors outside the principals' control to escalate the level of violence. Superpower confrontations in the Middle East therefore provide excellent opportunities to study how leaders of great powers act when they are forced to confront the contradictions between their regional interests and global ambitions.

Testing for the Effects of Value Conflict

The studies reviewed in the previous chapter suggest ways in which value conflict is likely to effect decision making during crises. However, the operation of cognitive biases and psychological coping mechanisms is not only subtle, but effectively invisible. If decision makers were aware that these biases were occurring, they would almost certainly act to stop them. Any effort to explore how value conflict influences Soviet decisions is therefore forced to derive its data from observable manifestations of phenomena that are permanently hidden from view. The analyst is thus in a position much like that of Plato's metaphoric prisoner in the cave, whose only information about the outside world comes in the form of shadows projected on the wall. Fortunately, while many of the details of decision making in the Brezhnev Politburo remain hidden, some glimpses of the process have come to light after the collapse of Soviet power, and the communications and actions that result from crisis decisions are readily apparent.

This study will test two hypotheses on the relationship between situational factors that increase the likelihood of decision makers' resorting to defensive means in coping with value conflict and Soviet behavior in crises:

Hypothesis One. In regional crises, Soviet risk-taking tends to increase when time pressure is high and decrease when time pressure is low.

Hypothesis Two. In regional crises, Soviet risk-taking tends to increase when autonomous risk is high and decrease when autonomous risk is low.

The concept of time pressure is fairly straightforward, but with regard to its use in this study it should be kept in mind that any crisis by definition entails some element of time urgency. The time pressure experienced by decision makers even during a period of "low" time pressure in one of the crises discussed in this book is considerably greater than that which attends routine policymaking. The other variables set forth in these hypotheses require some explanation, particularly the concept of risk, which is central to all of them.

Risk may be understood as a potential or possible loss and is a probabilistic concept involving uncertainty; if it is *certain* that an action will result in losses, those losses represent the *costs* rather than the risks of that action. Any kind of risk may thus be considered to be the product of two factors: *probability of loss* (the "odds") and *magnitude of potential loss* (or the "stakes" that are at risk). If risk is conceived of in this fashion, then in a conflict where vital interests are at risk (qualifying the conflict as a crisis), even a small probability of loss would create a situation of substantial risk. During the Berlin Airlift, for example, the probability of military conflict that could have resulted in losses by either side was quite low, but as both parties believed their vital interests to be endangered, the situation was regarded as a protracted crisis.[10] Conversely, a conflict where only peripheral interests are at stake, but that involves a very high probability of loss, also results in a substantial net risk. This type of conflict was faced by American leaders at the end of the irrepressible conflict in Vietnam in the period leading up to the fall of Saigon, when the probability of loss to U.S. interests was extremely high, but the extent of political losses was limited by "writing off" the Republic of Vietnam.[11]

Snyder and Diesing define *autonomous risk* as the danger that the parties to a conflict will lose control of events.[12] In a crisis, the ability or inability of the opponents to control events directly affects both the probability and magnitude of the potential losses they might suffer. Autonomous risk therefore represents the potential for the actions of entities or forces other than the principal opponents to affect either or both of the two components of risk. The potential for such actions abounds in crisis and war, particularly if third countries supported by one of the principals are engaging in or contemplating hostilities against the other's allies. Preparations by an American ally to attack a state allied to the USSR, for example, would serve to increase the probability of losses to Soviet interests and possibly to American interests as well, to a degree dependent on the likelihood of success of the attack. Similarly, the potential magnitude of loss to a superpower's interests could be affected by a number of events and decisions beyond either superpower's control, such as horizontal escalation of a conflict by a third party, imposition of or cancellation of bombing sanctuaries, or changes in war aims. The source of autonomous risk need not be a human agency, of course. Equipment failures, truly automatic defense systems (such as the U.S. *Aegis* air-defense system when operating in automatic mode), weather, and pure random chance can all act to increase the danger that the parties to a conflict will lose control of events.

Adomeit defines *risk-taking* as doing something or failing to do something that increases the probability of losses or disaster, disaster being an outcome that imposes heavy losses on both parties to a conflict or bargaining situation.[13] Under this definition, risk-taking does not necessarily have to involve anything that would normally be considered conflictual or dangerous. As Jack Snyder points out, cooperation with a potential adversary in a "prisoner's dilemma" game is risky, because if the opponent does not reciprocate, the cooperating player will suffer major losses.[14] This observation points out that in some situations, the choice of any course of action, including doing nothing, involves risks. In both the prisoner's dilemma and chicken games, both coercion and accommodation entail a probability of loss. In chicken, by contrast, only standing firm runs the risk of disaster, a risk that is not present in prisoner's dilemma.

In any U.S.-Soviet crisis, the possibility of escalation to a disastrous confrontation, no matter how low the probability of such a conflict may initially appear, must be taken into consideration by decision makers on both sides. For the purposes of this study, therefore, risk-taking will be defined as *intentionally* doing something (or intentionally *not* doing something) that increases the probability of losses or disaster. This analysis is primarily concerned with Soviet behavior that ran the risk of escalation of a conflict. While it can identify situations in which Brezhnev-era Soviet leaders were more likely to make concessions, it is designed to examine the circumstances under which they acted coercively. More specifically, it is designed to explore how value conflict may have prompted Soviet decisions to take risks in support of a strategy of compellence, in an attempt to force adversaries to make concessions on two conflicting Soviet objectives. In other words, the main task of this study is to explain why the Politburo acted more coercively than its bargaining power would have dictated in Middle East crises. For this reason, risk-taking will be defined in a manner that emphasizes the risks of coercion rather than accommodation. Only intentional acceptance of risks will be considered to fit this definition, to distinguish deliberate risk-taking from unintentionally or unknowingly placing Soviet interests "at risk." Of course, Soviet leaders' perceptions of the risks inherent in acting coercively may or may not have corresponded accurately to the risks their actions actually entailed. Postdecisional bolstering, in particular, may have acted to reduce the apparent risk in some Soviet maneuvers.

Time pressure and autonomous risk are clearly related, but they are separable phenomena, and they have varied separately in many crises. For example, during the Berlin Airlift, a considerable degree of autonomous risk was present because of the possibility of incidents between Soviet and Western aircraft, particularly after Marshal Sokolovskiy's announcement that large-scale Soviet air maneuvers would extend into the air corridors between the Western-occupied zones and Berlin. Time pressure, however, remained relatively low from the American perspective, after it became evident that the airlift could supply Berlin's civilian population with the bare essentials of sustenance for a prolonged siege.[15] Conversely, during the prelude to the fall of Saigon, autonomous risk was quite low, as it was fairly clear that the Viet Cong and the North Vietnamese Army intended to pursue their military objectives and there was little that South Vietnamese forces could do to stop them on their own. The probability of American military intervention in this case was low, but the option was considered, and President Ford and his advisors had a short time span to arrive at a decision when Saigon's capture became imminent.[16]

These examples of crises where time pressure was high while autonomous risk was low, or vice versa, illustrate two important points about the assessment of time pressure. First, time pressure must be valued according to a comparison of the time needed to reach a decision with the time perceived to be available, not according to a fixed scale of days and hours. Brecher emphasizes that "crisis time," which can adversely affect decision making, differs from clock time. If 48 hours are required to arrive at and implement a decision, the time pressure felt by decision makers will be low if leaders feel they have 72 hours in which to act, but high if only 24 hours are available.[17]

Second, the principal actors in a crisis will not necessarily be subject to the same level of time pressure at the same moment. In many situations, such as the Berlin Airlift referred to above, some decision makers may feel that the time available for them to make decisions is adequate because "time is on their side," while their opponents may feel that, as their position is deteriorating, "time is working against them" and the probability of losses or their likely extent increases with time.

It might appear at first glance that autonomous risk should not vary independently for each decision unit involved, as autonomous risk by definition represents the potential for action of forces independent of both main opponents. In *crises*, however, decision makers' *perceptions* of autonomous risk and its inherent uncertainties can vary greatly between the principal opponents, particularly if allied third parties are involved. For example, while both major nations may assess the probability of accidents equally, leaders in one nation may regard their own ally's government as rational and prudent, while their adversaries view the same allied state as an unpredictable loose cannon.

This study's hypotheses on the relationship between time pressure and autonomous risk, on one hand, and Soviet risk-taking, on the other, contradict both intuitive expectations and the findings of several empirical studies. For example, George's distillation of the Bolshevik operational code predicts that Soviet leaders are more likely to take risks when they believe they are able to control the events that could create a sequence leading to war.[18] Adomeit, examining the Berlin and Cuban crises, concludes that Soviet leaders are likely to take risks only after careful preparation and construction of fallback positions.[19] Likewise, Fukuyama finds that the USSR has threatened military intervention in Middle Eastern conflicts only after the peaks of the crises had already passed and it was clear that the threats would not have to be carried out.[20] As noted earlier, these analyses predict a pattern of Soviet risk-taking completely opposite from that hypothesized here.

Part of this difference in expectations is due to differences in emphasis between this study and some of its predecessors. Most of Adomeit's work is primarily concerned with direct confrontations between the USSR and the United States, while Fukuyama concentrates on threats of military intervention rather than the whole spectrum of risk-taking behavior. Nevertheless, an analytical framework based on observations of the effect of value conflict on decision making yields expectations for Soviet behavior that run contrary to the conclusions of studies that find that the Politburo sought to control risks whenever possible. Certainly, Soviet leaders have shown strong tendencies toward risk aversion in most international conflicts, and this study does not dispute that Soviet decision makers generally display great reluctance to take risks. If conditions are favorable (in terms of the framework's independent variables, if time pressure and autonomous risk are low), the most likely Soviet course of action is a low-risk strategy of moderate compromise on regional and global goals. The hypotheses developed in this section thereby fulfill Snyder's requirement that in order to be analytically useful, explanations based on the effects of value conflict must identify when decision makers are most likely to make value trade-offs as well as when they are most likely to avoid them.[21]

Alternative Explanations

Empirical studies of Soviet behavior in crises suggest that both time pressure and autonomous risk would decrease the likelihood that Soviet leaders would take risks in support of their allies. Time pressure would make it more difficult for Soviet leaders to engage in sequential analysis of the risks and opportunities involved in the conflict, would reduce the time available for careful preparation for forward operations and a fallback position, and would shorten the time span over which damage to Soviet interests could be expected, and so would tend to dissuade Soviet leaders from accepting risks in support of their objectives.[22] Autonomous risk would decrease the Politburo's confidence that the chain of events that could lead to a major confrontation or war could be controlled and thus have a similar deterrent effect on risk-taking.[23] As these expectations are diametrically opposite to those of the two hypotheses derived in this section, the chicken game model, embellished by empirical surveys of Soviet risk-taking and actions in crises, will be used as an alternative explanation of Soviet behavior in the Middle Eastern conflicts that serve as test cases for this study's analytical framework.

In a chicken game, disaster for both players occurs when both stand firm. Submitting to the opponent's demands is therefore preferable to the "collision" that results if neither player backs down. Conceding, however, always entails some losses, and winning (standing firm while the opponent concedes) is always the most favorable outcome. In such a situation, choice of a strategy depends heavily on two factors: the credibility of the opponent's threat to stand firm and the costs of making concessions. The player who stands to lose more by making unilateral concessions has an inherent advantage in the chicken game, because his critical risk, the maximum risk of war the player can afford to accept, is higher. (In other words, the player can accept a greater risk of disaster in standing firm, as concessions would impose a greater penalty than the opponent would suffer if he conceded.)

Consequently, if both players believe each other's threats to stand firm are equally credible, the player having more to lose by conceding has higher bargaining power, and thus is more likely to stand firm, while the player who would lose less by backing down is more likely to offer concessions.[24] Perceptions and signals of resolve are especially important in a chicken game, because a player who believes that the opponent is bluffing will be much more likely to pursue a coercive strategy, which risks disaster if this perception of the adversary's lack of resolve is incorrect. Snyder and Diesing conclude that in a typical chicken crisis, both parties act coercively at first, until relative bargaining power is established. When one party realizes that the opponent's bargaining power is greater, it backs down. The stronger party can facilitate the weaker's surrender by offering a minor concession "which the loser can use and magnify afterward to obscure the extent of his defeat."[25]

In U.S.-Soviet conflicts over the Middle East in the 1960s and 1970s, the balance of interests and of bargaining power clearly favored the United States. Although Soviet strategic nuclear forces attained rough parity with U.S. forces in the late 1960s, the United States retained greater "power projection" capabilities though air- and sealift capacity and so could bring greater conventional military capability to bear in the region to support allied forces, which usually enjoyed superiority over the questionably reliable forces of the USSR's regional allies.[26] While Soviet analytical writings and statements for public consumption challenged the legitimacy of American influence in the area, and it was emphasized that the USSR was concerned with conflicts in a region "close to its borders," the strength of America's commitments to Israel was tacitly acknowledged and the reliance of the West on Middle Eastern oil was well understood.[27] The United States, as an established power in the region, would suffer substantially greater political losses than the USSR would incur by withdrawing its challenge. The domestic political losses that any U.S. president who failed to support Israel would have suffered, and of that both American and Soviet decision makers were cognizant, would have further reinforced the likelihood of a firm American stand and grudging Soviet concessions.

Because Washington's bargaining power in Middle East crises was demonstrably greater than Moscow's, the Politburo would be likely to "swerve" at the critical point in the crisis if Soviet decision making were best explained by the chicken game. Providing that the United States initially signals its resolve to stand firm in support of its regional allies (through such measures as bilateral and public communications and timely provision of military aid), the chicken model predicts that Soviet leaders would allow their allies to be defeated, perhaps making some face-saving gestures to cushion the blow.

Fukuyama offers a similar explanation for Soviet behavior from a holist rather than a positivist perspective. Examining six different Middle Eastern crises, he finds that in each case the USSR threatened to intervene only after the point of highest tension and uncertainty had passed and a resolution was already in sight.[28] Like Snyder and Diesing, Fukuyama argues that Soviet threats issued after tensions had clearly began to de-escalate were used to preserve the USSR's reputation as the guarantor of its regional allies' vital interests without risking a major confrontation with its principal global opponent. According to this interpretation, the Politburo adhered to a predetermined strategy of risk-avoidance while the issue was still in doubt, followed by coercive threats after the conflict had basically run its course, when there would be no need to carry them out.

A chicken game is not the only possible alternative explanation for Soviet behavior in regional crises. Snyder and Diesing, for example, structure Soviet decision making during the 1967 war as a game of "protector," played between the USSR and Egypt, in that the dominant Soviet strategy is one of failing to support the Arab allies until the war is lost, then stepping in to protect them from further humiliation.[29] This explanation is consistent with Fukuyama's analysis of the Soviet threat to intervene in the Six-Day War.[30] If either game is advanced as an explanation of Soviet decision making in regional crises, the resultant expectation is that Soviet leaders will tend to avoid rather than take risks when time pressure and/or autonomous risk are high. Both the chicken model and the value-conflict approach used in this study hypothesize that Soviet leaders will act to avoid losses in situations of high time pressure and autonomous risk, but the chicken game predicts they will do so by making concessions, while this study expects they will act forcefully in an attempt to force concessions from their adversaries.

Testing this study's hypotheses on Soviet risk-taking in regional crises against the alternative explanation suggested by the chicken model and empirical studies requires a means for assigning values to both independent and dependent variables. This requirement will not always be easy to meet, considering that perceptual variables are involved, that variation will occur not only between but within crises, and that sensitivity to levels of crisis-induced stress must be maintained. This chapter's final section will discuss how these difficulties may be overcome.

Measuring Variables of Risk and Risk-Taking

This study will test its two hypotheses by examining Soviet decisions made during three conflicts in the Middle East. The Six-Day War of 1967, the War of Attrition of 1969–1970, and the October War of 1973 offer opportunities to study Soviet decision making in a variety of regional crises. These cases include a crisis that led to a major war within the region (1967), a crisis precipitated by a protracted low-intensity conflict that did not lead to an all-out war (1969–1970), and a deliberately initiated war that led to an intrawar crisis and a superpower confrontation (1973). These conflicts display a great deal of variation, both in Soviet risk-taking and the independent influences on Soviet behavior. This variability contrasts with the continuity and stability of the USSR's top leadership during the space of time spanned by the cases, which was the beginning of the "period of stagnation" *(zastoi)*. The dreary consistency of this period enables us to observe how the same key group of leaders dealt with a variety of crisis situations.[31] This section outlines the methods that will be used to test the hypotheses on the effects of value conflict on Soviet crisis decision making in the Brezhnev era.

The two independent variables to be used in this study are both perceptual variables and as such present unavoidable difficulties of measurement. Fortunately, some useful measures of each are available for the cases under consideration. As discussed earlier in this chapter, time pressure represents the availability of sufficient time to make a decision. In a case where leaders had infinite time to make a decision, time pressure would be zero (and the leaders would probably never choose a course of action, especially if all possible options involved value trade-offs). If, on the other hand, decision makers had no time to arrive at a decision, time pressure would be infinite.

In actual crises, of course, this variable would never reach either of these extremes, but it is possible to assign ordinal values to a range of levels of time pressure between the two. If leaders believed that they faced a deadline by which a decision had to be made, but perceived this deadline to be comfortably beyond the time necessary to choose a course of action, the situation would qualify as a crisis due to the finite response time, but time pressure would be very low. If, on the other hand, every hour that passed before the USSR acted threatened additional losses to Soviet interests, time pressure would be very high. Several sorts of indicators enable the analyst to approximate where on this continuum the time pressure operating in each phase should be placed. The limitations on response time created by factors such as the speed of movement of forces, their proximity to actual or potential objectives, or the rate of loss of soldiers and equipment can be estimated fairly accurately.

The second independent variable, autonomous risk, represents the perceived likelihood that the level of conflict will escalate or the risks to Soviet interests will increase due to causes that are beyond the control of Soviet or American leaders. If the principal adversaries had absolute control over every possible event, autonomous risk would be zero, and the "chess game named disaster" would contain no random elements. Alternatively, if the main opponents had no control over anything, autonomous risk would be infinite, but the leaders involved could not be considered decision makers, as nothing they did could influence the outcome of the conflict in a predictable manner.

Factors that can create autonomous risk include accidents, unauthorized action, or the implementation of standard operating procedures (such as attempts to destroy aircraft believed to be hostile) by the forces of the decision makers' nation or their main opponents, and actions by other actors involved in the conflict. Like time pressure, this variable represents decision makers' perceptions or assessments of the situation. These perceptions may be measured by objective indicators if it appears likely that decision makers were aware of them. Indicators of autonomous risk include the intensity and change in intensity of ongoing combat, the alert levels of allied and hostile forces, and strategic or tactical warning of escalatory actions planned or contemplated by the parties to a conflict, when these cannot be controlled by Soviet or American leaders. As discussed earlier, Soviet leaders exhibited great sensitivity to political signals of strategic warning, so the case studies cannot fail to take these into account when evaluating autonomous risk. Political signals of autonomous risk that might unsettle the Politburo would include credible threats to take military action issued by Soviet or American allies or statements indicating a pronounced increase in the mutual hostility of the direct participants in the regional conflict.

The nature of crises is such that the two independent variables are likely to exhibit significant covariation. The case studies must therefore include attempts to determine if time pressure and autonomous risk have quantitatively or qualitatively different effects or if the influence of one factor appears to cancel out or reinforce the effects of the other. For example, a given level of autonomous risk may prove to be linked to increased Soviet risk-taking only when a certain threshold level of time pressure is also present. If this were the case, both variables could be seen as necessary but not sufficient causes of a heightened tendency toward coercive risk-taking. On the other hand, the Politburo may appear to take risks during periods when the combination of the two independent variables adds up to an identifiable threshold when both are moderately high or even when the independent factors vary inversely (i.e., when autonomous risk is very high when time pressure is low, or vice versa). If this were observed, both independent variables could be regarded as equivalent and mutually reinforcing influences on Soviet risk-taking.

The dependent variable, coercive risk-taking, can be measured by Soviet statements and actions. Because many indicators of risk-taking were intended to be signals, they are readily visible to the analyst even if they were overlooked by their intended targets. These indicators include public statements, diplomatic correspondence, and movements and alerts of forces. However, these indicators alone are not sufficient proof that value conflict had an effect on Soviet decision making. The effects of cognitive bias can only be measured in controlled psychological experiments, if even then. Nevertheless, evidence that Soviet decision makers were tending toward one of the patterns of coping with value conflict identified by Janis and Mann can serve to indicate that cognitive bias influenced Soviet decisions and actions.

Indirect indicators of cognitive bias can be found in a variety of sources, including public statements, private communications, memoirs, published and translated documents, and press sources. Care must be taken in using press sources to distinguish between evidence of an ongoing "debate" in Soviet policymaking circles and indications of a course of action actually adopted by the Politburo. The existence of "debates" on Brezhnev-era Middle East policy is itself a matter of debate. Spechler and Kass, for example, find that the positions of individual Politburo members on Middle Eastern affairs may be discerned from items in the press organs of government institutions that they control or influence.[32] Lilita Dzirkals, Thane Gustafson, and Ross Johnson, on the other hand, conclude from a survey of Soviet émigrés who held positions in press organizations that foreign policy was not a subject of factional communication in the press.[33] Regardless of the position taken on the issue of factional conflict and debate, statements in the Soviet press can serve as indicators of consensual Politburo positions on and decisions regarding ongoing conflicts, particularly when newspapers run unsigned editorials (or pieces over the pseudonyms "V. Petrov" and the *Pravda* "Observer") on the conflict in question on their front pages.[34] Commentaries by academics and journalists may be regarded as less authoritative, but still provide important clues to the policies and perceptions of Soviet leaders, particularly when the commentator has close ties to the Foreign or Defense Ministry, the Main Political Administration, or departments of the CPSU responsible for foreign and defense policy.

Intragovernmental communications would, of course, be the best sources of data for examining the effects of value conflict, but precious few of these are available, as Soviet decisions made during Middle East crises are still politically sensitive. In any event, indirect indicators can yield evidence of the ways in which Soviet decision makers attempt to accept or avoid value conflicts. For example, vigilant information processing and acceptance of value conflict could be indicated by evidence that the Politburo considered the matter in question in several meetings, contacted allied states in an effort to achieve consensus or present a united front, and actively searched for information from a variety of sources before announcing a decision. Precipitate action without evidence of consultation with allies, the United States, or Soviet personnel in the area, on the other hand, would indicate hypervigilance. Finally, evidence of defensive avoidance would include the disregard of relevant information, a lack of attempts to gain more information (particularly if it is likely that the information gained would be disconcerting), and repeated assertions that the actions of others left the Soviet government no choice but to act as it did.

Particular caution must be exercised in interpreting Soviet protestations that their leaders had restricted options or no choice. Decision makers' assertions that adversaries forced them into their own actions must be distinguished from attempts to disavow responsibility for the possible *consequences* of an action, which may actually be beyond the decision makers' control, especially under conditions of high autonomous risk. The intended audience for statements of "no choice" can reveal much about the degree to which Soviet decision makers may have felt their freedom of action was restricted. Internal communications, again, would be the most powerful indicators of feelings of "no choice" as part of a resort to defensive avoidance, but even the most open and democratic governments show great reluctance to declassify such communications or grant researchers access to them. Statements for public consumption are probably least indicative of actual perceptions of "no choice." Diplomatic correspondence with adversaries and nonaligned states offers weightier evidence in this regard.

Confidential communications with allies, when their authenticity can be trusted, are perhaps the best readily available evidence of perceptions of restricted options and of defensive means of coping with value conflict in general. Several accounts confirm that the following exemplary interchange took place between Syrian President Shukri al-Kuwatly, Soviet Marshal Zhukov, and Khrushchev during the Suez Crisis of 1956:

> Kuwatly was in a highly emotional state. He insisted that Egypt must be helped. "But what can we do?" asked Khrushchev. "Is it for me to tell you what to do?" shouted Kuwatly. "Egypt is being attacked, and Egypt believed

you were going to come to her aid. If you do nothing your position in the Arab world will be utterly destroyed." Khrushchev repeated, "But what can we do?" "Why don't you ask Marshal Zhukov?" said Kuwatly.

So Zhukov produced a map of the Middle East and spread it on the table. Then, turning to Kuwatly, he said "How can we go to the aid of Egypt? Tell me! Are we supposed to send our armies through Turkey, Iran and then into Syria and on into Israel and so eventually attack the British and French forces?"[35]

If the available evidence is evaluated with care, the way in which Soviet leaders dealt with the inescapable value conflicts created by their Middle East policies in the Brezhnev era can be linked to Soviet actions in the regional crises examined in this study. The evidence also allows the expectations of an alternative explanation of Soviet risk-taking in regional crises to be matched against the expectations of this study's analytical framework. The conventional interpretation of Soviet decision making as a game of chicken played by risk-averse leaders would expect greater risks to be taken in periods of low time pressure or autonomous risk, and both Fukuyama and Adomeit contend that Soviet risk-taking behavior follows this pattern.[36] Conversely, Soviet decision makers would be expected to take fewer risks when time pressure or autonomous risk were high. Representing Soviet decision making as the necessity to balance two conflicting goals yields directly opposite expectations: coercive risk-taking is hypothesized to be more likely when time pressure or autonomous risk are greater and less likely when these pressures are less intense.

What This Approach Can Teach Us about Decision Making

The case studies in the following three chapters will employ the method of structured, focused comparison to test the utility of the analytical framework developed in this chapter.[37] This method stresses the need to concentrate on a consistent set of independent and dependent variables in all cases so that analysis of them may be more useful for the development of theory. The examination of each case will begin with an explication of the value conflict that confronted Soviet leaders prior to each of the three crises, including a brief outline of Soviet interests in the region and the contradictions between these objectives and Soviet global interests. Following this, the crises will be divided into phases demarcated by "break points" identified in secondary literature or determined by examination of the most important events in the conflict. Usually, the boundaries between phases will be occurrences or actions that resulted in changes in the values of the two independent variables, time pressure and autonomous risk. Breaking each crisis into phases enables the analysis of Soviet behavior to take into account variations in the likely influences on Soviet decision making that are observable not only between the cases but within each individual case.

The values of the independent variables will be assessed for each phase and expectations for the dependent variable, risk-taking, will be drawn based on these values. Indicators of the coercive risk-taking will then be examined to determine if the pattern of Soviet behavior exhibited in the crisis matches the expectations of the hypotheses being tested or fits better with the alternative explanation. Next, a summary of findings from all phases of the crisis will attempt to discern the overall effect of value conflict on Soviet actions during the confrontation. Finally, the case studies will evaluate the efficacy of Soviet coercive and accommodative moves in furthering the Politburo's regional and global objectives in the near term and determine how Soviet actions affected the context of successive conflicts.

In addition to indicating whether Soviet leaders accepted or denied the necessity of value trade-offs during regional conflicts, examination of Soviet crisis behavior from a value-conflict perspective can help determine whether the Politburo attempted to manipulate autonomous risk in its efforts to employ coercive diplomacy. The Middle East is a region where fervor frequently erupts into violence and conflicts all too quickly invoke the logic of war. In such an environment, regional actors often have insufficient control over the forces they employ, and external powers attempting to cooperate with, deter, or manipulate them can exercise even less control over the forces in conflict. The following case studies will look not only at the timing of Soviet coercive risk-taking but also the tactics employed, to see if the Politburo tended to increase the risk of loss of control of events or to decrease it. George and Adomeit conclude that Soviet leaders attempt to control risks insofar as possible even when challenging or trying to coerce an adversary in direct confrontations.[38] This study can help ascertain whether, in acting coercively in regional crises, the Politburo let slip the dogs of war or tried to keep them chained.

Finally, the intention in testing the hypotheses advanced in this chapter against the expectations of an alternative conception of crisis decision making is not to assert that the approach described here is superior to the rational-actor or Kremlin politics perspectives, but to provide additional insight into the way in which leaders make decisions in crises. The value-conflict perspective is designed to complement, rather than supplant, the rational-actor model by explicating how decision makers may act more coercively than their relative bargaining power would dictate, and to identify situations where they are more likely to avoid value trade-offs and hold their adversaries responsible for conflicts between their own goals.

The following three studies of conflicts in the Middle East will be tests of a new approach to opening the "black box" that still surrounds Soviet crisis decision making during the Brezhnev years. If it is successful, this approach may be applied to other instances of great-power behavior in regional crises, but it is not advanced as a self-contained alternative conception of decision making. Rather, it is intended to help us understand how the pressures of conflict and crisis constrict the bounds of rationality.

THREE

The Six-Day War, 1967

I think the Soviet Union has to bear a large share of responsibility for what happened. Given our influence with Nasser, given our ability to exert pressure on Egypt, we should have restrained the Egyptians from demonstrating their belligerence. . . . I think our military men, more than our diplomats, are to blame. They should never have let the Egyptians force Israel into betting everything it had on a preventive attack.

—Nikita Khrushchev
Khrushchev Remembers: The Last Testament[1]

How much responsibility for the Six-Day War rests with the Soviet Union? This chapter does not claim that the USSR was primarily responsible for the outbreak of the war; all parties to that conflict must share the blame for it. Rather, this chapter contends that the Soviet Union made a probably unintentional but nevertheless crucial contribution to the escalation of violence and that an examination of the effects of value conflict on Soviet decision making can help explain how and why this occurred.

The chapter begins with a brief outline of Soviet interests in the eastern Mediterranean in 1967, showing how the pursuit of regional objectives risked a global confrontation, in order to illustrate the dilemma that Soviet leaders were forced to deal with when the ongoing Arab-Israeli conflict reached crisis proportions. The political and military weakness of the Syrian Ba'ath regime, in particular, made it extremely difficult for the Politburo to protect its regional allies without running the risk of turning the Soviet-American competition for influence in the Middle East into an acute U.S.-Soviet crisis.

Next, it will show that conventional explanations of Soviet coercive risk-taking in the crisis do not adequately deal with the Soviet actions that entailed the highest degree of risk. Analyses of Soviet behavior based on both game-theoretic and empirical models produce the expectation that the Politburo should have acted most coercively after the crisis was essentially resolved and little danger of escalation remained. These perspectives contend that Soviet leaders made coercive moves primarily as face-saving gestures when the risk of events getting out of control had subsided. In the actual crisis, however, the Politburo issued coercive threats or encouraged their allies to act most forcefully when they had reason to believe that a substantial degree of autonomous risk existed. Essentially, the balance between coercion and accommodation in Soviet actions tipped toward coercion at points when conventional models of the crisis would not expect it to.

To determine more precisely when those points occurred, the 1967 crisis will then be divided into six phases demarcated by critical events in the war and the tense period that preceded it. As most of these phases are characterized by changes in the two independent variables used in this study, time pressure and autonomous risk of escalation, values for these variables will be assessed and corresponding expectations on the likelihood of Soviet coercive risk-taking will be derived for each phase. Soviet statements and actions during each phase will then be examined to evaluate the level of risks taken and for evidence of value conflict effects on decision making. A comparison of Soviet behavior in each of the phases shows that Soviet leaders tended to avoid risks in periods where decision makers are hypothesized to be more likely to accept the conflict between their regional and global goals, but took greater risks at times when attempts to deny the contradictions between goals were most probable. The chapter's conclusion will show how focusing on the effects of value conflict on decision making helps explain how Soviet decisions in 1967 contributed to the disastrous defeat of the USSR's Arab allies.

Conflicting Soviet Objectives in the Middle East, 1967

This section will not attempt a comprehensive discussion of Soviet interests in the Middle East at the time of the Six-Day War. Instead, it will outline the general objectives of Soviet policy toward its allies in the eastern Mediterranean, the interests that were most threatened by escalation of the Arab-Israeli military conflict, and the potential for regional conflicts to result in a direct Soviet-American confrontation.[2]

In the most general terms, the USSR sought to increase its political influence in the region and reduce that of the Western powers, particularly the United States. Nikita Khrushchev inaugurated the Soviet "opening to the Third World" in 1955 by arranging for Czech armaments to be sent to

Nasser's Egypt, and economic and military aid was subsequently extended to nonaligned nations in attempts to break up the Western-leaning Baghdad Pact and exploit anticolonial sentiment to Soviet advantage.[3] The USSR supported the partition of mandated Palestine in 1947 and the creation of the state of Israel in 1948, but it subsequently avoided openly taking sides in the Arab-Israeli conflict until the Czech Arms Deal. As would soon become apparent, that intractable dispute offered both opportunities and dangers for the Soviet Union as it strove to attain recognition as a world power.

Egypt and Syria were the USSR's main Middle Eastern allies in 1967, but each was important to Soviet regional interests for different reasons. Egypt possessed major strategic significance because it was the most populous Arab state, it controlled the Suez Canal, and it had excellent port facilities, to which the USSR repeatedly attempted to gain access.[4] Egypt also played a leading role in the Non-Aligned Movement, and Nasser's stature as the most charismatic leader in the Arab world lent his country added political importance.[5] Syria, on the other hand, was probably more important to Soviet interests for its weaknesses rather than its strengths. While the USSR regarded the coup that brought the left wing of the Syrian Ba'ath to power in 1966 as a major victory for socialism in the developing world, Soviet leaders were fully cognizant of the regime's vulnerability to its internal and external enemies.[6]

The Politburo and the Ba'ath disagreed on a number of issues, especially since the Ba'ath refused to acknowledge the need for an independent Syrian Communist Party, but a joint CPSU-Ba'ath communiqué issued after the visit of a Ba'ath delegation to Moscow in January 1967 papered over these differences and stressed agreement on the "main questions of the struggle against colonialism and imperialism."[7] The need to bolster the Syrian regime against internal and external enemies was clearly recognized, and the Politburo's perception of the regime's vulnerability was acute.[8] Increased deliveries of armaments after the 1966 coup and reports of plots against the Syrian government by internal reactionaries in collusion with American and Israeli agents indicate that the USSR was keenly aware that the sole example of left-wing Arab socialism was fragile and had to be protected.[9]

It is not possible to determine whether the Politburo considered Syria or Egypt to be the most valuable Soviet ally in the Middle East. Egypt had greater potential for military power, economic strength, and political influence, but Syria was more dependent on Soviet support for the survival of the left-wing Ba'ath regime and therefore likelier to be a more reliable partner for Soviet policy in the region. Dependence, however, frequently increases the dependent's influence over the benefactor, and by 1967 both Egypt and Syria were able to exploit the USSR to advance their own regional ambitions.[10]

This relationship of mutual dependency would soon become the central factor in the contradiction between Soviet regional and global interests. While the term détente had not yet gained widespread currency in discussions of U.S.-Soviet relations, avoidance of a direct confrontation with the United States, especially a military confrontation, was clearly of paramount interest to the Soviet leadership. Soviet writings repeatedly warned that conflicts in the Middle East could ignite a nuclear war that would be catastrophic for the entire world.[11] Similarly, while America's commitment to Israel was not as strong as it would later become, President Johnson and Congress were in agreement that "the Arabs should not be permitted to drive the Israelis into the sea."[12] This study is not the place for debate on whether the USSR's regional allies were seeking to destroy the state of Israel in 1967. It suffices to say here that Soviet officials were well aware that many political leaders among their Arab allies were striving for the annihilation of Israel. Soviet leaders who were opposed to or ambivalent about this objective could not have been reassured by their allies' rhetoric.[13]

While the vital interests of their allies were thus diametrically opposed, U.S. and Soviet vital interests were not in direct conflict in the Middle East in 1967. Moscow and Washington were clearly engaged in a political struggle over the region, and both wished to avoid the possibility of military conflict. Soviet decision makers, however, had especially strong incentives for seeking to forestall an acute Soviet-American crisis, because the "balance of interests" as well as the balance of conventional forces in the region did not favor the USSR. The political and strategic situations in the Middle East in 1967 resembled the "correlation of forces" that prevailed in the Caribbean in 1962. The Politburo had neither a superiority in conventional arms nor a recognized claim of vital interests to strengthen its bargaining power.[14] Any direct confrontation would have been far more likely to end in humiliation for the Politburo rather than a political victory.

As a result, while the Soviet leadership was not prepared to abandon its global political competition with the United States, it was in the USSR's interest to avoid a confrontation over the Middle East. Consequently, when the violence of the Arab-Israeli conflict escalated, the objective of maintaining relations with and influence over Syria and Egypt began to clash with the need to avoid a Soviet-American confrontation.

Interpretations of Soviet Behavior

Most explanations of Soviet actions in the 1967 crisis contend that the general pattern of Soviet behavior was somehow predetermined, either by the structure of the conflict or by the Politburo's predisposition toward risk-avoidance. Snyder and Diesing, for example, argue that the crisis is best described by a "protector" game matrix in which the dominant Soviet strategy is to withhold strong support from its regional allies until the Arab states meet with disaster. The USSR then steps in after the crisis has passed to protect its clients from destruction or total humiliation.[15] If Soviet decision makers followed the strategy prescribed by the protector game, they might make some coercive moves that did not involve substantial risks while hostilities between U.S. and Soviet allies continued, but would take a primarily accommodative course of action until the crisis was resolved. After the peak of the crisis had passed, coercive moves would serve as face-saving gestures and as means to prevent the elimination of their regional allies while maintaining them in a state of subordination and dependency. Fukuyama offers a similar explanation, using empirical methodology rather than formal modeling.[16] In 1967, according to these interpretations, the Politburo adhered to the preferred Soviet strategy of risk-avoidance while the issue was still in doubt. Empty coercive threats were only issued after the conflict had basically run its course, when there was no need to carry them out.

Both of these explanations are consistent with the expectations of a chicken-game matrix in which the balance of bargaining power favored the Soviet Union's opponent. If Soviet decision makers were playing a game of chicken in 1967, their best strategy would have been to make an initial display of firmness, but then to avoid coercive risk-taking when time pressure or autonomous risk remained high. They would issue threats or bluffs only when escalation of the crisis into a superpower confrontation became a remote possibility, just as Khrushchev did in the 1956 Suez Crisis. Early commitment in the form of a threat to intervene at or before the peak of the crisis would avail the Politburo little, as any such threat would be a bluff that the United States could easily call. After the crisis was resolved, the Politburo could threaten intervention in order to prevent Israel from expanding the scope of its victory, and thereby claim that it had saved its Arab allies from annihilation. This strategy would allow Soviet leaders to minimize the risk of conflict with the United States and to maximize the opportunity to increase the defeated allies' dependence on, and hopefully obedience to, the USSR.

If Soviet behavior in the crisis were best explained by a U.S.-Soviet game of chicken, therefore, Soviet actions that entailed the highest degree of risk would be taken when the war was essentially over. Consistent with this explanation, the action that most conventional analyses focus on as an example of Soviet risk-taking is the hot-line message of June 10, which was received in Washington after Israel had agreed to a cease-fire.[17] (The actual timing of the message with regard to the cease-fire will be discussed later in this chapter.) The message contained a vague threat of Soviet military action if Israel continued its offensive against Syria, which by the time of its receipt in Washington, the Israeli cabinet had decided not to do.[18] According to the conventional consensus, this was a coercive gesture that did not involve any real risks, as it represented a threat that would never have to be carried out, intended to deter an action no longer being contemplated. This perspective thus contends that the hot line message should be regarded as a "threat which left nothing to chance."

The hot-line message, however, was not the Soviet Union's riskiest move in the crisis. The Soviet action that involved the greatest degree of risk was the encouragement of Egypt to mobilize its forces to meet an Israeli attack on Syria in mid-May, when no such attack was yet planned.[19] This action, which will be discussed in detail later, came during a period of high autonomous risk and at a point when Soviet decision makers were likely to have felt intense time pressure. Explanations based on the chicken model cannot easily account for this action, because if Soviet decision makers behaved as their relative bargaining power would dictate, they would have attempted to avoid losses through accommodative bargaining, with a leavening of firmness added to save face and discourage their adversaries from taking too great an advantage of the situation. In actuality, however, the Politburo opted to coerce its allies into coercing their opponents, an action that is inconsistent with the predetermined strategy suggested by the chicken model.

Analysis of the value conflict that confronted Soviet leaders in May 1967 suggests a different explanation. Acceptance of a value trade-off by the Politburo in May 1967 would have entailed clear and substantial losses to the compromised objective. A Soviet deterrent threat of intervention at that point would have necessitated an American response, increasing the probability of a confrontation that would most probably end in a called bluff and humiliation, resulting in significant losses to Soviet global interests. On the other hand, sacrificing regional interests for global objectives by doing nothing risked grievous damage to the USSR's relationships with Egypt and Syria if Israel were to carry out successfully a major offensive.

Faced with these unpalatable options and having no time available to accept or resolve this value conflict, the Politburo adopted a chimerical compromise and attempted to manipulate its allies into an action that seemed to offer a possibility for avoiding losses to Soviet regional and global interests. This possibility was realized in the short run, as the effort to encourage an Egyptian mobilization was successful, but it set in motion a chain of events that led to disaster for the USSR's regional allies. In an effort to limit risks and deter further escalation, Soviet decision makers tried to put out the fire with gasoline, with predictable results.

Phases of the 1967 Crisis

The 1967 crisis may be divided into six phases, each of that is bounded by key events generally recognized as turning points in the conflict.[20] As will be seen with all three crises considered here, most of these events were actions or decisions taken either by local actors (usually Israel or Egypt) or the USSR. In general, these key events resulted in major changes in the independent variables used in this book.[21] The phases thus constitute periods of time within which the values of the independent variables remained relatively stable, but between which the factors of time pressure and the autonomous risk varied significantly. For clarity, each phase will be assigned a name based on a key event or dominant characteristic of the phase.

Once these phases have been defined, Soviet actions in each phase may be examined for evidence that suggests how Soviet decision makers dealt with the conflict between regional and global objectives. This section outlines the six phases of the crisis from April 7 to June 10, 1967, and assigns appropriate values to the two independent perceptual variables. These values will be determined both inductively, by examining Soviet statements made during the crisis, and deductively, by noting events that significantly changed the perceived threat to the Soviet interests outlined in the previous section. Government statements offer the most authoritative evidence for inductively determining the levels of time pressure and autonomous risk perceived by the Politburo, but these are not available for every phase and, as might be expected, are generally absent when the actions of third parties did not create the urgent need for a Soviet response. Most of the events that can be used deductively to assign values to the independent variables are actions of third parties, especially alerts and movements of forces, escalation and deescalation of low-intensity military conflict, and developments in the course of conventional military operations.

Two points should be noted before proceeding. First, the independent variables are designed to represent assessments of time pressure and autonomous risk from a Soviet perspective, as best as this may be determined by an outside observer. Attempts to analyze the conflict from an Egyptian, Syrian, Jordanian, Israeli, or American perspective would assign values to the independent variables depending on threats to the interests of each individual state, and these values would not necessarily be the same for all the parties involved. At a given point in the crisis, for example, Israeli and Egyptian decision makers might be likely to perceive vastly different levels of time pressure. Because this study is primarily concerned with Soviet perceptions and behavior, the following account of the conflict's six phases does not attempt to present a complete historical narrative of the crisis that led to the Six-Day War, but instead focuses on the events that this study hypothesizes as most likely to have had a significant impact on Soviet perceptions of the situation.

Second, the effects of time pressure on decision makers' abilities to manage value conflicts in 1967 may have been heightened by the offense-dominant environment in which the conflict took place. Jervis notes that when offensive operations are believed to have advantages over the defensive, "defensive aggression" and preemptive strikes become more attractive, and leaders are more likely to interpret ambiguous information as evidence that other parties have aggressive intentions.[22] Stephen Van Evera concurs that the risk of preemptive or preventive war rises in an offense-dominant strategic environment, but also finds that "windows" of vulnerability and opportunity open wider in such situations, reducing the time available for leaders to make decisions.[23] The events of 1967 illustrate how the rapid operational movement capability of armored forces and the short distances between the front lines and strategically vital rear areas, particularly in Israel and Syria, heightened perceptions of vulnerability on all sides and lessened the time available for decision makers to react to events.

Clashes between *fedayeen* guerrillas and Israeli forces became more frequent after the Ba'ath coup in Syria in February 1966 and progressed until fighting near Lake Tiberias (Sea of Galilee) on April 7, 1967, involving Israeli and Syrian tanks and aircraft, raised the violence on the Israeli-Syrian border to a new level and signaled an increase in the possibility of further escalation. This possibility began to be realized, as *fedayeen* activity subsequently increased after the Lake Tiberias clash.[24] Soviet concern about the likelihood of larger-scale fighting is reflected in the official protest sent to the Israeli embassy in Moscow on April 21, which warned Israel against "playing with fire" in an area "close to the borders of the Soviet Union."[25] These standard expressions indicate that the incident raised the perceived probability of an escalation of conflict in the region. The delay in issuing the protest, however (two weeks had elapsed since the protested incident occurred), betokens a lack of perceived time pressure. For the purposes of this study, therefore, April 7 will mark the start of the first phase of the 1967 crisis, which will be referred to as the Border Clashes phase. It continued until May 6 and is characterized by moderately high autonomous risk and low time pressure.

The boundary between the first and second phases is demarcated by an event of which the Politburo may or may not have been aware. On May 7, Israel's cabinet took a decision to launch a limited retaliation raid against Syria if public warnings did not result in a decrease in the incidence of terrorism and sabotage.[26] Nadav Safran speculates that Soviet intelligence agencies subsequently learned of an Israeli contingency plan for an attack on Syria, suggesting that an Israeli General Staff document must somehow have fallen into Soviet hands, but does not offer any evidence on when or how this might have occurred (though he does conclude that the USSR passed on some information to Nasser before May 13).[27]

Regardless of the success of Soviet intelligence in uncovering Israeli plans, political warnings of the possibility of a serious escalation in the fighting were available to the Politburo through open sources. Prime Minister Eshkol, addressing a Labor Party meeting on May 11, stated that if fedayeen activities continued, Israel would be forced to take retaliatory measures "no less drastic than those of 7 April."[28] He repeated this warning in stronger terms in a speech on May 13:

> We have furnished proof that we shall not permit our borders to be open to attack. We have proved that, to their attempts to pick easy and exposed targets, we were able to respond at a place, time and by a method of our own choosing. . . . If they try to sow unrest on our borders—unrest will come to theirs.[29]

Eshkol's speech was probably very alarming to a group of leaders sensitive to political signals of the risk of escalation. Kosygin, in his June 19 speech to the United Nations, stated that the USSR had learned that Israel was planning to attack Syria on May 9.[30] Continued threats of some form of retaliation by Israel, in the absence of any attempts at restraint by the United States, must have created the impression that a major escalation of the conflict that neither the United States nor the USSR could control was highly probable. Regardless of the provenance or accuracy of Soviet intelligence reports, it is clear that the Politburo became very concerned in early May that an attack on Syria might be imminent. As it is not possible to determine exactly when reports of the Israeli contingency plan reached the Politburo, the adoption of the plan will serve as the start of the second phase of the crisis, May 7 to May 14, which will be referred to as the Israeli Warnings phase. Kosygin's speech strongly indicates that the Politburo perceived a high level of autonomous risk and very urgent time pressure during this period.

The third phase begins with the activation of the Egyptian-Syrian mutual defense treaty on May 14 and the subsequent mobilization of the Egyptian armed forces.[31] While the Egyptian mobilization increase heightened the risk of war, it served temporarily to relieve Syria of the immediate threat of Israeli attack. Several Soviet commentators soon emphasized that even though Syria was still menaced by Israeli aggression, the regime in Cairo was a reliable ally that would aid Damascus in the Ba'ath's hour of need.[32] Nasser's placement of Egyptian forces on a higher state of readiness meant that if Israel were to attack Syria, Egypt's not inconsiderable conventional forces would be capable of rendering prompt assistance to the imperiled Ba'ath. Any need for urgent Soviet action to protect Syria would thereby be reduced. Israel's need to fight a two-front war would increase the time available for defusing the crisis, or at worst obtaining a cease-fire, before Damascus could be seriously threatened. Consequently, the level of time pressure felt by Soviet decision makers was likely to be lower. The alert could not be expected to completely deter Israeli military action, however, and could raise the likelihood of Israeli-Egyptian military conflict, so autonomous risk remained high. The third phase of the crisis may therefore be regarded as a period during that time pressure was moderately low while autonomous risk remained high,. Because this phase began with the Egyptian mobilization order on May 14, it will be named the Egyptian Mobilization phase.

This less tense period, however, lasted only until May 20, when UAR forces began preparations to blockade the Strait of Tiran. An Egyptian parachute battalion dropped that day at Sharm el-Sheikh, and the United Nations Emergency Force contingent occupying the area completed its evacuation the following day.[33] By the time Nasser's speech announcing the blockade of the strait was broadcast in the early morning of May 23, it became apparent to the USSR that Egypt's action, and Israel's mobilization in response to it, had created a situation where war could break out at any moment. The Soviet press carried commentaries warning that tensions in the Middle East had reached a dangerous level and that there was an urgent threat of an Israeli attack, probably against Syria and possibly abetted by collusion with America.[34] The Tiran Blockade phase from May 20 until June 5 can therefore be said to have been characterized, from a Soviet viewpoint, by high time pressure as well as high autonomous risk.

The events of June 5 proved that Soviet expectations of an Israeli attack were well founded. The Politburo was probably surprised and somewhat relieved, however, to find that Egypt and Jordan, rather than Syria, were the targets of the initial ground offensives. The USSR's stronger allies had been attacked first, relieving the pressure on Syria, at least for the moment. Soviet official statements issued during the first four days of the war sharply condemned the Israeli attack and emphasized that the USSR and its "fraternal socialist" allies "reserve[d] the right to take all necessary steps" to halt aggression in the region, but they did not mention the need for immediate action.[35] By the morning of June 9, Egypt, Jordan, and Syria had accepted the cease-fire called for in two U.N. resolutions (a third would be passed that afternoon) and land combat had virtually stopped.[36]

Until the Israeli offensive against Syria began in earnest, the USSR might well have entertained hopes that the war could be ended without a renewed threat to the Ba'ath. Because a serious threat to Syria did not manifest itself until nightfall on June 9, when Israeli troops reached the edge of the Golan Heights, the Sinai Offensive phase of the Middle East crisis from the morning of June 5 until the evening of June 9 should be regarded as a period in which autonomous risk was very great, but pressure for rapid Soviet action was temporarily reduced because Syria was not immediately threatened.

The success of the Golan Heights offensive posed a serious threat to the USSR's most vulnerable interests in the Middle East. Soviet decision makers could not be certain that Israeli forces would stop at the edge of the heights until Israel accepted a cease-fire on the afternoon of June 10. The fall of Damascus would have had disastrous consequences for the Ba'ath and for Soviet influence in the region, and any actions intended to forestall an attack on the Syrian capital would have to be taken with all possible speed. What the Soviet leadership did, could have done, or threatened to do to protect Damascus will be discussed later. The possibility of a continued Israeli offensive indicates that autonomous risk was high during this phase. This is supported by the language of the Soviet note announcing the breach in diplomatic relations between the USSR and Israel, delivered on June 10, which states that "Information was just received to the effect that Israeli troops . . . are proceeding in the direction of Damascus."[37] TASS reported in dispatches datelined June 10 that Israeli tanks had captured Qunaytira and would continue on to Damascus.[38]

The hot-line message that Kosygin sent to Johnson on the same day, before the cease-fire became effective, warns that a "very crucial moment" was at hand and that the USSR would act unless military operations ceased within the next few hours.[39] The message conveys the perception of very high time pressure. The final Golan Offensive phase of the crisis, from the evening of June 9 until the cease-fire on the afternoon of June 10, was therefore a period of both great time pressure and very high autonomous risk from a Soviet perspective.

Table 2 summarizes the values of the independent variables this study expects to have influenced Soviet decision making during the six phases of the 1967 crisis. During the Border Clashes and Sinai Offensive phases, time pressure was relatively low, while the level of autonomous risk was relatively high. The Egyptian Mobilization phase was a period of moderate to low time pressure and high autonomous risk, while the Tiran Blockade phase was characterized by high values for both independent variables. During the Israeli Warnings and Golan Offensive phases, high levels of time pressure were combined with very high autonomous risk and serious perceived threat to the Soviet Union's vulnerable Syrian allies. Because a pronounced element of autonomous risk ran throughout the 1967 crisis, the case of the Six-Day War and the events leading up to it can serve to test the effect of variations in time pressure on the ability of Soviet leaders to cope with value conflict in a situation involving a relatively high degree of uncontrollable risk.

With the independent variables valued as in Table 2, the value conflict approach would expect that Soviet leaders would be least likely to take risks in support of a strategy of coercion in phases 1 and 5, the Border Clashes and Sinai Offensive phases. Coercive risk-taking would be more likely in phase 3 (Egyptian Mobilization) and still more likely in phase 4 (Tiran Blockade). Phases 2 and 6, the Israeli Warnings and Golan Offensive phases,

Table 2   Time Pressure and Autonomous Risk in the 1967 Crisis

Phase	Date	Time Pressure	Autonomous Risk	Likelihood of Risk-taking
1. Border Clashes	April 7–May 6	Low	Moderately High	Moderately Low
2. Israeli Warnings	May 7–May 14	High	Very High	Very High
3. Egyptian Mobilization	May 14–May 20	Moderate	High	Moderately High
4. Tiran Blockade	May 20–June 4	High	High	High
5. Sinai Offensive	June 5–June 9	Low	High	Moderately Low
6. Golan Offensive	June 9–June 10	High	Very High	Very High

are the periods when this study expects the Politburo to have been most likely to take risks in an attempt to pursue simultaneously the USSR's conflicting regional and global objectives. During these two phases, when conditions were least favorable for successful value integration and trade-off between global and regional objectives, the Politburo would be most likely to tilt the balance between coercion and accommodation in favor of increased coerciveness, and consequently greater risk-taking.

An explanation of Soviet behavior that structures the crisis as a game of chicken, on the other hand, would expect that the USSR would be least likely to take risks in phase 2, more likely in phases 3 and 4, still more likely in phases 1 and 5, and most likely in the final phase, following Israel's acceptance of a cease-fire. A logical strategy for a chicken game would prescribe coercive opening moves followed by a swing toward accommodation, with an empty coercive gesture made after the conflict was resolved.

The next section will look at actual Soviet behavior during the crisis in order to determine when the Politburo adopted more accommodative courses of action and when it acted most coercively, and in so doing accepted greater risks. A pattern of greater coercive risk-taking when time pressure and autonomous risk were lowest would indicate a strategy determined by relative bargaining power; a strategy of greater risk-taking when time pressure and autonomous risk were highest, however, would indicate increased coerciveness due to defensive avoidance and other effects of value conflict. In order to obtain collaborating evidence of the role played by value conflict in the Politburo's decisions during the crisis, the next section will also look for textual indicators in Soviet communications that suggest how Soviet decision makers resolved, accepted, or attempted to deny the contradictions between their regional and global goals.

Soviet Communications and Actions in the 1967 Crisis

This section will examine each phase of the 1967 crisis for evidence of cognitive effects on Soviet decision making. More evidence is available for the later phases of the conflict than for the early periods, but the published documents, public and private statements, and press commentaries issued throughout the Arab-Israeli confrontation give indications that varying levels of time pressure and autonomous risk had a noticeable impact on Soviet decisions and actions during the crisis. This impact may be seen not only in the content of messages, but in their tone and means of delivery as well as timing.

The most important point about the official Soviet response to the Lake Tiberias clash, which began the crisis' initial Border Clashes phase, may be that it was not issued until 14 days after the event. This indicates that the Politburo took advantage of the time available to discuss the situation before deciding to deliver an official protest, which warned that "Israeli aggression" would have "serious consequences" and suggested that Israel consider its actions carefully, but did not threaten to take any action.[40] This protest was read out to Israeli Ambassador Katz on May 21 by Deputy Foreign Minister Malik in Moscow, who refused to tender a written copy at the time, and the note was not published until April 26.[41] This may indicate an unwillingness to commit the USSR publicly to any course of action at this stage of the conflict. A subsequent message to Katz cautioned Israel to "not allow external forces to play with the fate of its people and State," but did not say that Soviet action would be part of the consequences of military operations against Syria.[42]

Commentators in the Soviet press during this period charged that the United States and other "imperialist" powers were conspiring with Israel to destabilize Egypt and Syria and stressed that Syrian-Egyptian solidarity or unity of progressive forces in the Arab world would oppose such plots.[43] No hint of Soviet involvement in the conflict was in evidence other than affirmation that "the people of the USSR are with Syria" in its struggle with "imperialism."[44] Because the situation did not demand immediate Soviet action, and because suggestions that the USSR might become more closely involved could have adversely affected both regional and global interests, it is hardly surprising that no effort was made to advertise the possibility of Soviet intervention in the conflict. In general, communications from Moscow during this first phase suggest that the Politburo was concerned, but would try to keep its options open.

In the second phase, by contrast, the USSR played a crucial role in the escalation of the conflict. Some time before May 11, Soviet officials began sending the UAR warnings of an imminent Israeli attack on Syria. David Kimche and Dan Bawly report that an "urgent Soviet message" of an impending attack was delivered to Cairo and Damascus before Israeli Prime Minister Eshkol's speech on May 11.[45] This message may have been prompted by the interception of Israeli General Staff documents, as Safran postulates, but this possibility cannot be confirmed until and unless the relevant Soviet documents are declassified.[46] Regardless of whether Soviet intelligence had learned of the cabinet's contingency plan, it is easy to understand why the Politburo might have been concerned by the implications of Eshkol's speech, in which he said that "drastic measures" might be required to respond to Syrian actions.[47]

Subsequent Soviet communications became more specific about the timing of the upcoming Israeli strike. A second message through diplomatic channels warned that the attack would commence at 0400 on May 17.[48] Details on the provenance or exact date of this message have proven elusive, but several other sources report Soviet efforts to pass warnings of an imminent Israeli attack. Anwar Sadat's memoirs include a firsthand account of one such communication. He reports that on May 13, as he was preparing to return to Cairo after heading an official visit of a delegation from the Egyptian National Assembly to Moscow, he was given an alarming message:

> I was seen off at Moscow airport by Mr. Semenov, the Soviet Deputy Foreign Minister, who was accompanied by the Speaker of the Soviet Parliament. The plane was more than an hour late, that gave us a chance to talk at length, mostly about the Syrian situation. They told me specifically that ten Israeli brigades had been concentrated on the Syrian border. When I arrived back in Cairo, I realized that the Soviet Union had informed Nasser of this.[49]

This "confirmed" a message from Syrian Defense Minister Assad to Egyptian Marshal Amer, sent the same day, that Israel was massing its forces.[50]

In fact, however, Israeli forces were making no such preparations at the time, and one account claims that the Egyptian General Fawzi reported as much to Nasser.[51] While the exact source of the information that led Soviet leaders to expect an Israeli attack cannot be determined, Eshkol's May 13 speech was one of several signals that the Politburo may have interpreted as political warnings of an Israeli offensive. In a speech before the United Nations after the war, Kosygin claimed that the Knesset had given the Israeli Government the go-ahead for an attack against Syria.

On 9 May 1967 the Israeli Parliament authorized the government of Israel to carry out military operations against Syria. The Israeli troops began concentrating at the Syrian borders, and mobilization was carried out.... At that time, the Soviet government, and I believe others also, began receiving information to the effect that the Israeli government had chosen the end of May as the time for a swift strike at Syria in order to crush it and then planned to carry the fighting over into the territory of the United Arab Republic.[52]

This "authorization" may refer to the Israeli cabinet decision, taken on May 7, to develop a contingency plan for a strike against Syria, of which Soviet intelligence may have apprised the Politburo.[53]

Richard B. Parker has recently suggested that Soviet leaders may have actually believed Israel was concentrating its forces for an attack, despite all the evidence to the contrary that was made available to them.[54] (Prime Minister Eshkol even invited Chuvakhin to tour the area to see for himself that Israeli troops were not massing for an attack on Syria, but the Soviet ambassador refused, saying that his function was to "communicate Soviet truths, not to put them to the test.")[55] Parker concludes that the Politburo believed reports of Israeli preparations to attack Damascus were plausible enough to be passed on to Egypt and that the Egyptians seized upon them because they fit with their perceptions of Israel.[56] As he acknowledges, however, there is no direct evidence to support this interpretation, and given the refusal of Soviet officials to verify the facts, the conclusion that the Politburo deliberately passed on false reports appears more plausible.

In any event, Soviet warnings appear to have had a major impact on Nasser's decision to mobilize. Referring to Sadat's meeting with Semenov at the airport, Heikal contends that these warnings were the primary reason for the Egyptian mobilization:

Not a great deal of credence had been attached to the Syrian reports, but now that they were confirmed by the Russians Sadat naturally felt they must be taken extremely seriously.... It was on the basis of these warnings that on May 16 [sic] Nasser proclaimed a state of emergency and decided to send troops into Sinai.[57]

Because one of the objectives of Heikal's version of the events leading up to the Six-Day War is to blame the USSR for the UAR's defeat, it is likely that he exaggerates the impact of the Soviet reports.

It is clear that Soviet reports of preparations for an attack on Syria were not the only factors that prompted the Egyptian mobilization. It is not clear whether the overestimation of Israeli belligerence reflected in the reports was deliberate or unintentional. Georgii Mirskii attributes it to a desire by Soviet intelligence analysts to err on the side of caution.[58] If this was in fact the case, Soviet caution served to facilitate Egyptian reckless-ness. While the Soviet warnings temporarily alleviated the danger to Syria, in the following weeks they would strongly contribute to a dangerous es-calation of the conflict.

Very little about the situation in the Middle East appeared in the Soviet press during the Israeli Warnings phase of the crisis, although *Izvestiia* re-ported that the United States and Israel were planning a coup against the Ba'ath, which was to be signaled by an Israeli attack.[59] Accounts of troop concentrations on the Israeli-Syrian border did not appear until May 16.[60] When Katz called at the Foreign Ministry in Moscow on May 22 to protest the portrayal of Israeli actions toward Syria in the Soviet press, his inter-locutor responded, "We cannot be responsible for what is happening in the atmosphere which was poisoned by your leader's statements."[61]

Predictably, reportage in the third or Egyptian Mobilization phase cen-tered on the UAR's mobilization in response to the threat of an Israeli attack. Israel was again admonished against "playing with fire," and a fresh round of accusations of a plot against Syria appeared.[62] Most reports stressed, how-ever, that the UAR and other Arab countries would come to Syria's aid if Is-rael were to launch an attack.[63] While the press was full of nebulous references to "imperialist plots," *Pravda* and *Izvestiia* did not emphasize the possibility of direct American military intervention in the conflict, while *Krasnaia zvezda* and *Trud* specifically mentioned that the Sixth Fleet, a "gen-darme" force, could be preparing to participate actively in Israeli machina-tions against Syria.[64] This could indicate that some differences of opinion on the likelihood of American action existed within the Politburo during this period, but the evidence for this is inconclusive. In general, communications from Moscow conveyed the message that "Arab solidarity" would be suffi-cient to meet the Israeli threat. This formula may have been a signal that the Politburo was not prepared at that point to commit the USSR to interven-tion in the conflict.

The start of the fourth phase of the crisis was marked by the UAR's preparations to blockade the Strait of Tiran, which appears to have taken So-viet decision makers by surprise.[65] The Politburo was well aware that the blockade greatly increased the possibility of armed conflict, but it could not publicly blame Egypt for the heightened danger of war. Therefore, when re-ports of the blockade began to appear in the Soviet press, commentators speculated that war might begin with an American attempt to break the blockade. *Krasnaia zvezda* reported on May 26 that the United States was threatening to use naval forces to break the blockade.[66] Other papers ran items the next day that said that the "interventionist" Sixth Fleet, "the har-binger of previous invasions," was menacing Egypt and Syria.[67] These re-ports were premature, however, as major units of the Sixth Fleet did not actually begin concentrating in the eastern Mediterranean until May 30, while the aircraft carrier *Intrepid* passed through the Suez Canal on June 1.[68]

Most Soviet diplomatic activity during the Tiran Blockade phase sought to avoid war. A Soviet government note issued on May 23 warned of the danger of war and stated that Israeli aggression would meet a united front of Soviet, socialist, and Arab resistance:

> [L]et no one have any doubts about the fact that should anyone try to unleash aggression in the Near East he would be met not only by the united strength of Arab countries but also by strong opposition to aggression from the Soviet Union and all peace-loving states. . . . Taking due account of the situation, the Soviet Union is doing and will continue to do everything in its power to prevent a violation of peace and security in the Near East and safeguard the legitimate rights of peoples.[69]

Kosygin mentioned this note to UAR Defense Minister Badran, who arrived in Moscow on May 24, and told him that Egypt must avoid giving Israel or the United States any pretext to launch an attack.[70] Sadat recalls that "the Soviet Union consistently warned that the tempo of events was moving faster than it should."[71] Early in the morning of May 26, Soviet ambassador Pozhidaev implored Nasser not to attack in dramatic fashion:

> [T]he Soviet Ambassador went to Nasser's house without an appointment. It was three o'clock in the morning of May 26. He asked for the President to be wakened. The Ambassador explained to Nasser that he had received orders from the Soviet leadership to see him immediately. He had to tell Nasser that the Americans had contacted the Kremlin and told the Russians that the Israelis had information that the Egyptians were going to attack at first light. He said that if that was true, the Soviet Union urged the President not to go ahead with his plans because whoever fired the first shot would be in an untenable political position. As friends, they advised Egypt not to fire that shot.[72]

Heikal also contends, however, that some Soviet back-channel communications conveyed a different message. He reports that on May 29, as Soviet Defense Minister Grechko saw Badran off on his return to Cairo, Grechko told Badran, "Stand firm. Whatever you have to face, you will find us with you. Don't let yourselves be blackmailed by the Americans or anyone else."[73] Heikal also relates that Nasser received reports from Syrian President Atassi that said "various Soviet sources" had told Atassi during a visit to Moscow that "everything would turn out all right" without a lessening of Egyptian pressure on Israel.[74] (Again, it should be noted that Heikal sought to implicate the Soviet Union in the defeat of its Arab allies.)

In any case, a preponderance of evidence indicates that the Politburo genuinely attempted to reduce tensions during the Tiran Blockade phase, but some conflicting signals sent by Soviet officials may have worked to undermine its efforts. Throughout the phase, the Soviet press reported that America and Israel were preparing to attack.

The reports were half right. The crisis' fifth phase began with devastating Israeli air attacks that were immediately followed by rapid advances in the Sinai and the West Bank. As Egypt and Jordan bore the brunt of the initial ground offensives on June 5, however, Syria was not in immediate danger. The Soviet government made good use of the time made available by the fact that Damascus was not Israel's first target. Soviet diplomats repeatedly pressed for a cease-fire at the United Nations.[75] A Soviet official statement issued on the day the war began condemned the Israeli attack, demanded that Israeli forces immediately withdraw to the prewar armistice lines, and in closing, combined an appeal for multilateral action with a vague hint that the USSR might eventually find it necessary to act unilaterally.

> The Government of the USSR expresses the hope that the Governments of other States, including the Great Powers, will on their part do everything in their power to extinguish the military conflagration in the Near East. The Soviet Government reserves the right to take all steps that may be necessitated by the situation.[76]

A note to Israel sent on June 7 used similar language, but neither communiqué was specific about what those "necessary measures" could involve.[77] In addition to using the U.N. Security Council and bilateral diplomacy to attempt to secure a cease-fire, the Politburo sought to create a united socialist front in opposition to Israel's actions by convening a meeting of leaders of the Warsaw Pact countries and Yugoslavia in Moscow on June 9.[78] The joint communiqué issued that same day stressed the unity of the socialist states and "progressive" movements worldwide in opposition to Israeli aggression.

> Today more than ever firm and united action is needed on the part of all peace-loving and progressive forces and of all who value the cause of national freedom and independence.
>
> Unless the Government of Israel halts its attack and withdraws its troops behind the armistice line, the socialist States which have signed the present statement will do everything necessary to help the peoples of the Arab countries give a firm rebuff to the aggressor, to protect their lawful rights, to eliminate the hotbed of war in the Near East and to restore peace in that area.[79]

The effort reflected in the communiqué to display socialist unity against Israel was not entirely successful, however, as Rumania refused to sign it.

The USSR's Egyptian allies were not satisfied with these diplomatic efforts and were angered when more concrete Soviet support was not forthcoming. Marshal Amer upbraided the Soviet ambassador to Cairo on June 6, claiming that Pozhidaev's late-night call on Nasser was evidence of a Soviet-American conspiracy: "It is you who prevented us from making the first strike. You deprived us of the initiative. That is collusion!"[80] Soviet military forces scrupulously avoided provocative activity during this phase of the crisis. The Soviet navy's Mediterranean squadron slightly increased its shadowing of Sixth Fleet vessels, and a Soviet cruiser approached within five miles of the carrier *America* on June 8, but there is no evidence that Soviet military units attempted a show of force in the region or elsewhere during this period.[81]

The Soviet press resounded throughout the Sinai Offensive phase of the conflict with condemnations of the Israeli attack. Many commentators predicted that Israel's actions would bring disaster upon itself.[82] The United States was frequently accused of knowing of and encouraging the surprise attack. Vishnevetskiy, possibly the most vehement denouncer of U.S. policy during this period, charged America with "pouring gasoline on the flames" of the conflict.[83] Israel's methods and tactics were described as inspired by, or designed to be direct copies of, American actions in Vietnam.[84] Britain, West Germany, and Western oil companies were also accused of complicity in the Israeli attack.[85]

Despite these denunciations, the Soviet press indicated that Soviet intervention to halt the Israeli offensive was not likely. Items referred repeatedly to Soviet government statements and Soviet calls for a cease-fire in the U.N. Security Council as evidence of the "resolute support" of the USSR and other socialist countries for the Arab cause.[86] One writer in *Krasnaia zvezda* did say that "urgent steps are necessary to put an end to aggression," but he did not elaborate on the measures he felt the situation demanded.[87] For the most part, however, Soviet press reports and commentaries stressed during this phase of the crisis that although Egypt and Syria might lose the war, "Arab solidarity" would eventually defeat Israel and restore peace.[88] "V. Petrov" summed up the prospects for an ultimate Arab victory by observing that Israel could not hope to fight 100 million Arabs or the "stream of history."[89]

It soon became obvious, however, that Israel had won a major victory, and near the end of the crisis it may have appeared to Moscow that Israel would attempt to deal Syria a crushing blow. The sixth and final phase of the crisis began on the night of June 9, when Israeli forces began positioning themselves for an assault on Qunaytira, a strategically important city overlooking the Damascus plain and a primary objective of the phase's eponymous Golan offensive. Soon after Syrian troops abandoned Qunaytira, in the morning of June 10, Soviet diplomatic activity showed signs of expectation that the worst was yet to come.

After the U.N. Security Council had received reports that Qunaytira had been taken, but before Israeli forces had actually occupied it, Soviet U.N. Ambassador Fedorenko told the Council that the Soviet government had decided to break off relations with Israel.[90] That same day, Katz was summoned to the Soviet Foreign Ministry to receive the note that announced the severance of relations. The note began by claiming that Israeli forces were advancing toward Damascus and then issued a stern warning:

> The Government of the Soviet Union warns the Government of Israel that it will bear the full weight of responsibility for its treachery, for the flagrant violation of the Security Council resolution.
>
> If Israel does not immediately cease military operations, the Soviet Union, together with all peace-loving countries, will apply sanctions against Israel with all the consequences resulting therefrom.[91]

Soviet Ambassador Chuvakhin delivered an identical message to Israeli Foreign Minister Abba Eban in Tel Aviv that afternoon. Eban does not give an exact time for the receipt of this message, but indicates that Chuvakhin arrived after Israeli forces occupied Qunaytira. He also relates that the Soviet ambassador's eyes filled with tears after he read out the communiqué.[92]

It is impossible to say whether the break in relations with Israel was intended to show support for the USSR's Arab allies without making definite commitments, to save face and transfer the blame for policy bungling, to prepare the way for possible military action, or all of the above. In any case, the language of the note indicates an attempt on the part of Soviet leaders to transfer the onus of responsibility for subsequent developments from themselves onto their opponents. Any signal intended to demonstrate resolve during a crisis, of course, does this to some extent, so this external communication does not by itself constitute strong evidence that defensive avoidance was influencing Soviet decision making. About the same time as the message was delivered, however, Israeli forces were continuing to move into Qunaytira.[93] The decision to break relations must have been made, therefore, while some possibility of continued fighting still existed. The timing of the message and the political cost of the severance of relations suggest that it was more than an empty face-saving gesture.

Another communication from the Politburo sent that same day, whatever its intention, caused considerable consternation in Washington. The Soviet action during the crisis that most alarmed the United States was the transmission of the hot-line message on June 10. The message, signed by Kosygin, said that a "very crucial moment" that threatened a "great catastrophe" had arrived, and warned that unless Israel halted all military operations within the next few hours, the USSR would take "necessary actions, including military."[94] Johnson ordered the Sixth Fleet closer to the Syrian coast in response to this communication.[95]

Fukuyama describes Kosygin's message as a bluff designed to display support for the USSR's allies after the real danger of an Israeli attack on Damascus had passed.[96] The chronology of events on June 10 casts doubt on this interpretation. Israeli Prime Minister Eshkol and Defense Minister Dayan met with the United Nations Truce Supervision Organization chief of staff, General Odd Bull, at 1200 GMT and agreed to a cease-fire as of 1630.[97] Johnson received the hot-line message only one hour after this meeting, at 1300 GMT.[98] It is not likely that a report of this meeting could have been sent to Moscow (either through the U.N. or Soviet intelligence), the information communicated to the Politburo and verified, and a hot-line message composed and sent to Washington, all within the space of one hour. Furthermore, there were also indications that Israeli forces were still advancing both before and after the time Kosygin's message was received in Washington. Israeli troops had not secured Qunaytira until 1230 GMT, shortly before the hot-line message was received, and additional forces were arriving at the city at 1400 GMT.[99] These troop movements could easily have raised suspicions that the announced cease-fire might not hold. The American reaction to the message increased the possibility of a U.S.-Soviet or U.S.-Syrian incident, raising the risk of a confrontation that the USSR had sought to avoid.

Kosygin's message therefore heightened the risk of escalation while the war was still hours away from its end. Both the short time between the acceptance of the cease-fire and the hot-line message as well as the developments in the Golan Heights, which probably appeared threatening from a Soviet viewpoint, strongly suggest that the hot-line message was not a face-saving gesture made after the crisis was over, but an action that Soviet leaders knew to involve a significant element of risk.

As the Golan Offensive phase of the crisis lasted less than 24 hours, the Soviet press had only a short time in which to comment on the Golan Heights fighting and the threat to Damascus. Commentaries appearing during and shortly after the last stage of the fighting, echoing the language of the June 9 joint communiqué, called for "resolute joint action" to rebuff Israeli aggression.[100] Dymov, in *Krasnaia zvezda*, excoriated Israel for "trying to take the opportunity to advance as far as possible" into Syria and argued that the "widest support" from socialist countries, especially the USSR, had great bearing on the situation.[101] It is difficult to determine whether this comment should be interpreted as a call for greater Soviet support of its Arab allies or an attempt to take credit for halting the Israeli offensive.

After the war, Soviet leaders claimed repeatedly that support from the USSR and the socialist community played a decisive role in bringing the conflict to a close. The CPSU plenum held on June 20 and 21 debated Soviet policy during the crisis and reaffirmed Soviet solidarity with the UAR, Syria, Algeria, and progressive forces within the Arab world, while calling for a political solution to the Arab-Israeli conflict. The resolution adopted at the plenum credited the "united front" approach with achieving the cease-fire that ended the war.

> The plenary session notes that the swift, resolute, and joint actions of the Soviet Union and other socialist states played an important role in the cessation of hostilities in the Near East. . . . The Central Committee plenary session states with satisfaction that the fraternal socialist states that signed the Statement of 9 June 1967 acted together, shoulder to shoulder, at a crucial moment in the development of international affairs. It was confirmed once again that the joint action of socialist countries is a potent factor in the struggle against the aggressive schemes of international imperialism.[102]

The resolution also warned against allowing the People's Republic of China (PRC) to expand its influence in the Middle East, a concern voiced earlier by "V. Petrov" in *Izvestiia.*[103] Brezhnev sounded similar notes in his speech to graduates of Soviet military academies on July 5, in which he praised the role played by Soviet-led joint action in resolving the conflict:

> In the very first days of the Israeli aggression, the Soviet Union, in close unity with other socialist states and in constant contact with the Arab countries, took energetic measures to stay the hand of the aggressor, protect the lawful interests of the Arab peoples, terminate the armed conflict and prevent it from increasing to proportions endangering all of mankind. Looking back today, we can say confidently that our actions in the critical days of the Near East crisis were correct.[104]

There is, nevertheless, some evidence of recriminations following the crisis. The removals of Nikolai Yegorichev (from the leadership of the Moscow CPSU Central Committee) and Aleksandr Shelepin (from the Ministry of Light Industry) may have been linked to their policies on the Middle East during the war, and Ambassadors Pozhidaev and Chuvakhin were replaced without receiving new appointments.[105] These personnel changes cannot be taken as indications of post-decisional regret, however, because dismissals and demotions are normal consequences of policy failures and do not necessarily reflect on the process by which the regretted decisions were made.

Value Conflict and Soviet Decision Making in 1967

What do Soviet statements and actions in the 1967 crisis reveal about the effects of value conflict on Soviet decision making? In phases 1, 3, and 5, Soviet communications and actions indicate that the Politburo accepted the contradictions between its global and regional objectives and acted to limit risks. Soviet behavior in phases 2 and 6, on the other hand, provides evidence of increased coercive risk-taking in attempts to simultaneously avoid confrontation with the United States and maintain Soviet influence over regional allies. The evidence from phase 4 appears mixed.

In the phases of the crisis where autonomous risk was high while time pressure was at low or moderate levels, Soviet decision makers made gestures in support of both regional and global objectives, but did not take great risks in pursuit of either. Israel's actions of April 7, at the start of the Border Clashes phase, were answered only with an official protest on April 21.[106] The delay indicates that the Politburo used the time available to make compromises between its contradictory goals and achieve consensus on a response to the Lake Tiberias incidents. Similarly, when the initial Israeli offensives on June 5 (during the Sinai Offensive phase) were directed against Egypt and Jordan rather than Syria, Soviet leaders took advantage of the brief period when the Syrian Ba'ath was not in immediate danger to convene a meeting of other socialist states in an effort to build a united front in support of its Arab allies. Although the resulting Moscow Declaration indicated some dissension in the socialist camp (from Rumania), the meeting offered the opportunity for Soviet decision makers to gauge the strength of support that the USSR's Eastern European allies were willing to extend before engaging in more forceful actions.[107]

While the views of Yugoslavia and the USSR's Warsaw Pact allies may have had little influence in the decision adopted, the effort to show socialist solidarity offered a means to display political support for the Arab allies without making a commitment to intervene in the war. Throughout the crisis, the theme of solidarity and joint action appeared in official communications and the press as a signal that strong material or military support would not be immediately forthcoming. During the Egyptian Mobilization phase (May 14–20), commentators stressed that Arab solidarity, backed up by Soviet support, would be sufficient to deter an Israeli attack.[108] After this deterrent failed, the Politburo convened the June 9 Moscow conference (during phase 5) to assess and rally the support of its Warsaw Pact allies for "resolute joint action" to stop the fighting.[109] Press commentaries in the fifth phase likewise conveyed the message that unity among progressive forces in the Arab world, reinforced by Soviet support, would eventually turn the tide and erase the gains made by the Israeli offensive.[110]

While the emphasis on solidarity seems to indicate a lack of Soviet willingness to take risks in support of the Arab allies, efforts to depict the United States as an imperialist aggressor and portray Israel as its lackey—intended as music to Arab ears—continued during the Border Clashes, Egyptian Mobilization, and Sinai Offensive phases.[111] The goal of maintaining Soviet influence in the region was thereby not completely abandoned, and political conflict with the United States was heightened somewhat during the first, third, and fifth phases. This indicates that while avoidance of a Soviet-American confrontation was probably valued higher than increasing Soviet influence in the Middle East during these periods, risk-limiting compromises were made on both regional and global Soviet objectives. In addition, measures intended to insure that the USSR's allies were "on board," to obtain information (including dissenting views) from a wide variety of sources, and to secure cooperation from many groups that could affect, or must implement, decisions were key components of vigilant information processing. There is no direct evidence that the Politburo actively sought out opposing viewpoints during any phase of the crisis, but it nevertheless received one from Rumania at the June 9 Moscow conference. These statements and actions indicate acceptance of a value conflict and achievement of a compromise between opposing goals.

The evidence of the effect of value conflict on Soviet risk-taking in the fourth or Tiran Blockade phase (May 20–June 4) is not clear. Heikal's accounts indicate that Soviet behavior in this period was characterized by contradictory signals. On May 29, three days after Pozhidaev demanded to see Nasser in the middle of the night to plead with the Egyptian president not to attack, Marshal Grechko, the Soviet defense minister, told his Egyptian counterpart to "stand firm" and resist American pressure to deescalate the conflict.[112] Similarly, while Badran was being told by Kosygin not to give the United States or Israel any pretext for an attack, Atassi received assurances in Moscow that continuation of the Egyptian blockade would result in a favorable resolution of the crisis.[113] These accounts, however, are not confirmed by other sources.

The reports of mixed signals may reflect differences within the Soviet leadership on how to proceed, but there is insufficient evidence to determine whether this was the case. By the same token, the Soviet press exaggerated the danger of Western naval intervention during this phase.[114] However, it is impossible to determine if these statements reflect deliberate inflation of Western belligerence for propaganda purposes or a genuine concern over the possibility of an American attack or U.S.-Israeli collusion. In any event, Soviet leaders generally did not exhibit an increased propensity to accept risks during the Tiran Blockade phase.

In phases 2 (Israeli Warnings, May 7–14) and 6 (Golan Offensive, June 9–10), on the other hand, Soviet actions indicate a significantly greater willingness to make coercive maneuvers and accept risks. In the second phase, the Soviet government engaged in a concerted effort to warn the UAR through multiple channels that an Israeli attack was imminent, when in fact it was not.[115] Soviet officials provided erroneous starting times for a mid-May offensive and expressed alarm at troop concentrations that did not exist.[116] These reports of Israeli preparations for an offensive had the desired effect on Nasser and the UAR's leadership, in that they increased Egyptian readiness to come to the defense of Syria. However, Soviet leaders could not have been ignorant of the risk that Nasser would order a further escalation of the crisis. Sadat relates how Nasser seized the opportunity for war with Israel in a meeting of the UAR Supreme Executive Council near the end of May:

> Nasser said, "Now with our concentrations in Sinai, the chances of war are fifty-fifty. But if we close the Strait, war will be a one hundred percent certainty." Then, turning to Amer, he asked: "Are the armed forces ready, Abdel Hakim?" Amer pointed to his neck and said: "On my own head be it, boss! Everything's in tiptop shape."[117]

Everything wasn't, of course, and it did fall on Amer's head: he was arrested on August 25 for allegedly plotting a coup, and committed suicide on September 14.[118]

Deterrence is a coercive strategy that requires both capability and commitment in order to attain a high probability of success. In early May 1967, the Politburo did not have Soviet conventional forces in place in the region capable of backing up a deterrent threat directed at Israel, and any move to introduce Soviet forces there would have lacked credibility due to the certainty of an American response. Deterrence of Israel, therefore, required the use of allied forces, that carried with it a heightened risk of loss of control. This risk would have been increased further if Nasser perceived the pressure for a defensive mobilization as an endorsement of military provocations or war against Israel. The Politburo therefore accepted a great risk of uncontrolled escalation of the regional conflict by attempting to deter a threat to its regional interests indirectly, in hopes of avoiding a confrontation with its primary global adversary. As the crisis unfolded, the potential for creation of an escalatory spiral inherent in the Politburo's strategy of coercion by proxy was realized. Their encouragement of an Egyptian mobilization, made on the basis of false or exaggerated information, served only to hamper both regional and global objectives and ultimately backfired catastrophically.

The hot-line message sent near the end of the crisis also involved a significant degree of risk. Kosygin's mention of the possibility of Soviet military intervention on June 10 (during the Golan Offensive phase) led to American actions that increased the chances of an accidental Soviet-American confrontation, although the chance of direct military conflict was never great. Eshkol and Dayan had stated that Israel would accept a cease-fire shortly before Johnson received the message.[119] Nevertheless, the situation on the Golan front may have been very worrisome for Soviet decision makers at the time the message was composed. The timing of the hot-line message is consistent with Snyder and Diesing's characterization of it as an effort to protect defeated allies from total humiliation, and such was clearly one of its objectives.[120] Another probable objective was to obtain greater American pressure on Israel to stop its offensive against Syria. Both of these possible goals for the hot line message involve strong elements of coercion at a time when the outcome of the conflict was still in doubt. Less risky face-saving measures, such as the draft U.N. General Assembly resolution condemning Israel that was proposed by Kosygin, were available to the Politburo and were adopted after the war's conclusion.[121] The hot-line message clearly represented an attempt at coercion in what proved to be (but might not have been) the final hours of the Six-Day War.

It is certainly unlikely that the Politburo planned to carry out the threat of military action the hot-line message implied. It is equally unlikely, however, that Kosygin's message was entirely bluff and bluster, as Fukuyama argues.[122] The Politburo's real intentions, which may remain forever undisclosed, most likely lay somewhere between these two extremes. The issuance of the message during a period when it was not at all clear that the just-agreed-upon cease-fire would be observed suggests that it was probably not an empty gesture made to give the Politburo political cover. It is more probable that this vague threat of Soviet intervention, issued during a period of intense time pressure and high autonomous risk, intentionally risked heightened U.S.-Soviet conflict in order to limit the losses to Soviet regional allies and interests.

Although the Politburo displayed greater willingness to accept risks during the Israeli Warnings and Golan Offensive periods (phases 2 and 6), it appeared unwilling to abandon either regional or global objectives. In the second phase, it attempted to use Egyptian forces to deter an expected attack on Syria without direct Soviet involvement, which would have provoked a U.S.-Soviet confrontation. The attempt to get the UAR to mobilize succeeded, but the effort to deter war failed. In the final phase, the hot-line message may have been an attempt to use American diplomatic pressure to dissuade Israel from advancing on Damascus, again avoiding direct commitment of Soviet forces. A stronger show of support for the USSR's regional allies was another likely goal of that communication, that in the short run served only to raise tensions unnecessarily.

Essentially, Soviet actions during these phases attempted to pursue both conflicting goals by attempting to manipulate other actors into working toward Soviet objectives. The attempt to manipulate Egypt succeeded in the short run but led to a disastrous failure, while the attempt to manipulate the United States did nothing but further antagonize Washington. Soviet actions in these phases did involve lower risks than direct intervention would have entailed. In both instances, however, Soviet behavior indicates that denial of value conflict prompted efforts to pursue contradictory goals, but these efforts were worse than useless.

To recap the empirical findings of the 1967 case, Soviet actions and statements indicate that Soviet decision makers acted more coercively and took greater risks during the phases 2 (Israeli Warnings, May 7–14) and 6 (Golan Offensive, June 9–10), when time pressure was high and autonomous risk was very high, than in the other phases of the crisis. The Politburo did not exhibit an enhanced tendency toward coercive risk-taking in the Tiran Blockade period (phase 4, May 20 - June 4), when indicators of both independent variables were high. In 1967, therefore, both Hypothesis One (Soviet risk-taking increases with time pressure) and Hypothesis Two (Soviet risk-taking increases with autonomous risk) are supported most strongly when the two independent variables vary together and when a very high level of autonomous risk is present (phases 2 and 6), and are also supported when time pressure is low but autonomous risk is moderately high or high (phases 1, 3, and 5). Curiously, the hypotheses are not supported in phase 4, where both are high. There is also significant evidence that Soviet decision makers compromised both regional and global goals during periods of moderate to low time pressure and high autonomous risk, but attempted to pursue both objectives by manipulating other actors when time pressure was high and autonomous risk was very great. This evidence is also consistent with the expectations of this study's analytical framework.

With regard to alternative explanations, Soviet behavior in 1967 runs contrary to the conventional wisdom produced by conceiving of Soviet crisis decision making as a U.S.-Soviet chicken game. This explanation predicts that coercive risk-taking will be greatest in periods of low time pressure and autonomous risk and least in evidence when time pressure and autonomous risk are high. Representing Soviet crisis decision making as a process driven by the acceptance and avoidance of value conflict therefore affords a better explanation of Soviet behavior, if not a perfect one.

Finally, an explanation that focuses on conflict between objectives can account for Soviet actions throughout the crisis, while contentions that the USSR had a predetermined strategy of stepping in to limit damage to its allies only after the crisis was resolved cannot adequately explain the variations observable in Soviet risk-taking behavior before and during the Six-Day War. The Politburo did act coercively near the end of the war to protect the USSR's Arab allies from complete destruction or humiliation, but its attempts at coercion earlier in the crisis set in motion an escalatory spiral that ultimately led to its allies' disastrous defeat.

Conclusions: The Soviet Role in the Outbreak of the Six-Day War

The leadership of the USSR played a pivotal role in the escalation from crisis to war in 1967. This chapter does not suggest that war would not have broken out if the USSR had not acted as it did, as the Arab-Israeli conflict has generated violence and war with depressing frequency. Instead, it contends that a study of the effects of value conflict on Soviet decision making can help explain how and why the USSR inadvertently contributed to the defeat of its Arab allies.

The evidence from the 1967 crisis generally supports this study's hypotheses on the effects of value conflict. When Soviet leaders appeared to accept that their goals were mutually opposing, they tended to compromise their regional aspirations in favor of global objectives and succeeded in limiting risks. When both Soviet regional and global objectives were jeopardized, however, it appears that Soviet decision makers did not compromise one value in favor of the other, but instead took greater risks in support of coercive moves that attempted to achieve both.

Attempts to manipulate others into supporting one's own interests are common in international politics. Soviet decision makers may have simply seized the opportunities for manipulation available in the 1967 crisis in order to facilitate denial of the conflict between Soviet goals. In other crises, the Politburo may have used different means to make risks more palatable. In any case, Soviet actions before and during the Six-Day War show that in their efforts to maintain influence in the Middle East, Soviet leaders took significant risks at crucial moments.

At these critical junctures, when conditions for successful value integration were least favorable, Soviet leaders acted more coercively than their relative bargaining power would lead us to expect. Representing Soviet crisis decision making as an attempt to deal with conflicts between goals therefore provides a better explanation of Soviet risk-taking in 1967 than conventional game-theoretic or empirical analyses, which predict that the Politburo would follow a predetermined strategy of accommodation during the crisis followed by bluffing after the conflict was over. Although further testing of the two hypotheses on Soviet coercive risk-taking is clearly required, an examination of the events of 1967 strongly suggests that Soviet leaders' failure to resolve the conflicts between their goals helps to explain why the actions of the Politburo were instrumental in the outbreak of a war the Soviet leaders strove earnestly to prevent.

FOUR

The War of Attrition, 1969–1970

Over the decades, our leadership has got in a huddle and, without any hint of glasnost, taken the secret decision not just once, and not just twice, to employ our armed forces far beyond the state's borders. Sometimes, as in the case of Egypt, this was, to all intents and purposes, a secret operation involving what really was a limited contingent of our troops. But just remember Hungary 1956, 1962 and the Caribbean crisis, 1968 and Czechoslovakia. The habit of using force in foreign policy was formed.

—Yevgeniy Kiselev
7 Dnia television program
February 25, 1990

The deployment of Soviet pilots and air defense units to Egypt in March 1970 marked the first time since the Second World War that Soviet combat troops were committed to action outside of a socialist country. This "secret" military operation was detected immediately by Israeli and Western intelligence and caused great apprehension in Washington and Tel Aviv, but almost 20 years would pass before it was openly discussed in the USSR. Gorbachev-era Soviet commentaries draw parallels between the Politburo's decision to send Soviet forces to Egypt in 1970 and the intervention in Afghanistan in 1979, implying that in both cases, decisions taken in secret took into account neither the true interests of the Soviet people nor the possible consequences of military action.[1]

The situation faced by the Politburo in 1970 noticeably differed from the crises of 1979 and 1967 in that during the War of Attrition, Soviet leaders had more time to consider their options before taking action. Several Western analyses of Soviet behavior in the period between March 1969 and

August 1970 conclude that this difference in time pressure is largely irrelevant, because Soviet strategy was decided upon before the point of highest tension in the conflict.[2] This chapter argues, however, that the USSR did not adhere to a predetermined strategy, and that while the factors of time pressure and autonomous risk did not weigh as heavily on Soviet decision makers in 1970 as they did in 1967 or 1973, these elements had a significant impact on the decision to risk Soviet troops in defense of Nasser's Egypt.

Examination of Soviet risk-taking during the War of Attrition will begin with an overview of Soviet interests in the region and of the points of conflict and concord between Soviet and American objectives regarding the Arab-Israeli conflict. The ways in which the initial stages of détente affected the contradictions between Soviet global and regional interests will receive special attention. Following this, two alternative interpretations of Soviet behavior in the crisis, both of which say that Soviet strategy was predetermined, will be outlined. Next, the Israeli-Egyptian military confrontation will be divided into six phases bounded by crucial events in the conflict. Changes in the levels of autonomous risk and time pressure weighing upon Soviet decision makers will then be assessed, and expectations on the likelihood of Soviet risk-taking will be derived for each phase.[3]

An analysis of Soviet statements and actions in each phase of the crisis will then show that Soviet leaders made the decision to send combat troops to Egypt at the point in the conflict where time pressure and autonomous risk were highest. This commitment of Soviet forces at a juncture when the fighting threatened to topple Nasser's regime indicates that the Politburo again acted most coercively when the contradictions between Soviet regional and global objectives became most acute. The available evidence does not support the alternative arguments that Soviet strategy was determined long before the point of highest tension or that Soviet leaders accepted risks only when the apex of the conflict had already passed. The chapter will conclude with some observations on the efforts made by the USSR to limit the risk of escalation after the decision to commit Soviet troops was taken (most notably, the ambiguous warnings sent to the United states and its allies) and a discussion of how the beginning of détente may have influenced Soviet decisions to take a firm stand in order to protect the USSR's regional interests.

Soviet Interests in the
Middle East after the 1967 War

The Six-Day War transformed the political and military landscape of the Middle East. The CPSU Central Committee attempted to reassure the USSR's allies, and to claim credit for ending the war, with its resolution of June 22, 1967, which echoed the language of the June 9 Moscow Declaration:

The plenum notes that the swift, resolute and joint action of the Soviet Union and other socialist states played an important role in the cessation of hostilities in the Near East. . . . The Soviet Union, together with other socialist countries, will do everything necessary to help the people of the Arab countries deal a decisive rebuff to the aggressor.[4]

At the same time, Soviet propaganda efforts to proclaim the USSR as the sole champion of the Arab cause, exemplified by the following quote from *Pravda*, were stepped up:

The Soviet Union is on the Arab side! The Soviet Union demands the condemnation of the aggressor in the Security Council! The Soviet Union demands a cease-fire! The Soviet Union resolutely warns Israel of its responsibility for the crimes committed! The Soviet Union severs diplomatic relations with Tel Aviv! The Soviet Union and other socialist countries sign the Moscow declaration and participate in the Budapest Conference. They fully support the Arab countries fighting against Israeli aggression and demand immediate withdrawal of the invader's armies![5]

Israel's victory immediately deepened the USSR's commitment to supply arms to its Arab allies, and to Egypt in particular. Egyptian forces had suffered heavy casualties and massive losses in equipment, and with Israeli forces entrenched on the east bank of the Suez canal, resupply of weapons was urgently needed to prevent Egypt's strategic situation from deteriorating even further. Supreme Soviet Chairman Nikolai Podgorniy and Chief of the General Staff Marshal Zakharov visited Cairo from June 21 to 24 to mend fences and provide personal assurances that the Soviet Union would step up deliveries of military equipment. Many Arab leaders felt that the USSR had abandoned or betrayed its allies in the war, and Podgorniy knew that promises of Soviet aid would have to be generous and swiftly fulfilled if Moscow was to regain its credibility as a supporter of the Arab cause. The agenda for Podgorniy's meetings with Nasser also included the establishment of a Soviet military presence in Egypt by gaining access to Egyptian port facilities for the Soviet navy and dispatching military advisors.

The Politburo remained concerned, however, that Soviet weapons intended for defensive uses might be employed for offensive purposes. An account of the talks between Podgorniy and Nasser on June 23 relates that the Soviet leader questioned the Egyptian president on his ultimate intentions with regard to Israel, and received an evasive answer:

Podgorniy: As for the type of aircraft, I believe that the military people will determine the suitable types so that your armed forces may be able to repel any new attack against them and even be able to launch a counterattack. But there is a point in your statements that I want explained: Do you ask for more air-craft with the aim of annihilating Israel finally?

Nasser: Let us ask ourselves: What is defense and what is offense? What are defensive weapons and what are offensive weapons? When war starts, there are no so called offensive and defensive weapons.[6]

There is some evidence that Nasser may have misperceived or misrepresented the views Podgorniy expressed during the talks on the desirability of sending Soviet combat forces to defend Egypt. Farid reports that Podgorniy, implying that he spoke for the Politburo, specifically rejected the deployment of Soviet troops.

My comrades in Moscow have agreed to the need for Soviet participation with the greatest possible efforts to bolster the entire air defense of your republic. [However,] the presence of foreign military forces on the territories of a sovereign state is a sensitive issue in the domestic situation. Therefore, it is more befitting for the air defense to be Egyptian and that Soviet aid be advanced to it.[7]

However, the same source quotes Nasser as saying, at a meeting on April 7 1968, of the Egyptian Council of Ministers, that Podgorniy agreed on this visit to send Soviet pilots to Egypt:

Nasser: May I inform you that Podgorniy agreed during his presence in Cairo to send a number of Soviet pilots. But the Soviets later turned down the request and did not agree to send pilots.[8]

In any case, the USSR soon made good on its promises to supply its allies with war materiel and military advisors. By late autumn, Soviet arms deliveries replaced 80 percent of Egypt's aircraft and tank losses in the Six-Day War free of charge, and the quantity and quality of weapons sent to Egypt surpassed Soviet aid to North Vietnam.[9] Approximately 2,000 military "experts" were stationed in Egypt by 1968, and between 2,500 and 4,000 by the beginning of 1970.[10] Many Egyptian officers resented the authority these foreign advisors exercised over their troops.[11]

While many of the weapons supplied to Egypt after the Six-Day War possessed considerable offensive capability, their primary purpose was to bolster Egypt's defensive strength, and air defense in particular. Throughout the period between the Six-Day War and the War of Attrition, the Politburo repeatedly turned down Nasser's requests for weapons that would greatly expand the offensive capability of the Egyptian armed forces, and Egyptian officers complained about the defensive emphasis of Soviet military training and advice.[12] Heikal reports that, on a visit to Moscow shortly after the war,

Algerian President Boumedienne criticized the Politburo for Soviet parsimony in arms supplies, motivated by the doctrine of "peaceful coexistence." Brezhnev answered by asking him, "What is your opinion of nuclear war?"[13]

It should be noted that not all observers would characterize Soviet arms deliveries as defensive. Ra'anan, for example, contends that the only weapons the USSR refused to supply Egypt with were nuclear warheads and that all other weapons delivered possessed offensive capability.[14] While almost any weapon can be used offensively, and some exceptions were made to the Soviet policy of sending primarily defensive weapons (such as the agreement to provide a limited number of FROG rockets in October 1968), Arab leaders' dissatisfaction with the amount and type of weapons provided by the Politburo is evidence that the USSR's regional objectives conflicted with the aspirations of its Arab allies. Sadat, for example, charges that the Soviet leadership planned to send only enough arms to maintain their presence in the region, and that "it was not part of the Soviet leaders' plan to have Nasser fight another war; they supplied him with the weapons as a courtesy gesture . . . but never intended them to be used."[15]

The deepening of Soviet commitments to Egypt thus added another contradiction to Soviet interests in the Middle East, in that Soviet regional goals increasingly conflicted not only with Soviet global objectives, but also with the intentions of Arab leaders, many of whom sought increased offensive capability against Israel. Soviet policy toward the region after the 1967 war had two primary aims: to protect and maintain a pro-Soviet regime in Egypt, and to secure an Israeli withdrawal from the occupied territories on terms favorable to the USSR. The first objective entailed defending the Arab Socialist Union (Nasser's party) from internal enemies as well as external adversaries. Articulating a Soviet view of Nasser's political vulnerabilities, Georgii Mirskii blamed Egypt's defeat in the war on "reactionary forces," especially within the senior ranks of army officers who "did not support the revolutionary ideas of the UAR leadership."[16] Although Beliaev and Primakov concluded in May 1968 that the purge of Marshal Amer indicated that "progressive" forces were winning their struggle with the "military bourgeoisie," Mirskii cautioned in December that the "calculating, ruthless leaders" of the Muslim Brotherhood and other groups opposed to socialism were trying to take advantage of popular discontent.[17] Sadat acknowledges that the political position of the Arab Socialist Union was precarious after the 1967 war.[18] As will be discussed later, Nasser's waning political strength before and during the War of Attrition was a problem the Politburo could hardly ignore. Soviet military and economic aid to Egypt during this period therefore served three interrelated purposes: protecting the friendly Egyptian regime from foreign enemies, maintaining the regime in power, and insuring that it would stay friendly.[19]

The Soviet position on the territorial issue crystallized after the passage of U.N. Security Council Resolution 242 on November 22, 1967. Soviet commentators recognized that a complete settlement of the Arab-Israeli conflict would have to include mutual diplomatic recognition, territorial integrity, the refugee problem, and other issues, but unconditional Israeli withdrawal from the occupied territories was demanded as a necessary first step to any political resolution.

> Undoubtedly, however, the solution of these problems . . . is possible only as a result of elimination of the traces of the Israeli aggression, that is to say, pursuant to the withdrawal of all Israeli forces from all the occupied Arab territories. This is the first and indispensable step.[20]

Some Western analysts, including Rubinstein, contend that the USSR preferred the state of "no war, no peace" to any resolution of the Arab-Israeli issue, arguing that the constant state of low-intensity conflict furthered Soviet interests in the Middle East.[21] Others, including George Breslauer, conclude that the Politburo wanted a settlement of the conflict, but not at any price, and that continuation of the conflict was preferable to a settlement that damaged Soviet regional interests.[22] While this debate will be taken up again in Chapter Five, it suffices to say here that the present author agrees with Breslauer's position. Although some differences may be visible between elements of the Soviet leadership who insisted on a "political solution" to the conflict and groups who held that "all necessary means" were acceptable to force a resolution, Soviet policy statements, diplomatic demarches, and patterns of military and economic aid strongly indicate that the Politburo was genuinely interested in a solution to the conflict—so long as that solution enable the expansion of Soviet influence in the region.

Just as the Six-Day War profoundly affected Soviet goals and commitments in the Middle East, the beginning of détente changed the nature of Soviet relations with the West. The *Ostpolitik* treaties with Germany and the start of the Strategic Arms Limitation Talks (SALT) process were signs that a less confrontational relationship was developing between the USSR and the United States and its allies. While the Politburo displayed no intentions of moderating its goals of expanding Soviet influence in the Middle East, Soviet commentators observed that the time was ripe for moving away from the "confrontation era" of the Johnson administration toward an "era of negotiation" with the United States under Nixon.[23] The Soviet leadership initially hoped that the Nixon administration would be more conciliatory in the Middle East than its predecessor.[24]

This hope soon faded, however, and it became clear that Soviet-American rivalry in the Middle East would continue as each superpower sought to arrange a solution to the Arab-Israeli conflict that favored its own interests. The United States sought to minimize Soviet influence in the region and hoped to broker an Arab-Israeli settlement that would safeguard Israel's security. Henry Kissinger remarks in his memoirs that he had "always believed it essential to reduce the scope of Soviet adventurist policies in the Middle East."[25]

Therefore, despite détente, the danger still remained that the overlapping conflicts in the region might escalate in ways that would require intervention by either or both superpowers to protect their regional allies. Moreover, during 1969–1970, Washington labored under the misapprehension that Moscow could "deliver" its regional clients if the superpowers worked out a Middle East settlement among themselves, and Moscow tended to believe that Washington could similarly "deliver" Israel.[26] Both superpowers should have known better after the experience of 1967, but this classic mutual exaggeration of the degree to which the other side could control the situation made it all too easy to shift the responsibility for actions that escalated the conflict.

On balance, while the early stages of détente moderated the conflict between Soviet and American global interests, the changes wrought by the Six-Day War intensified the contradictions between the superpowers' regional interests as both became more closely tied to their key regional allies. The contradiction between Soviet regional and global interests in 1969 and 1970 was sharpened by the fact that in the initial stages of the War of Attrition, the USSR's ally was on the offensive. As later sections of this chapter will show, Soviet leaders frequently had to decide how much support should be given to the Egyptian offensive, and Egyptian leaders complained that they never received enough. Nasser also proved very skillful at manipulating his patrons, deliberately exaggerating the risk that his regime could collapse if his strategy failed. When Egypt lost the initiative and went on the defensive, the Politburo was forced to consider how to prevent the war from bringing down Nasser while minimizing the risk of confrontation with the United States. As in the 1967 war, the USSR's Middle East dilemma was most acute when its allies were losing, but it existed throughout the conflict.

An interesting feature of the War of Attrition from the standpoint of superpower crisis interaction is that both the United States and the USSR faced serious difficulties in other regional conflicts during the course of the war. The United States was heavily involved in the irrepressible conflict in Vietnam and Cambodia during this period. According to Kissinger, Nixon believed at the beginning of his administration that some sort of trade-off with the USSR between the Middle East and Vietnam was possible.[27] For its part, the Politburo was often preoccupied with its own "neuralgic area," the Sino-Soviet border, where fighting broke out intermittently between March and September of 1969. The Sino-Soviet dispute had already spilled over into Soviet Middle East policy before the 1967 war, and at the June 1967 Cairo meeting, Podgorniy warned Nasser of the dangers of allowing Chinese influence to expand in the region.

> China is engaged in propaganda attacks against us everywhere, alleging that the Soviet Union has betrayed the Arabs, as it had already betrayed the Vietnamese. We are well aware of their propaganda and their moves. They are trying now to make us lose Syria and they are pushing it toward an unequal fight, regardless of the results expected of such a fight.[28]

By "it," Podgorniy may have been referring to the Arab-Israeli conflict, but this is not clear. It is also not clear exactly how either the competition for influence with China or the need to deal with two crises at once may have affected the Politburo's strategy for dealing with the Arab-Israeli conflict when it reattained crisis proportions in 1969. Harry Gelman finds that the Politburo was "preoccupied" with China during 1969.[29] While later Middle East conflicts would display how obsession with a domestic political crisis severely reduced the ability of an American president to deal with an international crisis, it is difficult to find similar evidence of how the need to deal with two crises at once affected Soviet decision making.

Did the USSR Have a Predetermined Strategy?

Two currents of Western opinion on Soviet actions during the War of Attrition hold that Soviet decision makers adopted a strategy for pursuing Soviet interests in the conflict long before the crisis reached the critical stage. Both of these interpretations of Soviet behavior are consistent with the chicken-game model in that they contend that the structure of the conflict determined Soviet strategy early in the crisis. They differ in that one finds that the Soviet leadership viewed the war primarily as a danger to be avoided, while the other argues that the Politburo saw it as an opportunity to be exploited.

Fukuyama's analysis, exemplifying the first viewpoint, states that the engagements of Soviet-piloted MiG fighters with Israeli aircraft on July 25 and 30, 1970, represented the strongest Soviet intervention in the conflict. As these engagements occurred after Nasser had announced on July 23 his intention to accept a cease-fire, Fukuyama concludes that Soviet strategy in the crisis followed a pattern similar to other Soviet threats to intervene in Middle East conflicts, that of refraining from action until the crisis was essentially resolved and then threatening military action as a symbolic gesture.[30] The main flaw in Fukuyama's interpretation is that Soviet intervention, which entailed considerable risk of U.S. reaction and virtually guaranteed that the intervening forces would suffer casualties, had already occurred in early March, when the outcome of the conflict was very much in doubt.[31] The conclusion that the Politburo followed a strategy of avoiding substantial risks (playing "C" in the chicken game) until the crisis was resolved does not fit well with the actual timing of the decision to intervene and the dispatch of Soviet forces.

Ra'anan, on the other hand, argues that elements of the Soviet leadership, particularly military leaders, put forward a plan for military intervention sometime in the summer of 1969. According to Ra'anan, the decision to intervene was probably taken in November, and the plan was presented to Nasser urging his secret visit to Moscow in January 1970, when he appealed for Soviet aid at the moment when Egypt was most militarily vulnerable and his regime was weakest politically.[32] From this perspective, some Soviet decision makers viewed the War of Attrition as an opportunity to introduce a Soviet military presence into the Middle East, formulated a plan for intervention far in advance of Nasser's January visit, and persuaded the Egyptian president to come to Moscow so that he could be presented with this prearranged plan.[33] Rubinstein disagrees with some of the details of Ra'anan's position, but concludes that the "basic decision" to send Soviet troops had been made before Nasser's visit.[34]

Neither Rubinstein nor Ra'anan, however, present any convincing evidence in support of this argument, that Ra'anan admits is primarily conjectural. The limited evidence available on Nasser's secret visit contradicts Ra'anan's interpretation. According to Heikal, Nasser asked the Politburo for Soviet PVO (Air Defense Forces) troops when he was told that it would take months to implement the Soviets' initial proposal to train Egyptian crews to operate SAM-3 missiles, and Brezhnev called a special meeting of the Politburo to consider the issue before agreeing to send Soviet forces.[35] Sadat's memoirs concur that the Politburo was wary of dispatching Soviet troops to the conflict and agreed to do so only after a special meeting.[36]

The timing of Soviet actions and the available evidence on Soviet decision making lead most Western analysts to agree that the decision to intervene in the War of Attrition was made shortly after Egyptian air defenses collapsed in early 1970.[37] The following sections will argue that time pressure and autonomous risk influenced Soviet strategy throughout the conflict, including the decision to accept the unprecedented risk of sending Soviet troops into combat in defense of their beleaguered allies.

Phases of the Crisis, 1969–1970

Changes in the independent variables of time pressure and autonomous risk, as seen from a Soviet viewpoint, divide the War of Attrition into six phases.

As in the previous chapter, the objective here is to gauge the strength of situational influences on Soviet decision making rather than to present a complete history of the conflict.[38] The phases will again be named for clarity and ease of identification.

The first phase opened with duels between Egyptian and Israeli artillery along the Suez Canal on March 9, 1969. Soviet commentators predictably blamed Israel for the escalation of violence, contending that Tel Aviv's "provocations" were designed to frustrate efforts toward a peaceful settlement of the ongoing conflict (specifically the Four-Power talks and the Jarring mission).[39] As the fighting dragged on during the Artillery Duels phase for several months, Soviet press statements focused on the civilian casualties caused by Israeli shelling and the effectiveness of Egyptian retaliation. But although Koriavin accused Israel of "playing not only a criminal but a reckless game," there are few indications that the Soviet leadership felt a great sense of urgency or worried about rapid escalation of the conflict.[40] Perceptions of both time pressure and autonomous risk therefore appear low during the first or Artillery Duels phase.

The situation changed markedly when the Israeli air force began an intensive bombing campaign on July 20. Soon after the initial raids, Soviet press commentaries opined that the conflict had become more dangerous. Vladimir Yermakov wrote that the raids represented "a stage in the Israeli aggression on the way to a new anti-Arab war" and that "Israel is prepared to throw a flaming torch headlong into the powder barrel."[41] Egypt's military situation deteriorated sharply when Israeli aircraft completed the destruction of Egyptian surface-to-air missile (SAM) sites on November 10.[42] An unsigned front-page editorial in *Krasnaia zvezda* on December 3 said that Israel's actions were "extremely dangerous" and were "pushing the events in this region toward a new military conflict."[43] A UAR delegation headed by Sadat visited Moscow from December 8 to 12, but although the joint communiqué issued upon his departure said that talks had progressed in an atmosphere of "full mutual understanding and friendship" (a code phrase for mutual recognition of differences of opinion), significant increases in Soviet aid did not follow.[44] Egypt's defenses did not totally collapse during the second phase of the conflict, but the SAM sites that were rebuilt after the initial Israeli raids were destroyed again by December 24.[45]

Because the evidence indicates that Soviet leaders perceived an increased degree of autonomous risk during this second phase (that will be referred to as the Canal Raids phase, although Israeli raids during this period were not restricted to the Suez Canal area), the independent variable will be assessed as moderately high. Time pressure, on the other hand, remained relatively low, because the Israeli raids on the canal front did not yet pose an immediate threat to the survival of Nasser's regime.

The critical period of the crisis started on January 7, 1970, when Israeli aircraft began deep-penetration raids into the UAR's heartland. The bombing of Cairo and the Nile Delta was carried out with the stated purposes of breaking the Egyptian army's will to fight and of toppling Nasser, and the destruction caused by the raids seriously threatened to accomplish both objectives.[46] The UAR's air defenses were a shambles, and as Piotor Demchenko noted, Israeli bombs were falling upon Cairo for the first time since the disastrous 1967 war.[47] An unattributed *Izvestiia* editorial (indicating reflection of the views of senior leaders) warned that Israel's strategy was "fraught with the most dangerous consequences for the cause of peace."[48] The UAR's desperate situation prompted Nasser's secret visit to Moscow on January 22, which will be discussed in detail in the following section. The danger that the USSR might soon lose its most valued Middle Eastern ally created a situation of high time pressure and high autonomous risk during the third or Deep-Penetration Raids phase of the crisis.

Western estimates indicate March 1 as the approximate date when Soviet SAM first became operational in Egypt, so this date will be used as the beginning of the conflict's fourth or Soviet Deployment phase.[49] A *Krasnaia zvezda* commentary on that date declared that Israel's air superiority was decreasing, although it did not mention the USSR's role in shoring up Egypt's air defense capabilities.[50] The Israeli air force resumed raids on SAM sites on March 1, but in spite of these attacks, a Soviet air-defense system was largely in place in central Egypt by March 19.[51] An unsigned *Pravda* editorial on March 3 signaled the new state of affairs, proclaiming that "The time in that it was possible to talk to people, who were upholding their fundamental interests, in the language of guns and bombs has sunk into oblivion."[52] Until the final Israeli deep-penetration raid on April 17, however, Nasser's regime remained in significant danger, and the presence of Soviet troops in the combat zone increased the risk of an open Soviet-Israeli confrontation, from which the United States could not remain aloof. Time pressure in the crisis' fourth phase will therefore be rated as moderate, while autonomous risk is assessed as moderately high.

Although the first encounter between Israeli and Soviet-piloted aircraft took place on April 18, the cessation of Israeli air force deep-penetration raids demonstrated the success of the initial phase of deployment of Soviet air-defense forces. The penultimate phase of the crisis began with the halt of deep-penetration raids and continued through the implementation of the second stage of the Soviet deployment. This second stage began on the night of June 29–30 with the first reported Soviet "missile ambush," or attempt to emplace SAMs along the Suez Canal under cover of darkness.[53] The "SAM box" on the Canal front was complete by mid-July. The new strategic situation was reflected in a radio commentary by Vladimir Popov, in which he stated that Israel was reacting "hysterically" to the new effectiveness of the UAR's air defenses.[54] A glasnost-era Soviet source claimed that the first Israeli aircraft to be destroyed by a Soviet pilot was shot down on July 22.[55] Nasser again visited the USSR from June 29 to July 17 (spending a great deal of time being treated in a special hospital) and shocked his Politburo hosts by informing them that he planned to accept the U.S.-sponsored Rogers Plan for deescalating the Arab-Israeli conflict and would soon order a cease-fire.[56] The restoration of Egyptian air defenses along the Canal despite continuing Israeli raids during this period of the crisis (which will be referred to as the SAM Extension phase) indicates that time pressure should be rated moderately low, while autonomous risk declined to a moderate level.

Nasser announced his acceptance of the Rogers Plan on July 23, but the cease-fire did not go into effect until August 7. The War of Attrition therefore had a brief terminal phase in which the crisis was essentially over, but some potential for escalation remained until the cease-fire was fully implemented. Consequently, the sixth phase of the crisis will be termed the Disengagement phase. The encounter between Soviet-piloted and Israeli aircraft on July 25 and the dogfight on July 30 in which four Soviet-manned planes were shot down remind us that military conflict and the possibility of an open Soviet-Israeli confrontation continued during this phase.[57] Time pressure and autonomous risk were both present at low levels from Nasser's announcement until the final cease-fire.

Table 3 on page 81 shows the values of the two independent variables and the resultant expectations for Soviet risk-taking during the War of Attrition. The third or Deep-Penetration Raids phase of the crisis is clearly the period during which this study's analytical framework would expect Soviet leaders to be most likely to stand firm in support of the beleaguered Nasser regime. This expectation obviously differs from the predictions of one variant of the chicken model, which holds that the USSR's predetermined strategy of risk-avoidance would make the Politburo most cautious, most accommodative, and least likely to take risky actions during the third phase. Threats of intervention would be most likely in phase 6, the Disengagement phase, if the USSR followed a predetermined strategy of conciliation followed by face-saving after a cease-fire had been agreed upon.

The other variant of the chicken model contends that Soviet leaders were waiting for an opportunity to introduce a Soviet military presence into the region and so would be likely to exploit the situation in January 1970 by dispatching Soviet forces. The main difference between the expectations of this conception of Soviet strategy and those of this study's analytical framework is that this study suggests that the decision for military intervention was not predetermined, but was made under the pressures of the conflict's critical period. Evidence that showed that the

Table 3 Time Pressure and Autonomous Risk in the War of Attrition

Phase	Date	Time Pressure	Autonomous Risk	Likelihood of Risk-taking
1. Artillery Duels	March 9–July 19	Low	Low	Low
2. Canal Raids	July 20–January 6	Moderately Low	Moderately High	Moderate
3. Deep-Penetration Raids	January 7–February 28	High	High	High
4. Soviet Deployment	March 1–April 17	Moderate	Moderately High	Moderate
5. SAM Extension	April 18–July 22	Moderately Low	Moderate	Moderately Low
6. Disengagement	July 23–August 7	Low	Low	Low

decision to intervene was made extemporaneously would demonstrate the advantages of the value conflict perspective over the second variant of the chicken model.

Soviet Statements and Actions, 1969–1970

Indicators of Soviet leadership attitudes in the first or Artillery Duels phase of the War of Attrition reveal concern over the sharp escalation of violence, but provide little evidence that Soviet action was needed or contemplated. The *Pravda* "Observer" on April 30 reaffirmed the USSR's "solid support" for the Arab cause, but did not mention that urgent action by the Soviet Union or other socialist countries was necessary.[58] A commentary by Rumiantsev on the anniversary of the Six-Day War charged (correctly) that Israel was trying to overthrow Nasser, but contended that "maximum mobilization of all anti-imperialist segments" of the Egyptian people would thwart Tel Aviv's plans—in other words, that strengthening the UAR's "internal front" would protect Egyptian socialism.[59] Other press sources gave assessments that this strategy was working, claiming that the UAR's army was "growing closer to the people" and that Egyptian forces and Arab "partisans" were repelling aggression and carrying the war to Israel itself.[60]

The United States and other Western countries were derided for supporting Israel's ambitions. One radio commentary claimed that America was helping Tel Aviv develop nuclear weapons and had sent 1,000 volunteers to serve in Israel's armed forces.[61] The German government—the "Bonn revanchists" in Soviet parlance—was the target of especially vehement criticism during this phase and was repeatedly accused of cooperating with Israel to build nuclear weapons and of helping to construct a reactor in the Negev desert to provide a test facility for German nuclear weapons.[62] Despite these accusations, Soviet communications during the first phase did not warn that American intervention in the conflict was imminent or probable, although the United States was accused of "saber-rattling" with NATO naval maneuvers in the eastern Mediterranean.[63]

The joint Soviet-Egyptian communiqué issued after Gromyko's June 10–13 visit to Cairo, which reaffirmed the UAR's and USSR's willingness to carry out U.N. Resolution 242, did not contain language that hinted that the level or type of Soviet support would soon change.[64] Heikal claims that the USSR "begged Nasser to use every effort to halt the War of Attrition" during this period, relating that Kosygin admonished visiting Egyptian officials in June, "You must try to cool the situation. Don't let the situation get out of hand. . . . You must not do anything that can be taken advantage of by the Israeli warmongers."[65]

The Soviet press expressed great consternation over the intensified bombing campaign that marked the start of phase 2 (Canal Raids), but early reports stated that Egypt's land and air forces gave the offensive a "decisive rebuff."[66] A Beliaev commentary early in phase 2 indicated that while some causes for concern existed, the UAR was not in mortal danger either along the Suez Canal or on the domestic front. He reported that the air attacks had failed to demoralize the UAR armed forces, that land reforms were strengthening the Egyptian "internal front," and that Israel's "blitzkrieg doctrine" was futile.[67]

As the war progressed, Agaryshev wrote that Egyptian morale was improving while Israeli morale declined and that although the need for technical training remained a problem within the UAR's armed forces, a "solution is not far off."[68] Beliaev again noted that the war had not drastically weakened Nasser or the Arab Socialist Union politically, commenting that while "national liberation" was being enhanced within the UAR and that the "military bourgeoisie," who were responsible for the defeat in 1967, had been neutralized, the Muslim Brotherhood and other reactionary forces remained active.[69] The Cairo conference of Arab League ministers was held up as evidence that Arab unity and cooperation with the USSR were growing, and German Ryzhikov asserted that "strengthened unity and determination of the Arabs" would repel the Israelis.[70] Near the end of the Canal Raids phase, Demchenko pointed to pledges of assistance to Egypt from Libya and Sudan as evidence that Arab unity was expanding and that continued Israeli attacks would not solve the crisis.[71]

There were indications during this phase, however, that the conflict was perceived to be growing more dangerous. Primakov declared at the end of August that a fire at the Al-Aqsa mosque in Jerusalem exposed Israel's true anti-Arab designs, and he warned that if Israel did not withdraw from the occupied territories soon, a new war, which could spread beyond the Middle East, would result.[72] Warnings that the United States was planning to intervene in the region multiplied in September and October. Nikolai Kupenko claimed that the United States wanted to establish bases in southwest Asia to protect the West's oil lifeline and to "penetrate the bounds of the continent" with its aggressive designs.[73] Georgii Ratiani cited a "secret study by the Pentagon and the RAND Corporation" that explored the possibilities for using nuclear weapons in the Middle East.[74] Koriavin commented that because the coup led by Muhammar Qadaffi had deprived the United States of its bases in Libya, America wanted to turn Lebanon into a new base in a region where the situation was now "explosive."[75]

The Politburo's surrogates in the press sounded notes of growing alarm throughout the crisis' second phase. An unsigned *Krasnaia zvezda* editorial in early September quoted Brezhnev to reassert that the USSR was providing and would continue to extend "comprehensive assistance" to its Arab allies.[76] The *Pravda* "Observer" used more forceful language in a September commentary on Israeli Prime Minister Golda Meir's visit to the United States, saying that "the Israeli extremists have clearly lost their heads" and that the Soviet Union is "doing everything necessary to secure a liquidation of the results of the Israeli aggression."[77] A radio commentary had already asserted that the sailing of the Soviet aircraft carrier *Moskva* in the Mediterranean belied NATO claims that the Soviet Mediterranean squadron could be sunk in a matter of minutes.[78]

The Soviet Government statement of October 31 began by stating that "The situation in the Near East is worsening seriously," and went on to detail the failure of diplomatic initiatives intended to stop the fighting. Declaring that Israeli extremists and their coconspirators in the United States and elsewhere were the only obstacle to a political settlement, the pronouncement pledged that Soviet aid to the UAR would continue, reiterating the "comprehensive assistance" formula.[79]

By December, when Nasser's situation had deteriorated dangerously, a front-page *Krasnaia zvezda* editorial said that Israel's "extremely dangerous" actions were "pushing events in this region toward a new military conflict" and that Soviet forces were "attentively following the dangerous actions of the U.S. and its clients." It cautioned that the USSR and other socialist countries were "filled with the firm resolve to do everything incumbent upon them" to help their Arab allies repel aggression.[80]

The expressions of increasing concern and urgency may indicate that stronger Soviet support for Egypt was contemplated near the end of the Canal Raids phase. If the purpose of Sadat's December visit to Moscow was to secure new types of weapons, however, the visit failed, for although the communiqué issued on his departure called for "urgent and constructive steps" to resolve the crisis, the Politburo was not prepared at that time to risk sending more advanced weapons or Soviet forces into the conflict.[81]

When Israel began an intensive campaign of bombing Cairo and the Nile valley and delta on January 7, 1970, the UAR's military situation became increasingly desperate. The Soviet press quickly blamed the escalation of the war on the United States; Demchenko charged that "the United States is assuming a considerable portion of the responsibility for Israel's continuing aggression and the exacerbation of the situation in the Near East."[82] American and British naval exercises were portrayed as portents of aggression and efforts to raise tensions in the Arab-Israeli conflict and on Cyprus.[83] The deep-penetration raids continued while Egyptian air defense capabilities eroded, although some Soviet articles denied the reports of Israeli successes early in this period.[84] Sadat relates that after Nasser summoned the USSR's ambassador and chief of the military advisor group to ask that SAM-3 missiles be delivered in advance of their planned arrival date in June, the Politburo invited the UAR's president to the USSR to discuss the issue.[85] Nasser secretly flew to Moscow on the morning of January 22.

Several partial accounts of Nasser's momentous "secret visit" are available. Each is sketchy, as would be expected with any high-level secret meeting, but all are generally in agreement on the key points of the talks between the Egyptian president and the Politburo. According to Heikal's report, the discussions about supplying Egypt with SAM-3s were "heated" and almost ended in "complete deadlock," but Brezhnev finally agreed on January 22 to send the missiles and train Egyptian crews in their use.[86] However, when Nasser learned that training Egyptian crews to employ SAM-3s would take months, he asked on January 23 that Soviet crews be sent with the missiles as soon as possible.[87] When Grechko reportedly said that aircraft would be needed to complete the air-defense system, Nasser asked him to send planes and pilots as well. When Brezhnev reportedly expressed concern over the risks involved in committing Soviet troops to Egypt, Nasser responded by raising the political stakes:

> Let me be quite frank with you. If we do not get what I am asking for everybody will assume that the only solution is in the hands of the Americans. . . . We are not asking you to fight for us—we want to keep our independence. But as far as I can see, you are not prepared to help us in the same way that America helps Israel. This means that there is only one course open to me: I shall go back to Egypt and I shall tell the people the truth. I shall tell them that the time has come for me to step down and hand over [power] to a pro-American President. If I cannot save them, somebody else will have to do it. That is my final word.[88]

Nasser's threat had its desired effect, although one cannot but wonder if the Politburo recalled his resignation and rapid reinstatement after the Six-Day War in responding to his ploy. Heikal recounts that a special Politburo meeting was held to discuss deployment of Soviet troops, that Nasser was told that stationing Soviet air-defense forces in the UAR would have "grave consequences," and cautioned Nasser to exercise great restraint. Nevertheless, over Kosygin's reservations, the Politburo finally presented Nasser with a detailed plan for using Soviet crews and pilots to shore up Egypt's defenses.[89] Sadat recalls that Nasser gave him an essentially similar (although abbreviated) account of the meeting's events upon his return from Moscow on January 25.[90]

Soviet reportage on the secret Soviet-Egyptian summit began appearing in 1988. A *New Times* article by Igor Timofeev contains a sequence recalled by retired Colonel-general Katyshkin, who was chief Soviet military advisor in Egypt at the time and who was present during the talks. Katyshkin's recollections indicate that serious differences existed within the Politburo on the issue of deployment of Soviet troops into an ongoing combat.

> "Can you guarantee that these missiles will provide 100 percent cover for Cairo?" Prime Minister Kosygin asked Defense Minister Marshal Grechko. "No," replied Grechko. "You can never be a hundred percent certain in a wartime situation."
>
> The sharp exchange between Kosygin and Grechko was interrupted by the General Secretary of the CC CPSU, Leonid Brezhnev. "Stop arguing," he said. "Obviously we must adopt a constructive decision."[91]

Katyshkin continues to say that the "constructive decision" Brezhnev demanded was finally taken at a Politburo meeting on January 25 and that Brezhnev informed Nasser that same day that the USSR would soon dispatch SAMs to Egypt to cover Cairo and the Nile delta. His account suggests that the addition of aircraft to reinforce the SAMs may have been decided upon after the original decision, but is not specific on this point.[92]

All the evidence available on the decision to send Soviet troops thus indicates that the Politburo was well aware that the deployment risked a Soviet-American confrontation. As a result, Soviet communications through a number of channels began "preparing the ground" for the deployment of Soviet troops soon after the decision was made in an effort to control the risks inherent in the move. Press commentaries described the conflict as extremely dangerous; Koriavin wrote that "the situation in the area is nearing the critical point," and Yevgeniy Maksimov warned that the threat to peace was not confined to the Middle East.[93] America was charged with greater responsibility for Israel's "aggression" after Nasser's visit. Beliaev commented that the United States insisted on the overthrow of progressive Arab regimes, while Glukhov claimed that Washington was "prepared to urge Tel Aviv to new adventures against the Arab peoples."[94]

Most dramatically, Kosygin dispatched separate letters to the leaders of the United States, Britain, and France, calling upon the four powers to compel Israel to cease its attacks on Egypt. Kissinger reports that the letter to the United States, delivered by Dobrynin on January 31, demanded the "speediest withdrawal of Israeli forces from all the occupied Arab territories" and warned that if the raids continued, "the Soviet Union will be forced to see to it that the Arab states have means at their disposal, with the help of which a due rebuff to the arrogant aggressor could be made."[95] Nixon relates that Kissinger considered the Kosygin memorandum to be the first Soviet threat of his administration, but because the letter made no mention of Soviet troops, he replied on February 4 with a note warning the USSR that the

United States would match any new level of arms shipments and proposing negotiations on limiting arms supplies to the region.[96]

Kissinger recalls that Kosygin's letter made him suspect that the USSR would become more deeply involved in the conflict, but that the possibility that Soviet troops would be sent was not seriously considered until early February. Soviet specialists at both the State Department and CIA regarded Kosygin's letter as a bluff, noting that it was not reinforced by high-level contacts.[97] Kissinger recalls further that as no one in the administration wanted to create a confrontation with a formal communiqué, he told Dobrynin on February 10 that the introduction of Soviet troops into the Middle East "would be viewed with the gravest concern."[98]

The Soviet press predictably criticized the United States for its unenthusiastic response to Kosygin's appeal for joint action. The bombing of a factory at Abu Zabal on February 12 was presented as further evidence of Israel's barbarity and that urgent steps were necessary to compel Israel to cease its attacks and fulfill the Soviet interpretation of U.N. Resolution 242:

> The longer the fulfillment of this resolution is dragged out, the greater the responsibility for the dangerous state of affairs in the Near East will rest, along with the Israeli ruling circles, on the ruling circles of those powers which are in fact supporting this aggression. The big and small aggressors will not escape from their responsibility.[99]

When asked if he would accept the stationing of Soviet pilots in Egypt if the air war continued, Nasser disingenuously replied that he would have to think about it.[100]

As the first Soviet crews began arriving in Egypt, marking the beginning of the fourth or Soviet Deployment phase of the conflict, criticism of American support for Israeli policy continued. After Soviet SAMs became operational around Cairo and in the Nile delta during the early days of phase 4, Aleksei Vasiliev charged that U.S. pilots who had served in Southeast Asia were flying Israeli aircraft and that Israel was using the same bombing tactics in Egypt that the United States employed in Vietnam.[101] Other press statements claimed that the United States hoped that Israel's military pressure on the UAR would change the balance of power in the Middle East in favor of imperialism; that America sought to use Israel as a satellite to further its regional goals as it was using the Republic of Vietnam; and that the United States and Israel provoked clashes between the PLO and Phalangist forces in Lebanon as a pretext for an American invasion.[102] Tsoppi held the United States responsible for the April 8 bombing of an elementary school at Bahr al-Baqar and declared, "This is why we are firmly resolved to help with all our means the Arab peoples in their just struggle."[103]

The United States did not display an equally firm resolve to oppose the Soviet deployment. Kissinger relates that Israeli Ambassador Rabin informed him on March 17 that a major shipment of Soviet arms had arrived in Egypt, including SA-3 missiles (which had never before been given to any other nation), and accompanied by 1,500 Soviet troops. He recalls thinking that the deployment represented the initial phase of a significant new Soviet commitment and that a strong U.S. reaction was called for, the initial installment of which he delivered to Dobrynin shortly afterward.

> On March 20 I called in Dobrynin for a tough dressing down. . . . The troops had been sent despite my explicit warning of the dangers of such a step. The tactic, I said, was reminiscent of the Cuban missile crisis. We had no choice except to terminate all our efforts for the cease-fire and to inform Israel accordingly.[104]

To Kissinger's dismay, however, the United States did not follow up his meeting with the Soviet ambassador with a formal protest, increased military aid to Israel, or any other unambiguous gesture of firmness. Kissinger attributes the lack of a clear demonstration of American resolve to preoccupation with Southeast Asia (particularly the actions planned in Cambodia) and the tortuous process of policymaking in Washington, but he can hardly be considered an impartial observer.[105] Whatever the reason, although the United States was aware of the Soviet deployment in its early stages, a strong American response was not forthcoming.

Brezhnev's speech in Kharkov on April 14 did not acknowledge that Soviet forces had been sent to Egypt, but nevertheless signaled that the Soviet Union had taken on a new commitment in the Middle East. Predictably blaming the conflict in the region on Israel and its "imperialist" supporters, he departed from the "comprehensive assistance" formula in declaring the level of support the USSR was disposed to extend to its Arab allies.

> The socialist countries are true friends of the Arab peoples and are prepared to extend the necessary assistance to thwart the plans of the aggressors in the Near East. Together with the other socialist countries, the Soviet Union will *do everything in its power* to facilitate a settlement in the Near East that would ensure the restoration of justice and would bring peace and security to all the peoples of this region.[106] [Emphasis added.]

It was by then clear to the USSR's allies and adversaries that "everything in its power" included committing Soviet combat troops to the defense of Egypt and of Nasser's regime. The message was not lost on Israel. Soviet efforts on their allies' behalf achieved their primary goal by mid-April, when the Israeli deep-penetration raids were halted. Air attacks along the Suez

Canal continued, however, and prevented Egyptian forces from reconstructing an air-defense system on that front as the Soviet Deployment phase ended.[107]

Soon after the start of phase 5, the SAM Extension period, Soviet press sources began denying that the USSR was taking a new role in the conflict, but did not do so with their normal vigor. Beliaev wrote that the "false assertions concerning the Soviet Union are groundless," but did not specifically mention pilots.[108] Kosygin, during a news conference, responded to a direct question about Soviet pilots fighting in Egypt by saying that Soviet advisors were "attached to UAR troops," but neither confirmed nor denied that Soviet forces were involved in combat.[109] Yurii Tyssovskiy stated that Soviet strengthening of the UAR's defenses by "rendering extensive assistance" did not threaten Israel.[110] By mid-July, however, Soviet commentators had repeatedly and directly denied that Soviet forces were engaging in combat in Egypt.[111]

No references were made to the encounters between Israeli and Soviet-piloted aircraft on April 18 and June 22, but radio commentaries claimed that the tide of the war was turning by early June.[112] Tyssovskiy trumpeted that the United States and Israel had obviously miscalculated the strength of Arab forces and that Israel was forced to give up the deep-penetration raids in the face of an "insurmountable barrier" of UAR air defenses.[113] By the time that barrier was extended to the west bank of the Suez Canal by "missile ambushes" in late June and early July, Glukhov had reported that the Tripoli summit of the Arab League showed that unity among "progressive" Arabs was strengthening and broadening.[114]

The outcome of Nasser's visit to Moscow at the end of the SAM Extension phase was as surprising to the Politburo as the result of his secret visit in January was to the U.S. government. Heikal summarizes a memorandum prepared for Nasser by senior UAR military, intelligence, and Foreign Ministry officials just before he left on June 29, which outlined the conflicts between Soviet and Egyptian interests in termination of the military conflict:

> What would then be the situation, should a settlement be reached? The U.S. would emerge as the power that, by its pressure on Israel, had achieved a settlement. This it would have done without spending a dollar, while the other superpower, that had initiated the process, and in so doing spent its treasure and even its blood, would be left on the sidelines. This consideration . . . accounts for the hostility shown by the Soviet Union to the idea of direct talks between Egypt and the Americans.[115]

The outstanding issues were apparently not resolved at the June 29 meeting between Nasser and Brezhnev, where the Egyptian president requested more arms. All available accounts agree that Nasser told Brezhnev that he intended to accept the Rogers initiative. Nasser then spent two weeks receiving special medical treatments in Bervikha hospital, where he was visited by various Soviet leaders but did not discuss any matters of substance with them. Finally, on July 16, Nasser met with Brezhnev one last time, received a reply to his request for more arms, and restated his intention to accept the Rogers Plan and call for a cease-fire.

Sadat wrote that "Brezhnev was beside himself with rage" when he received this news.[116] According to Heikal, who accompanied Nasser on this last mission to Moscow, the Soviet leader was clearly stunned.

> Brezhnev pushed his spectacles down his nose and stared at Nasser over the top of them. "Do you mean to tell me you are going to accept a proposal with an American flag on it?" he asked. Nasser said: "Exactly. I am going to accept it just because it has an American flag. . . . We need a cease-fire, and the only cease-fire the Israelis will accept is one proposed by the Americans. But I don't think the initiative stands any chance of success. I wouldn't rate its chances at more than half a percent." Brezhnev was surprised, but I think he understood.[117]

Nasser's acceptance of the plan represented a significant political defeat for the Soviet Union. The USSR had consistently denounced the Rogers Plan as an American attempt to codify Israel's occupation of most of the occupied territories and to exclude the USSR from the process of resolving the Arab-Israeli conflict.[118] Acceptance of the plan by all parties to the conflict would recognize the leading role of the United States as the superpower guarantor of the peace process. Soviet opposition to the plan is thus understandable even though the Politburo's fears and characterization of it both appear exaggerated. It is, therefore, not difficult to see why Soviet leaders might well perceive Nasser's acceptance of the Rogers initiative, after the USSR took the unprecedented step of committing military forces to combat in defense of his country, as a major setback and an ungrateful betrayal.

In any event, Nasser's public announcement on July 23 that the UAR would accept the Rogers Plan began the terminal or Disengagement phase of the crisis. Soviet commentaries initially said that American diplomatic offensives and military support of Israel were designed to pressure the Arab states to accept the "pseudosettlement" offered in the plan.[119] Soon afterward, however, the Soviet press attempted to capitalize on this development, or at least control the damage it caused, by portraying Nasser's acceptance of a cease-fire as a courageous step on the road to peace. Glukhov referred to the cease-fire as an Egyptian initiative that was not easily taken but that did not betray weakness.[120] Radio Peace and Progress reported that Egypt's acceptance of the "American so-called peace proposal," despite continued U.S. military support of Israel, placed Washington and Tel Aviv in a difficult position, a line Vishnevetskiy echoed.[121]

The Soviet press said nothing about the clashes between Soviet and Israeli pilots on July 25 and 30, and most commentators waited until the cease-fire came into effect on August 7 to assess the state of affairs in the region. Medvedko claimed that the UAR's agreement to the plan forced Israel to agree, and correctly observed that "peace has a hard road ahead."[122]

Despite the surprise and anger with which the Soviet leadership greeted Nasser's acceptance of the American peace plan, Soviet analysts claimed that the USSR deserved credit for bringing about the halt in military action. Koriavin declared that the Soviet Union played a "large role in creating the prerequisites for settlement" of the conflict.[123] Beliaev's article in *Novoe vremia,* published on the last day of the crisis, claimed that Egyptian military strength forced Israel to accept a cease-fire, that the Rogers Plan offered nothing new and was an American attempt to legitimate Israeli occupation of Arab territory, and that the involvement of Soviet troops in the war was "mythical."[124] This would remain the official Soviet position on the War of Attrition until the era of glasnost 20 years later.

Value Conflict and Soviet
Decision Making, 1969–1970

Soviet coercive risk-taking during the War of Attrition followed clearly discernible patterns. The Politburo accepted the risk of placing Soviet air-defense troops in harm's way in Egypt during the Deep-penetration Raids phase, when both time pressure and autonomous risk were high. Conversely, in the Artillery Duels and Disengagement phases, when the independent variables that this study expects to influence the willingness of Soviet leaders to take risks were both low, Soviet leaders avoided actions that could have escalated the conflict, despite the danger in the first phase that the war would go badly for Egypt and the possibility in the final phase that the cease-fire would not hold. The extension of the Soviet air defense system to the Canal front in phase 4, when the likelihood of risk-taking is rated as moderate, probably represented the implementation of the strategy adopted at the peak of the crisis rather than a new decision to accept greater risks. In phases 2 and 5 (Canal Raids and SAM Extension), when the probability of risk-taking was respectively moderate and moderately low, the Politburo avoided taking risks in support of the USSR's main regional ally and thereby jeopardized Soviet influence in the Middle East.

Two features of Soviet behavior in phase 3 (Deep-penetration Raids, January 7–February 28, 1970) indicate that inability to resolve the conflict between regional and global objectives influenced the decision to deploy Soviet forces. First, although Moscow consistently accused Washington of exacerbating the crisis, charges that the United States would intervene to impose its version of peace, betokening attempts to shift responsibility for the USSR's actions onto the USSR's global adversary, peaked during this period.[125] Second, Kosygin's attempt to secure American, British, and French support for joint intervention is an example of an effort to pursue simultaneously regional and global interests by proposing joint action with the opponent. Unlike the peak of the 1967 crisis, the point of highest tension in the War of Attrition offers little evidence that the Politburo filtered out or minimized the risks of an attempt to pursue simultaneously global and regional interests during this phase. On the contrary, Soviet leaders appeared acutely aware of the risks involved and tried to get the United States to share in their actions, or at least the blame for them.

The differences in Soviet coerciveness during the high points of tension in the two crises may be explained by two factors. The first is the absence in 1970 of the intense time pressure created by the Israeli attack on Syria in 1967. The real threat to Nasser's control over Egypt in 1970 was internal. His inability to cope with the Israeli raids was undermining his authority and legitimacy as president. He believed that Israel's primary aim in fighting the War of Attrition was to destroy Egyptian morale, and by January 1970 it appeared very close to achieving this goal. Nasser expressed this concern clearly during his "secret visit" to Moscow, when he said that the Israeli deep-penetration raids

> were aimed at breaking the morale of the home front. Israel had failed to force Egypt into surrender in 1967, but was determined to do so now. Nasser said that the whole of Egypt felt unprotected—naked.[126]

The political crisis that Nasser and the Politburo feared could erupt suddenly, and it might come at any moment, but at the time of Nasser's secret mission to Moscow, it remained a potential rather than an actualized threat.

Additionally, political developments would most likely give the Egyptian and Soviet governments some time to react. Nasser's regime had forces available to deal with the possibility of a wave of riots or a military coup. Their success in suppressing a revolt could not be guaranteed, but the regime's foes could hardly be assured of rapid success themselves. In short, no foreseeable political threat in 1970, except perhaps an assassin's bullet, could move so fast that a decision could not be made on how to deal with it. In 1967, by contrast, forces sufficient to deal with a possible Israeli advance on Damascus were not in place, and the Israeli Defense Force had just demonstrated its rapid offensive capability. While the time pressure weighing upon Soviet decision makers was therefore high at the peak of the crisis in 1970, the 1967 crisis had been an order of magnitude higher.

Second, American behavior prior to the introduction of Soviet troops into Egypt gave little indication that the Soviet move could precipitate a Soviet-American confrontation. The Nixon administration did not perceive Kosygin's letter of January 31 as a threat of direct Soviet military action. American decision makers believed the note threatened an expansion of Soviet arms shipments to Egypt and responded specifically to that threat.[127] It might be argued, with the benefit of hindsight, that the United States should have perceived the threat of military action implicit in Kosygin's letter, but this contention would be unfair. Unlike similar Soviet communications in 1967 and 1973, the note did not mention military action, only provision of unspecified "means." As every warning is ambiguous to some degree, any threat analysis must take some element of deliberate ambiguity into account, but if the note did not refer to action by Soviet forces, it is difficult to see how it could have been automatically construed as an unequivocal warning that the Politburo was planning to introduce Soviet troops into the conflict. American policymakers did suspect that this meant the USSR was preparing to provide its allies with new types of weapons, and this suspicion proved correct when Soviet SA-3 missiles arrived in Egypt. The Soviet troops that accompanied them, and their subsequent commitment to combat, came as the surprise, and Kosygin's letter cannot be regarded as a warning clear enough to have made them less surprising.

Given the lack of a firm American response to Kosygin's letter, what does subsequent Soviet behavior represent in terms of the effect of value conflict on acceptance of risks? George argues that Nixon's response to Kosygin's letter may have encouraged the Politburo to believe that the USSR had no choice but to proceed with direct intervention and that the risks of intervention could be calculated and controlled. In his analysis, the United States miscalculated the pressure the Israeli raids created on Nasser and the Politburo, and the whole incident exemplifies the difficulty of establishing "ground rules" for limiting U.S.-Soviet competition in nonvital areas.[128] George concludes that the Politburo went ahead with deployment of Soviet troops because of mutual misperceptions: Soviet leaders believed Kosygin's letter to be a clear signal of their intentions, but the United States did not perceive this, and the Politburo interpreted the lack of a firm response as a failure to demonstrate resolve and therefore an acquiescence to their planned action. Value conflict plays no part in this explanation—misperception of an opponent's communication, not inability to resolve conflicts between objectives, lead to an overestimation of bargaining power.

This interpretation, however, places the cart before the horse. Less metaphorically, it focuses on the implementation of a decision rather than on the decision itself. All accounts agree that the Politburo's decision to commit Soviet troops to the ongoing conflict was made during Nasser's secret visit to Moscow, which ended on January 25. Reneging on their promise to support Nasser would have been disastrous to Soviet interests in the Middle East and deleterious to the USSR's global reputation and political influence, as it would have been a failure to fulfill a commitment made to a valuable ally in its hour of greatest need. The note was intended as a signal to the United States that the Politburo would fulfill this commitment to Egypt (of which the United States was unaware) and an attempt to reduce the risks involved in fulfilling it, not as a trial balloon for a course of action still under consideration. By the time Kosygin's note was sent, Soviet weapons and personnel had already started on their way to Egypt.[129] Vehement American opposition to the actions referred to in the note might have caused the Politburo to reconsider their decision if they perceived a risk of a serious confrontation, but the lack of an American response did not precipitate a Soviet decision. It only served to validate a decision taken previously, although a significant part of this validation rested on misperception.

Thus, when Kosygin sent his memorandum, he was not testing the waters, but trying to smooth the ripples he knew that the Politburo's forthcoming action would cause. The decision in favor of the most concrete and forceful gesture of firmness the Politburo would make in any Middle East crisis had been made earlier, in the atmosphere of high time pressure and autonomous risk caused by the impending collapse of Egypt's air defenses and the possible collapse of its government. Soviet leaders decided to accept the risks involved in committing forces armed with advanced weapons into the ongoing combat before any attempt to assess the probable American reaction had been made. Soviet leaders acted most coercively in the War of Attrition before they had any reason to believe that American acceptance of the deployment of troops as a *fait accompli* would have changed the balance of bargaining power in the region in their favor. After the decision was taken, efforts were made to implement it in secret (which quickly proved futile), and the signal sent to Washington to prepare the ground for it did not reveal its precise nature. This ambiguity and attempted secrecy indicates that the Politburo did not feel it had the upper hand, but was determined to stand firm regardless.

Soviet decision makers, therefore, chose a coercive course of action at the point of highest tension during the War of Attrition, in spite of the unfavorable balance of bargaining power vis-à-vis the United States. When American responses to this strategy appeared to indicate that the United States was not prepared to risk a confrontation, the strategy of coercion was implemented with increased assuredness, but the option was chosen at a time when the facts on the ground in the Middle East could hardly inspire confidence. The Politburo decided upon a coercive means of resolving the crisis at a point when value trade-offs were least likely. By attempting to create a *fait accompli* by deploying PVO forces into Egypt, Soviet leaders sought to buttress the toppling regime of an allied leader without risking a confrontation with the USSR's principal global opponent.

One account of the talks during Nasser's secret visit suggests that Kosygin was uncomfortable with the decision to deploy Soviet troops.[130] When his ambiguous note to Nixon did not provoke a confrontational response, the perceived lack of American firmness may have bolstered the chosen option and convinced the Politburo that it was safe to proceed. If the Politburo did intend to create a *fait accompli* in 1970, the attempt essentially succeeded. If in acceding to it, or seeming to do so, the United States enabled the success of a coercive strategy designed to pursue simultaneously Soviet regional and global objectives.

Careful examination of Soviet behavior in phase 3 also refutes contentions that the USSR followed a predetermined strategy in the crisis. No available evidence indicates that the Politburo had already decided on intervention and was waiting for an opportune moment. While some Soviet political and military leaders may have favored such a strategy, the decision to dispatch Soviet forces was made only after considerable deliberation during Nasser's secret visit.[131] The deployment of Soviet troops thus does not appear to be an opportunistic execution of a predetermined strategy of intervention. By the same token, Soviet efforts to limit the risks entailed by this decision, especially Kosygin's letter of January 31, show that the Politburo did not attempt to implement a long-planned encroachment into the Middle East, but rather sought to control the risks of a course of action intended to pursue simultaneously both global and regional interests.

The most forceful evidence against the other variant of the chicken model, which holds that the Politburo threatened forceful action only as a face-saving gesture after the peak of the conflict was past, is the timing of the Soviet decision to intervene. The riskiest Soviet action during the War of Attrition was taken in January, at the peak of the crisis, rather than in July, after Nasser announced that the UAR would accept a cease-fire.[132] In the period after the crisis was essentially resolved (the Disengagement phase, July 23–August 7) and before the conflict had escalated to a dangerous level (the Artillery Duels phase, March 9–July 19), Soviet leaders had scant need to take risks in pursuit of their regional objectives, and did not do so.

The extension of the area covered by Soviet pilots and SAM crews from the interior of Egypt to the Suez Canal front in the SAM Extension phase (April 18–July 22), though it involved greater hazards for Soviet personnel, did not entail any new political or military risks. The possibility of combat between Israeli aircraft and Soviet pilots or SAMs existed throughout phases

4, 5, and 6. There is also no evidence that Soviet decision makers consulted with their Egyptian allies before extending the area covered by Soviet air defense troops. This study, therefore, agrees with Bar-Siman-Tov that the "missile ambushes" in late June and early July were probably steps in fulfillment of the original Soviet air-defense plan for the UAR rather than the result of a new decision to extend the scope of Soviet intervention.[133] Similarly, Soviet behavior during phase 4 (Soviet Deployment, March 1–April 17) does not include acceptance of new risks, because it was essentially a period of implementation of the decisions made in the Deep-penetration Raids phase. The decision to take risks had already been made at the peak of the crisis.

Soviet actions in phases 2 (Canal Raids, July 20–January 6) and 5 (SAM Extension, April 18–July 22) display the risk-aversion characteristic of Soviet behavior in many crisis confrontations, and evidence indicates that this reluctance to take risks resulted from the resolution of value conflicts. In both phases, Egyptian delegations came to Moscow to request new weapons, and the Politburo refused both requests. Sadat and Heikal describe the strains in relations between the USSR and its primary regional ally that these denials generated. Indeed, repeated refusals to fulfill the UAR's demands for military hardware were primarily responsible for the anti-Soviet tone of their works.[134] In both phases, where time pressure was moderately low and autonomous risk was moderate (SAM Extension) or moderately high (Canal Raids), Soviet leaders made clear value trade-offs, compromising their regional interests in order to pursue their global objectives. The Politburo's surprise and anger at Nasser's plans to accept the Rogers initiative indicates that the cost of this trade-off to Soviet regional interests was greater than they expected to pay.

Overall, the evidence from all phases of the 1969–1970 crisis supports the hypotheses on Soviet risk-taking advanced in this study. The two independent variables exhibited substantial covariation throughout the crisis, both generally rising until the Deep-penetration Raids phase (January 7–February 28) and declining thereafter until the cease-fire. Nevertheless, Soviet risk-avoidance in the Canal Raids phase, despite moderately high levels of autonomous risk, and efforts to control risks in the Deep-penetration Raids phase suggest that time pressure influences the resolution of value conflict more strongly than does autonomous risk. The evidence also shows that the value-conflict perspective provides a more thorough explanation for Soviet decisions at the peak of the crisis than either variant of the chicken model.

Conclusions: Risk-taking and Risk-avoidance in the War of Attrition

As its name implies, the War of Attrition was a protracted conflict. Soviet decision makers therefore had a relatively generous amount of time to formulate and implement plans for protecting their regional interests and clients. However, a new factor affecting their global interests, the beginning of détente, placed constraints on their regional strategy. This final section discusses how these two elements may have affected Soviet decisions to accept or avoid risks during the war.

The Soviet military intervention in Egypt exhibited many of the characteristics described in operational code models of Soviet decision making. The deployment of Soviet air-defense troops was planned and executed with great care, and attempts were made to lay the groundwork for this challenge to U.S. interests (with Kosygin's letter and other communications) as if the Politburo were operating according to Adomeit's operational principles of Soviet crisis behavior.[135] The USSR's regional allies did not have time for this deliberate maneuvering, however, and repeatedly expressed their frustration and impatience, eventually by accepting an American peace proposal. Soviet efforts to control risks during the crisis' critical third phase thereby pose an important question: Did Soviet decision makers move carefully because of the time available, or did Soviet tendencies toward caution delay their actions?

While this question may resemble a moot "chicken-and-egg" debate at first glance, Soviet actions at the peak of the crisis suggest that it has an answer, and the answer shows how the analytical framework developed in this study can complement existing models of Soviet behavior. Because Soviet leaders did not face the intense time pressure they experienced in 1967 and would face again in 1973, they were able to exert efforts to minimize the risks of their attempt to pursue simultaneously regional and global objectives. The value conflict perspective expects that the Politburo would challenge the United States in order to avoid the necessity to choose between regional and global goals, while the operational code model describes how that challenge was likely to be made. To their transient good fortune, the Politburo's challenge succeeded, and Soviet efforts to control the risks inherent in a coercive strategy facilitated its success. Soviet actions in early 1970 are therefore consistent with both analytical perspectives, and although neither provides a completely satisfactory explanation by itself, both can be combined to gain additional insight into Soviet behavior.

The impact (or lack thereof) of détente on Soviet decisions during the war is more relevant to policy analysis issues than to theory-building, but the question of whether détente encouraged or discouraged risk-taking is nevertheless important. On one hand, while the détente relationship had not fully matured by 1970, many Soviet leaders had already developed a significant political stake in a relaxation of East-West tensions.[136] The Politburo as a whole also had important interests in the SALT process, *Ostpolitik,* and other aspects of improved relations. These considerations may have acted to raise the value of avoiding a confrontation with the United States over regional issues. On the other hand, Soviet leaders may have felt that U.S.-Soviet political conflict over the Middle East was less likely to escalate into a dangerous confrontation because of the reduced level of global antagonism. There is insufficient space here for a complete discussion of the effect of détente on Soviet policy in the Third World.[137] For the purposes of this chapter, it might be speculatively concluded that in 1969 and 1970, détente probably did not encourage Soviet leaders to challenge the United States out of perceptions of American weakness, but may have raised the likelihood of Soviet risk-taking in regional conflicts by fostering perceptions that a political confrontation was less likely to explode into military conflict. Kissinger, for his part, believed that the lack of a forceful U.S. response to Kosygin's letter encouraged the Politburo to act boldly in 1970.[138] In a subsequent crisis, as we will see in the next chapter, he made sure that the USSR would not get the same encouragement.

In some ways, Soviet decision making during the War of Attrition is an example of the "inverted 'U' phenomenon," when leaders perform best when under a moderate, but not excessive, amount of stress. Although the Politburo's actions at the peak of the crisis displayed significant evidence of value-conflict effects, and risks were taken in an attempt to defend regional allies without jeopardizing the development of détente, Soviet leaders took steps to minimize and control the risks inherent in their decision to send Soviet troops to Egypt. The main lesson of the 1969–1970 war may therefore be that if decision makers have days rather than hours to formulate and implement strategy, they may still seek to avoid making value trade-offs, but will be more able to limit risks by engaging and testing their opponents without directly threatening them. In periods when time pressure was still more moderate, the Soviet leadership consistently compromised its regional objectives to pursue the primary goal of avoiding confrontation with the United States. Because the deployment of air-defense forces helped prevent Nasser's regime from collapsing under the Israeli attack, Soviet strategy was clearly a success in the short term. The USSR's Egyptian allies would not forget their patron's procrastination and parsimony, however, and their frustration and resentment augured poorly for the future of Soviet Middle East policy.

FIVE

The October War, 1973

In my opinion, the Soviet position regarding Arab plans to launch a war against Israel was not consistent. In fact, it was at times rather two-faced, ambiguous, and contradictory, as was the foreign policy of the Soviet Union in general.

—Victor Israelyan
Inside the Kremlin During the Yom Kippur War[1]

Though it may not have been a bona fide superpower crisis, the Yom Kippur War was an extremely serious regional conflict in that both Moscow and Washington played dangerous games of risk manipulation.[2] In late October 1973, in response to the critical military situation on the Suez Canal front, Soviet airborne troops were readied for action and American forces were on worldwide nuclear alert. Few observers, however, would rank the resulting Soviet-American crisis on a par with acutely dangerous confrontations such as the Berlin or Cuban crises. In October 1973, the leaderships of both nations made military preparations and threatened military actions for purely political purposes, and each knew that the other's military maneuvers posed little direct threat. The primarily political character of the sudden sharp rise in U.S.-Soviet tensions leads some analysts to question whether the incident should be considered a crisis, particularly if the Soviet threat to dispatch troops to the Sinai, to which the United States responded with a nuclear alert, is regarded as a transparent bluff.

Recently disclosed evidence indicates very clearly that the threat of Soviet military intervention near the end of the war was neither an ultimatum nor a prearranged empty gesture, but a coercive move designed to help the Politburo escape the conflict between its regional and global objectives. This chapter will show how examining Soviet statements and actions in 1973 for the effects of value conflict can help determine how serious the Soviet-American confrontation really was, whether the superpowers acted as collaborators or competitors during the conflict, and how the maturation of détente may have affected Soviet behavior.

Like the preceding case studies, this chapter begins with an overview of Soviet global and regional interests in 1973, which will outline how the USSR's relations with its Middle Eastern allies became more turbulent, while the U.S.-Soviet relationship became more cordial and structured. After this, two schools of thought on Soviet actions in the crisis, both of that hold that the Politburo followed a predetermined course of action before and during the war, will be summarized. The Arab-Israeli crisis and war will then be divided into eight phases according to the time pressure and autonomous risk faced by Soviet decision makers. The subsequent examination of Soviet communications and actions will show that Soviet actions in periods when the likelihood of risk-taking was high closely resembled Soviet behavior at similar moments in 1967 and 1969–70, but Soviet signaling in the phases preceding the war differs markedly from the pattern established in the two previous crises. This suggests that while Soviet and American interests frequently conflicted in 1973, the formalization of détente moderated Soviet behavior and dampened the intensity of a regional conflict that could easily have escalated into a major Soviet-American crisis.

Soviet Regional and Global Interests in 1973

Soviet policy toward the Middle East suffered several major reversals between 1970 and 1973, but eventually experienced a partial recovery. Nasser's death in September 1970 deprived Egypt of its most revered and dynamic leader, and the USSR of a charismatic figure who could greatly aid the Politburo in advancing its regional agenda. Soviet ties with Egypt became increasingly strained under Nasser's successor, Anwar el-Sadat. The USSR refused to completely satisfy Sadat's requests for arms and advocated a political solution to the Arab-Israeli conflict.[3] The Politburo's continued reluctance to supply Egypt with the quantity and type of weapons Sadat desired, coupled with the relaxation in Soviet-American tensions, led many Arabs to believe that détente represented a betrayal of Arab interests. Sadat's remarks to a meeting of his military advisors expressed his growing perception that Moscow had abandoned its Arab allies:

> The cold war between the blocs is over, and détente will work for twenty to twenty-five years at least. But détente means that small powers like us will be crushed. The Soviet Union does not want us to go to war. They want us to reach a peaceful solution, because they know war might drag them into confrontation with the Americans.[4]

Sadat was even more direct in a postwar interview:

> At the summit meeting between the two giants in Moscow, a statement was issued heralding the era of "military relaxation in the Middle East," which simply means the continued existence of the state of no peace, no war, which would insure that Israel would achieve, in the long term, all that it wanted without firing a single bullet.[5]

Sadat's dissatisfaction with his Soviet allies steadily increased, and in July 1972, after an Egyptian delegation returned from Moscow without promises for the delivery of the arms he demanded, he expelled Soviet advisors and troops from Egypt. Sadat later gave several reasons for the expulsion, other than frustration over the type and quantity of military aid Moscow provided to Cairo. He had come to resent the imperious attitude of senior Soviet advisors, and he likened the deportment of the Soviet ambassador to that of the British high commissioner during the British occupation of Egypt.[6] His memoirs reveal his belief that the presence of Soviet troops limited his strategic options versus Israel and infringed upon Egyptian sovereignty to a degree that became intolerable.

> I wanted to put the Soviet Union in its place—in its natural position as a friendly country, no more, no less. The Soviets had thought at one time that they had Egypt in their pocket, and that the world had come to think that the Soviet Union was our guardian. I wanted to tell the Russians that the will of Egypt was entirely Egyptian; I wanted to tell the whole world that we are always our own masters.[7]

Sadat may have been emboldened by the opening of a back-channel dialogue between the United States and Egypt at the latter's initiative in April 1972. Kissinger relates that he expected the Egyptian leader eventually to offer a Soviet withdrawal in exchange for a new American initiative for a Middle East settlement, but recalls that the expulsion came as a complete surprise.[8]

Whatever Sadat's motivations were in ordering it, the withdrawal of Soviet forces from Egypt dealt a major blow to the Soviet position in the region. Although Soviet diplomats tried to compensate by stepping up support for Syria, Iraq, and the PLO, the loss of the strategic and political advantages of the Soviet presence in Egypt meant that the high-water mark of Soviet influence in the Middle East had passed.[9]

The low ebb in Soviet-Egyptian relations proved to be relatively short-lived, however. Egyptian efforts to procure arms from European sources met with little success, and Cairo eventually concluded that the USSR was the only possible source of the weapons that would be needed for an attempt to retake the occupied territories.[10] Egyptian Premier Aziz Sidqi's visit to Moscow in October 1972 signaled a limited rapprochement, and soon afterward Soviet arms deliveries resumed at an accelerated rate.[11] New Soviet shipments included Scud missiles and substantial numbers of Sagger anti-tank guided missiles (ATGMs). "The Russians are providing us now with everything that's possible for them to supply," Sadat said in April 1973, "and I am now quite satisfied."[12] Heikal recalls that the Soviet's redoubled generosity prompted Sadat to remark, "They are drowning me in new arms."[13] The USSR's provision of guided missiles to its Arab allies illustrates the difficulty in distinguishing between offensive and defensive weapons. The ATGMs furnished to Egypt and Syria are generally regarded as primarily defensive weapons and were probably intended to be used as such, but during the opening stages of the coming war with Israel, they would be fired offensively with considerable effect.

The Soviet Union's relations with other Arab states changed as well after the end of the War of Attrition. The overthrow of the Jedid regime in Syria in November 1970, by a coup led by Hafez Assad, caused some consternation in Moscow, as Assad had opposed some aspects of Soviet policy. However, growing Syrian-Egyptian ties reassured the Politburo that the new Syrian government would not frustrate Soviet regional goals.[14] Partially as a result of the strain in Soviet-Egyptian relations, the USSR established closer ties with the ruling Ba'ath party in Iraq under Sadat's archrival, Hassan al-Bakr. When Saddam Hussein visited Moscow in February 1972 and asked for a "firm strategic alliance," the Politburo was concerned that a Soviet-Iraqi accord might encourage Iraq to attack Iran, but Kosygin nevertheless signed a treaty of friendship and alliance during his visit to Baghdad in April of that same year.[15] The USSR also attempted to appeal to the more conservative Gulf Arab states and encouraged the use of the "oil weapon" against the Western capitalist economies.[16] However, many in the Soviet elite had reservations about this tactic, as the USSR would have no control over its employment.[17]

Throughout this period, Sadat was under escalating pressure to launch an offensive aimed at recapturing the territory lost in 1967. He announced that 1971 would be the "Year of Decision" and made plans for an offensive, but soon determined that unilateral Egyptian efforts at retaking the territories had little hope of success; meanwhile, his domestic political weakness turned his ambition to reverse the outcome of the Six-Day War into an imperative.[18] El Shazly relates that the Egyptian high command made two plans for an offensive: "Operation 41," an ambitious plan made with the full knowledge and cooperation of Soviet military advisors, but designed as a long-term program so that the list of arms requirements would appear "less traumatic"; and a more limited plan, "The High

Minarets," drawn up according to actual Egyptian capabilities, that was kept secret from the Soviet advisors.[19] At a Syrian-Egyptian joint command meeting in Alexandria in April 1973, Sadat and Assad agreed to plan and execute a coordinated attack and appointed Marshal Ismail as overall commander for the operation.[20] As part of the Arab strategy for achieving surprise, war preparations were feigned in May and August, and both feints provoked an Israeli mobilization.[21]

The final decision to attack was made at a meeting between Assad and Sadat in Damascus on August 26.[22] Although the USSR would not be informed of the impending attack through diplomatic channels until October, the Politburo quickly became convinced that the USSR's regional allies were determined to unleash a new war that Moscow could not afford them to lose.

The turbulence in Soviet Middle East policy contrasted sharply with the steady development of superpower détente. The Moscow Summit in May 1972 included the signing of the Basic Principles agreement, that paved the way for Soviet-American security cooperation and that Raymond Garthoff calls a "charter for détente."[23] The summit also saw the signing of the ABM Treaty and the Interim Agreement on strategic offensive weapons that formed the core of SALT I, which gave *de facto* recognition to the existence of rough strategic parity between the Soviet and American nuclear arsenals. The formal structure of détente was further developed at the Washington Summit in May 1973, where the Prevention of Nuclear War agreement was concluded and a framework for cooperation on regional conflicts began to take shape in discussions between Kissinger and Kosygin.[24] These accords explicated the mutual interest of the two nations in crisis avoidance and in resolving regional disputes by political means.

Both Soviet and American political leaders developed personal stakes in the preservation of détente, reinforcing the value of the USSR's traditional interest in avoiding and limiting confrontations with the power that now recognized, at least implicitly, the Soviet Union's legitimacy as a global power and contributor to the preservation of peace. From the American viewpoint, however, this recognition carried with it a responsibility not to exacerbate tensions between U.S. and Soviet regional allies that unavoidably conflicted with the USSR's commitments to supply arms to Egypt and other Arab states. Kissinger succinctly expressed the American viewpoint shortly after the start of the October War: "Détente cannot survive irresponsibility in any area, including the Middle East."[25] As a result, the leaders of both nations would look upon each other's behavior in the 1973 crisis as evidence of their sincerity in adhering to the principles spelled out in the summit agreements.

Overall, although superpower détente blunted tensions, it also sharpened the contradictions between Soviet global and regional objectives.

Many Soviet allies in the developing world, Sadat included, worried that better U.S.-Soviet relations would lead to a decrease in Moscow's support for the USSR's regional allies. Victor Israelyan, a member of the team of Soviet experts put together in 1973 to advise the Politburo on the Middle East crisis, characterizes the Politburo's insoluble dilemma.

> The goal of Soviet policy was to implement simultaneously two incompatible principles: peaceful coexistence and proletarian internationalism. . . . During the Yom Kippur War the Kremlin tried to cooperate with the United States, the leader of the "imperialist camp," and at the same time did its best to help the Arabs defeat Israel and "those imperialists who were backing it"—the same United States. Such mutually exclusive, contradictory principles could not help but bring substantial losses.[26]

Along with changes in the climate of U.S.-Soviet relations at the global level, a singular factor at the individual level strongly influenced superpower interaction during the 1973 crisis. Just as the Politburo was required to deal with the distraction of the Sino-Soviet border crisis in 1969, the Nixon administration was deeply mired in the Watergate affair in the summer of 1973. Unlike the influence of the Politburo's "neuralgic area" on Soviet behavior during the War of Attrition, the effects of this domestic crisis on American decision making are well documented. As will be discussed below, the psychological strain Watergate placed on the U.S. president effectively removed him from the decision process when the crisis in the Middle East reached the point of highest tension.

Defection, Cooperation, or an Ad Hoc Strategy?

As with the 1967 and 1969–70 conflicts, two schools of thought on Soviet actions before and during the October War argue that the Politburo had a predetermined strategy. The analysis by Foy Kohler, Leon Goure, and Mose Harvey exemplifies the viewpoint that the Soviet leadership endeavored to exploit the crisis in the Middle East in order to increase the USSR's influence in the region. Because the Brezhnev Politburo tried to undermine the United States' position in the area and strengthen its own as part of a global zero-sum game, the USSR pursued a forceful strategy throughout the conflict, and Soviet actions "went beyond the bounds of prudence."[27] These scholars note that Soviet statements in the months preceding the war, which warned of an impending Israeli attack, closely resemble similar Soviet warnings issued before the Six-Day War, and they contend that these propaganda statements were part of a long-standing strategy designed to blame Israel for the war in order to obtain maximum benefits for Soviet influence in the region at the expense of the United States and its allies. Rubinstein likewise concludes that the Politburo had decided to stand firm in support of its ally before the war began and that meetings between Sadat and Soviet Ambassador Vinogradov assured the Egyptian leader that Soviet backing would be forthcoming.[28]

The opposite viewpoint is once again represented by Fukuyama, who observes that the timing and probable intention of the Soviet intervention threat falls into the pattern followed in the Six-Day War and the War of Attrition. According to his analysis, the peak of the crisis came on October 19, when Israeli forces crossed the Suez Canal, but the threat of intervention was issued on October 24, after Egypt and Israel had already agreed to two U.N. cease-fire resolutions. Fukuyama acknowledges that "some ambiguity remained as to whether the Israelis would be compelled to withdraw to their earlier position and release the [Egyptian] Third Army," but he contends that the USSR felt confident that the United States could pressure Israel to comply with the U.N. resolutions and halt its offensive.[29] Fukuyama concludes that Brezhnev's note to Nixon, which threatened to introduce Soviet troops to enforce the cease-fire, and the alerting of Soviet airborne divisions and stand-down of air transport aircraft were measures taken after the peak of the crisis that did not signal the serious possibility of Soviet intervention. From this perspective, the Politburo never had any intention of risking a Soviet-American confrontation and only issued threats of military action, which would never need to be carried out, to make doubly sure that their allies did not suffer a complete disaster. Snyder and Diesing, applying the protector-game matrix to the October War, reach a similar conclusion.[30]

Not all Western observers find that Soviet strategy in the 1973 crisis was predetermined. Breslauer concludes that the Politburo worked to advance Soviet influence in the region and capitalized upon developments in the conflict, but did not have an overriding commitment to either the pursuit of unilateral advantage or the preservation of détente.[31] In this interpretation, Soviet strategy was formulated *ad hoc;* the USSR improvised and reacted to events in order to further its regional interests. Stuart Britton terms this line of analysis the "improvisator" school.[32]

The final word on this issue should go to Israelyan, who witnessed Politburo meetings during the crisis and describes Soviet behavior as largely event-driven and reactive.[33] Nevertheless, this interpretation of Soviet behavior does not attempt to explain why the Politburo acted coercively at some points in the crisis and adopted a strategy of accommodation and risk limitation at other junctures. The value-conflict perspective helps explain the variations in Soviet risk-taking behavior more thoroughly. To see how, it is first necessary to divide the Yom Kippur War and the events that led up to it into periods defined by changes in the situational variables that made the conflict between Soviet global and regional objectives alternatively more and less acute.

Phases of the 1973 Crisis

As the Politburo knew that the USSR's Arab allies were planning an offensive against Israel for several years, the boundary between the normal state of tension in the Middle East and the crisis that led to war is less clear for the October War than for other regional conflicts.[34] On August 26, a decision was taken at the Arab joint command meeting in Damascus to launch an attack on Yom Kippur, which in 1973 fell on October 6.[35] This study will therefore use August 26 as the starting point for the first of the eight phases into which the 1973 crisis divides. (As before, each phase will be assigned a name for convenience.) Galia Golan suggests that the Soviet government suspected that its allies were planning an attack shortly after the joint command meeting.[36] Soviet commentaries on the September meeting in Cairo between Sadat, Assad, and King Hussein of Jordan mention that the Arab leaders "strive to use all means available . . . to resist the aggressor and the imperialist forces protecting him"—a clear reference to unprecedented military cooperation among the Arab states.[37] The USSR was reminded of its allies' deteriorating position when 13 Syrian aircraft were destroyed in a dogfight with the Israeli Air Force on September 13; Glukhov penned that the combat showed Israel was using "blackmail and intimidation" against its neighbors.[38] Soviet suspicions that a new war was being planned, coupled with uncertainty as to when it would begin (with no strategic warning that an offensive would be launched shortly), indicate that during the first or "Decision & Commitment" phase of the crisis both time pressure and autonomous risk should be valued moderately low.

Clear strategic warning came on October 1, when Sadat ordered the offensive to be set in motion.[39] Sadat's order will be used to mark the start of the crisis' second or "Attack Preparations" phase. It is impossible to know how quickly Soviet intelligence learned of this order, but any doubts than an attack was imminent would have vanished by October 3, when, according to his own recollections, Sadat summoned Vinogradov to inform him of the decision to attack Israel.[40] Sadat recalls that he did not tell the Soviet ambassador the exact date when it would commence, but preparations for an offensive (such as the alert of the Egyptian Second and Third armies and the closing of Cairo Airport) became evident soon after the order was given.[41] Israelyan relates that Gromyko knew on October 4 that the Arab attack would start on October 6.[42] Because the strategic warning the Politburo received allowed some time to prepare for the impending war, time pressure during this second phase may be rated as moderately high. As Sadat had planned, the Arab preparations did not provoke an Israeli mobilization, so the chance of successful preemptive action was present, but not great, indicating that autonomous risk should be valued moderately high as well.

When Operation *Badr* began at 1400 hours on October 6, the Soviet leadership had good reason to doubt that their allies' offensive would succeed. The initial Egyptian assault soon threw bridgeheads across the canal, and Syrian forces gained ground on the Golan front, but by October 8 or 9 the momentum of the offensive was being lost and Israel's reserve forces, which were mobilized more rapidly than expected, were turning back the Arab advances.[43] The Soviet press reflected the uncertainties and dangers of the fluid situation in the first days of the war, with Matveev warning that the ongoing combat was "fraught with serious consequences for the entire world situation."[44] Israeli counterattacks in the Golan began regaining ground from Syrian forces (and from the Iraqi units that had arrived at the front on October 11) and achieved a breakthrough on October 12.[45] (The Israeli cabinet had decided on October 10 to attack in the direction of Damascus, but did not plan to occupy the Syrian capital at that time, and it is impossible to know whether the Politburo was apprised of Israeli intentions.)[46] In any case, Israelyan reports that by October 7, the situation on the Syrian front was critical and that Assad was "beginning to panic."[47]

The danger to Soviet interests in the region was illustrated by incidents such as the bombing of the Soviet cultural center in Damascus on October 9 and the sinking of the merchant ship *Il'ia Menchikov* in Tartus harbor on the October 12.[48] The best available reports indicate that the Politburo had decided by October 7 to start airlifting arms, and Soviet aircraft began arriving on October 10.[49] Comparison of the number of reported SAM launches by Syrian forces on October 10 and 11 suggests that substantial numbers of air-defense missiles arrived with the earliest shipments.[50] The fluidity of the front lines and the risk that the conflagration would end with a major Arab defeat indicate that during phase 3 of the crisis, which will be named after Operation *Badr,* time pressure on Soviet decision makers should be valued high, as should autonomous risk.[51]

When Israel's counteroffensive on the Golan front stalled by October 13, and the second phase of the Egyptian attack in the Sinai similarly failed, the war entered a period of stalemate.[52] Press accounts of the fighting on the Golan front reported that the Israeli drive had been repulsed.[53] Glukhov indicated that Egyptian forces were prevailing on the Sinai front, writing that Israeli youths, "hirsute as hippies," surrendered at Port Tewfiq because they did not want to die fighting for foreign soil.[54] Algeria's President Boumedienne visited Moscow to ask for more vigorous Soviet support of the Arab war effort, but the "friendly and frank" discussions produced little noticeable increase in the amount of Soviet material assistance.[55] The stability of both fronts during the few days following the halt of the Israeli Golan counterattack and the success of Soviet resupply efforts in shoring up their allies' defenses mark the crisis' fourth or "Stalemate" phase as a brief breathing space for the Politburo and indicate that time pressure during this period fell to moderate levels while autonomous risk remained high.

The Politburo's respite proved short-lived. The next phase of the crisis began when Israeli forces crossed the Suez Canal near Deversoir in the early morning hours of October 16.[56] Phase 5 of the crisis will therefore be referred to as the "Counteroffensive" phase. Having shifted its main effort to the Suez front, the Israel Defense Force began posing an increasingly serious threat to Egypt after the capture of the Chinese Farm position on October 17 and the subsequent expansion of the bridgeheads on the canal's west bank. The Politburo's military advisors warned on October 16 that the Israeli offensive could lead to Egypt's complete collapse.[57] Kissinger flew to Moscow for meetings with Brezhnev and Gromyko on October 20 to work out a joint appeal for a cease-fire.[58]

Typically, the success of the canal counteroffensive went largely unreported in the Soviet press during this period, with commentators announcing that Arab forces continued to deal Israel a "resolute rebuff."[59] These reports notwithstanding, the success of Israel's cross-canal attack made the crisis' fifth phase a tense one for the USSR, with both time pressure and autonomous risk valued high, until Sadat informed Vinogradov on October 21 that he would accept a cease-fire.[60]

Sadat's announcement raised hopes that the war could be brought to a swift end and serves to mark the start of phase 6 of the crisis, which was characterized by vigorous diplomatic efforts while the fighting continued in fits and starts. The U.N. Security Council passed Resolution 338 on October 21, which was accepted by Israel, Egypt, and Jordan and provisionally accepted by Syria. At 1852 hours on October 22 a cease-fire was in effect on the Suez front. Phase 6 of the crisis will consequently be called the "First Cease-Fire" phase. The Soviet-American agreement on the terms of a cease-fire, followed by its acceptance in principle by most of the parties to the conflict, dropped the time pressure acting on the Soviet leadership during this phase to moderate. The Politburo's main immediate objective, a cease-fire that would end the war and begin the process of disengagement, had been acceded to by the USSR's principal global opponent as well as the primary local actors, and a Soviet decision on what to do next to resolve the crisis would not be immediately required if the cease-fire held.

It was far from certain during phase 6, however, that the cease-fire would in fact be observed, and hostile forces remained active and in close proximity to one another. By 1200 hours on October 22, the lines of communication to the Egyptian Third Army in the southern sector of the front were cut, and Israel continued to move troops across the Canal after the cease-fire.[61] By the early hours of October 23, the cease-fire had obviously broken down, and Israel was launching new attacks on the west bank of the canal.[62] U.N. Resolution 339, renewing the call for a cease-fire, was passed that same day and was due to come into effect at 0700 hours on October 24.

There was, therefore, a substantial risk of accidental or inadvertent conflict between Arab and Israeli military forces that could lead to renewed escalation, and the failure of the first cease-fire demonstrated that the potential for events to run out of control still existed during this phase. Israel's reinforcement of its positions west of the Suez Canal, which could indicate that Israel had little intention of observing the cease-fire, and the subsequent failure of the first cease-fire show that the autonomous risk remained high during this period despite the relaxation of time pressure on Soviet decision makers.[63]

Developments on the Sinai front on October 24 gave the Politburo good reason to doubt that the second U.N.-mandated cease-fire would hold. The encirclement of the Third Army was complete by midnight, and Egyptian counterattacks failed to break it.[64] Because this encirclement was the dominant factor in the strategic situation during this period of the conflict, phase 7 of the crisis will be termed the "Encirclement" phase. The cease-fire due to commence at 0700 was stillborn. Israeli forces attempted to capture the city of Suez and refused to allow the resupply of the encircled Egyptians after the appointed time had passed.[65] Golan relates that "the atmosphere in Cairo was one of mortal danger and near panic."[66] By the time Sadat cabled Nixon and Brezhnev with an invitation to send both U.S. and Soviet forces to enforce a cease-fire, Israeli forces had already violated two cease-fires and were continuing to press their advantage on the west bank.[67]

This was the situation facing the two superpowers when a note from Brezhnev to Nixon, accepting Sadat's invitation and stating that the USSR would act unilaterally if the United States did not agree to joint intervention, was sent early in the morning of October 25, Moscow time.[68] (It was received at 2135 hours on October 24, Washington time.)[69] The content of this note will be discussed in detail later. Kissinger recalls that a conversation with White House Chief of Staff Alexander Haig convinced him that Nixon was "too distraught" over the Watergate crisis to participate in preliminary discussions on a response to the Soviet message, so Kissinger convened a Washington Special Action Group meeting, and at 2341 Washington time Admiral Moorer, chairman of the Joint Chiefs of Staff, issued orders for all U.S. forces to go on Defense Condition (DEFCON) 3 alert.[70]

A few hours later, another cease-fire became a dead letter as Israeli forces mounted a third assault on Suez at approximately 0800 hours, but this proved to be the last major Israeli attack of the war.[71] Although fighting on the ground in Egypt was the main source of both time pressure and autonomous risk for Soviet decision makers, the American nuclear alert exacerbated them and caused a shock in the United States and the rest of the world. Kissinger admits that the alert was not called for strategic reasons, but as a means of political signaling to show that the United States "meant business." Kissinger further relates that DEFCON 3 was chosen because it was the lowest level of alert that the Politburo would notice, and additional measures (including alerts of U.S. airborne divisions) were taken because the nuclear alert alone would not be detected quickly enough.[72]

In the event, the American alert did not have to be maintained for long to serve its signaling function, as the "superpower crisis" ended late in the evening of October 25 (Moscow time), when Brezhnev cabled Washington to agree that no Soviet or American troops should be sent to observe the cease-fire.[73] Phase 7 of the crisis was a period of very high time pressure and high autonomous risk, not because of the alert from Washington, which both sides realized was a political signal, but because of the critical situation of the Egyptian forces on the canal front.

Brezhnev's communiqué disavowing the possibility of Soviet intervention served as a notice to all parties that a serious resurgence of fighting was unlikely in the final phase of the crisis, although sporadic combat could continue. The United States stood down from nuclear alert at midnight on October 25, and a final cease-fire was in effect by 1230 hours on October 28.[74] Soviet reportage of Kissinger's October 25 press conference did not mention the U.S. alert, though the version of the transcript published later in *Pravda* quoted him as saying that the two superpowers were not in confrontation.[75] The dangerous period of the crisis having passed, time pressure during phase 8, which will be referred to as the "De-escalation" phase (October 26–28) was low, and autonomous risk fell to moderately low levels but did not vanish entirely until the final cease-fire.

The Soviet media gave no indication that a superpower conflict had taken place, until October 27, when TASS reported that the United States, citing Soviet actions as a pretext, had briefly placed its forces on alert. TASS reassured its listeners that "such explanations are absurd since the actions of the Soviet Union are aimed solely at promoting the implementation of the decisions of the Security Council on the cease-fire and restoration of peace in the Middle East."[76]

Table 4 on the following page encapsulates the values of the independent variables in the eight phases of the 1973 crisis and lists the resulting likelihood of Soviet risk-taking during each phase. As the table indicates, the periods when the Politburo would be expected to adopt a strategy of coercion in an attempt to avoid the value trade-off between Soviet regional and global goals are phase 3, the initial period of the war (Operation *Badr*), and phase

Table 4   Time Pressure and Autonomous Risk in the October War

Phase	Date	Time Pressure	Autonomous Risk	Likelihood of Risk-taking
1. Decision & Commitment	August 26–September 30	Low	Moderately Low	Low
2. Attack Preparations	October 1–October 6	Moderately High	Moderately High	Moderately High
3. Operation *Badr*	October 6–October 12	High	High	High
4. Stalemate	October 13–October 15	Moderate	High	Moderate
5. Counteroffensive	October 16–October 21	Moderately High	High	Moderately High
6. First Cease-Fire	October 21–October 24	Moderate	High	Moderate
7. Encirclement	October 24–October 25	Very High	High	Very High
8. Deescalation	October 26–October 28	Low	Moderately Low	Low

7, the Encirclement, during which Israeli forces threatened to destroy the trapped Egyptian Third Army.

Kissinger concludes that Nixon's political weakness, attributable to the Watergate scandal, was in part responsible for the Soviet threat to intervene militarily in the conflict, recalling "We had no choice except to call the bluff, if that was what it was, or face the reality if it was serious"[77] As Israelyan relates, the USSR's top leaders were surprised and dismayed by the American reaction to Brezhnev's note of October 25. He quotes Podgorniy's reaction to the U.S. overreaction: "Who could have imagined that the Americans would be so easily frightened?"[78] An examination of Soviet statements and actions before and during the October War, with special attention to evidence of the effects of value conflict, may help determine how the superpowers moved from concord and cooperation to confusion and confrontation in less than 48 hours in October 1973.

Soviet Behavior in the 1973 Crisis and War

Soviet spokesmen devoted considerable energy during the first phase of the crisis to defend Soviet policy from charges that détente meant a betrayal of Arab interests. Many commentaries were rebuttals to editorials in Egyptian and other Arab papers. O. Orlov, for example, denied Egyptian charges that détente had weakened Soviet support for the struggle to "liquidate the consequences of Israeli aggression."[79] A Radio Moscow commentary similarly contended that Soviet oil exports to the United States did not indicate that the USSR was trying to lessen American dependence on Arab oil and claimed that those who said otherwise were "enemies of Arab-Soviet friendship."[80] Vitaliy Korionov argued that contrary to the anti-détente current of Arab opinion, the Algiers summit of the Non-Aligned Movement showed that détente and strategic parity had aided the "national liberation struggle."[81] Commentaries on the anniversary of Nasser's death pointed out that the fallen Arab leader had recognized that only Soviet assistance had enabled the Arab states to withstand imperialist intrigues and aggression.[82] *Za rubezhem* guest commentator Yassir Arafat defended Soviet policy toward its Middle Eastern allies:

> It is now obvious, as never before, that the leading role in world politics belongs to the USSR, which, performing its internationalist duty, supports the struggle for national liberation and social progress throughout the world. Zionist and imperialist propaganda about a compact between the superpowers is a slanderous fabrication.[83]

Soviet official pronouncements during the Decision & Commitment phase called for a settlement of the Arab-Israeli conflict by nonviolent means. The joint Soviet-Bulgarian communiqué issued on the occasion of Brezhnev's visit to Sofia proclaimed agreement on the need for a political settlement and implied that a resolution of the conflict should take at least some of Israel's vital interests into account:

> In connection with the Middle East situation, which remains complex and dangerous for the cause of peace, the two sides declared for the speediest political settlement of the problem on the basis of the well-known decisions of the United Nations, for ensuring the legitimate rights and interests of all countries and peoples of the area, including the Arab people of Palestine.[84]

Beginning in mid-September, warnings of an impending Israeli attack against Syria or Lebanon began appearing in the Soviet media. Many of these reports quoted Arab sources, as Radio Moscow did when it referred to reputed Israeli troop concentrations in the Golan Heights as "a prelude to large-scale operations."[85] TASS repeatedly echoed that Israel was beginning "military preparations" against Lebanon and Syria, and Koriavin charged that Tel Aviv was seeking to increase tensions and pursue an "expansionist course" in the Near East with renewed military provocations.[86] Reports of Israeli troop concentrations had appeared earlier in August, before the Damascus meeting of the Arab joint command, so the mid-September reports do not constitute a sudden, unique propaganda offensive against Israel.[87]

The new wave of accusations in September may represent a reaction to the September 13 battle between Israeli and Syrian aircraft, which A. Kurov claimed was a terrorist incursion designed as a distraction from Tel Aviv's domestic difficulties.[88] Alternatively, as Golan concludes, they may have been an attempt to prepare public opinion for the possibility of a new war, because the Politburo knew that their allies were planning an offensive but did not know exactly when it would begin.[89]

On October 3, two days after Sadat issued the order for final preparations for an attack to begin, he summoned Vinogradov and told the Soviet ambassador, "I'd like to inform you officially that I and Syria have decided to start military operations against Israel so as to break the present deadlock. I would like the Soviet leaders to give me an urgent answer to this question: What will the Soviet attitude be?"[90] Sadat recollects that Vinogradov replied the following day by asking permission for special flights to evacuate the dependents of Soviet citizens still in Egypt, and the evacuation was carried out on October 4. The next day, October 5, Soviet ships began moving out of Alexandria and Port Said.[91] George speculates that the evacuation may have been a warning to the United States that the indications of an impending Egyptian attack should be taken seriously.[92] If the evacuation was intended as a warning, Washington did not react to it.

The Soviet media, for their part, gave off conflicting signals during the second phase of the crisis. On October 4, for example, TASS broadcast that Israel was reinforcing its armored and airborne units on the Golan Heights, but Radio Moscow quoted Syrian denials that a crisis existed in the Middle East and blamed rumors to that effect on imperialist propaganda.[93] The October 6 morning edition of *Pravda* included an article by Glukhov that warned that Israel was planning a massive attack and compared the situation in the Near East to the period immediately before the Six-Day War.[94]

The Soviet government statement issued at the start of the war on October 6 showed none of the hints of evenhandedness contained in the prewar Brezhnev-Zhivkov communiqué. The statement placed the blame for the conflict "wholly and entirely" on Israel and "external reactionary circles" and reaffirmed the USSR's unequivocal support for the Arab cause, though it did not indicate the level of material aid the Politburo was prepared to extend to it.

> What is happening in the Near East confirms forcibly the immutable truth that the liquidation of the hotbed of constant tension and the establishment of a reliable and guaranteed peace for all the states of the area are unthinkable without the complete liberation of all the Arab territories occupied by Israel and ensuring the legitimate rights of the Arab population of Palestine. The Soviet Union, true to its principled policy of support for peoples striving for liberation and independence, consistently acts as a reliable friend of the Arab States. Condemning Israel's annexationist policy, the Soviet Union resolutely supports the legitimate demands of the Arab States for the liberation of all Arab territories occupied by Israel since 1967.[95]

Mention of the rights of "all peoples" in the area is conspicuous by its absence, as it would have been difficult to blame Israel for launching an aggressive war while intimating that it may have had legitimate interests to protect. Israel's leaders, the communiqué concluded, would bear full responsibility for that country's "unreasonable course."

In the Soviet press, Primakov claimed that Israel had been concentrating its forces for weeks to carry out a preplanned attack and warned that the Arab-Israeli conflict could only be solved by political means.[96] Koriavin, noting that Egypt was winning on the Sinai front, also observed that the prewar situation was "reminiscent" of 1967.[97] With the exception of a Radio Moscow report that "Algerian observers" were concerned over "suspicious" movements of the 6th Fleet, accusations of American complicity in the alleged Israeli "offensive" were conspicuously absent.[98] The *Pravda* "Observer," on the day Israeli counterattacks achieved a breakthrough on the Golan front, condemned Israel for using terror against civilians, but cited a surprisingly evenhanded passage from an October 8 speech by Brezhnev:

Naturally, all our sympathies are on the side of the victims of aggression. As for the Soviet Union, it has been and still is a convinced supporter of a just in lasting peace in the Near East and guaranteed security for all the countries and peoples of this area which is so close to our borders.[99]

In spite of the early successes of the Egyptian and Syrian offensives, the Politburo was not sanguine about the Arab's prospects in the first days of the war, and Soviet diplomatic activity during this period used duplicitous means to convince its allies to accept a quick cease-fire. Sadat writes that Vinogradov met with him at 1940 hours on October 6 and told him that, in an October 4 meeting between Assad and the USSR's ambassador to Syria, Mukhitdinov, Assad had asked the USSR to call for a cease-fire within 48 hours of the start of hostilities. Sadat did not believe Vinogradov and refused to consider halting the offensive.[100] Sadat queried Assad soon after the meeting, but did not receive a reply until the following afternoon, when the Syrian leader cabled his denial of Vinogradov's story. Vinogradov asked for another meeting a few hours later, and when Sadat told him that Assad had denied asking for a cease-fire, his face reportedly turned white.[101] He nevertheless relayed the message that Syria had asked for another cease-fire before outlining the USSR's plans for an airlift of war materiel.

The Politburo soon made good on its promises to resupply its embattled allies. After the Soviet leadership saw the military situation deteriorate by October 7, the decision was made to begin a massive logistics effort, with the first shipments to go to Syria. The first Soviet transport aircraft took off on October 8 and arrived in Syria on October 9 (after a stopover in Budapest).[102] Quandt estimates that the USSR sent 12,500 tons of supplies to Egypt, Syria, and Iraq by air, and 58,000 tons to Egypt and Syria by sea during the war.[103] The Soviet government also took some limited and probably precautionary military measures during the Operation *Badr* phase of the crisis. Seven airborne divisions were put on alert on October 8, and their alert status was upgraded on October 11.[104] Additionally, a cruiser and two destroyers were moved through the Dardanelles into the Mediterranean on October 10.[105]

By October 13, the situation had become much less tense from Moscow's standpoint. Fighting on both fronts had become stalemated, and Algerian President Boumedienne flew to Moscow on October 14 to convince the Politburo to increase arms shipments to levels sufficient to break the stalemate. The "friendly and frank" talks with Brezhnev, Kosygin, Podgorniy, Gromyko, and Grechko yielded a statement of the USSR's determination to "assist in every way" the liberation of all territories occupied by Israel, but few new arms.[106] According to Sadat, Boumedienne offered $200 million for new weapons, but his offer was refused, and upon his return to Algiers he told his advisors, "While the Americans and the Israelis are eager to defeat President Sadat, the Soviet Union is a hundred times more eager to defeat him."[107] Soviet air shipments to Syria were stepped up on October 15, however, probably in response to the Israeli drive toward Damascus.[108]

A Radio Moscow broadcast during the period of stalemate in the crisis' fourth phase stressed Arab unity in the face of aggression, contending that "Israel will inevitably face the entire Arab world with its huge human and natural resources."[109] Golan believes that this statement was intended as a further signal that large increases in Soviet military aid were not forthcoming.[110] Maevskiy's October 14 *Pravda* commentary reflected an indication that the Soviet government was not willing to jeopardize détente to secure an Arab victory, noting that although the fighting was becoming "increasingly fierce," growing Arab unity would carry the day.[111]

The clearest signal in the fourth phase that Soviet leaders were not prepared to allow the war to jeopardize détente came from Kosygin. In a speech made on October 15 during a visit to Denmark, Kosygin said that Israeli aggression, abetted by "outside support and patronage," was to blame for the current military conflict, and he argued that forces opposed to the relaxation in U.S.-Soviet tensions were unjustifiably trying to paint the USSR as the culprit.

> We cannot but see that the opponents of détente are trying to use every pretext to revive the atmosphere of the cold war and cause mistrust in the policy of peaceful coexistence. They are now trying in every was to exploit for these purposes the resumption of hostilities in the Middle East, whitewashing the aggressor and accusing the victims of aggression. They have gone so far in this that they are presenting the Soviet Union's solidarity with the victims of Israel's aggression—with the Arab countries—as all but the source of tension in the area. It is difficult to imagine anything further removed from reality.[112]

Kosygin went on to say that the USSR was ready to make its contribution to a settlement that guaranteed the security of all nations of the region, but did not specify what kind of support the USSR would contribute to its Arab allies. His speech indicates that during the first brief period of stalemate in the October War, the Politburo was not willing to jeopardize its global interest in détente to further its regional interest in a victory for Arab solidarity. Upon his return to Moscow, Kosygin reluctantly agreed to go to Cairo, with instructions to tell Sadat that the USSR would not intervene militarily in the war. Israelyan relates that Kosygin was not happy about his mission and felt that he had no clear message to convey to the Egyptian leader.[113]

The Soviet tone changed abruptly on October 16, the start of phase 5, when Israeli forces threw bridgeheads across the Suez Canal. A TASS broadcast reported that day that 30,000 American "so-called volunteers" to fight for Israel were waiting to be dispatched.[114] *Izvestiia* later quoted unnamed "news agencies" as its source for a similar report.[115]

Not all Soviet reports warned of the possibility of U.S. intervention, however. Mikhail Sagatelian defended détente in *Literaturnaia gazeta*, arguing that it had restrained American aggressiveness and reduced the likelihood that the United States would become directly involved in the Middle East conflict.[116] Some press accounts made no secret of the fact that the United States was not the only superpower backing the parties to the military conflict. Commentator Leonid Latyshev acknowledged that the USSR was rendering military assistance to its Arab allies.[117]

Execration of Israel continued apace during the Counteroffensive phase, as reports repeated the charge that Israel was preparing to invade Lebanon.[118] A. Urzov in *Trud* described Israel's leadership as increasingly desperate and barbaric, reporting that pilots were being chained inside their cockpits and that any who refused to bomb civilians were summarily executed.[119]

The airlift of war material to the USSR's Arab allies increased during the Counteroffensive phase, with a pronounced increase in the airlift to Egypt beginning on October 17.[120] It is unlikely that this is related to developments during phase 5, however, as some lead time would be required to make the necessary logistical arrangements. Quandt concludes that the increase in arms deliveries was prompted by the loss of over 200 Egyptian tanks in a failed Sinai offensive on October 14.[121] Soviet naval activity increased during the fifth phase as well. Soviet troop transports entered the Mediterranean on October 17, followed by two destroyers on October 19, although U.S. Admiral Bagley later described the behavior of Soviet naval units as generally "restrained and considerate," recalling, "It looked as though they were taking some care not to cause an incident."[122]

Soviet diplomatic activity continued to focus on gaining agreement to a cease-fire. Kosygin arrived in Cairo on October 16 to propose a peace plan, but his initial entreaties to Sadat met with little success. Sadat recalls that their first meeting became acrimonious over the perennial issue of Soviet arms deliveries:

[Kosygin's] main request was that we should have a cessation of hostilities on the existing lines. "I'm not prepared," I said, "to have a repeat of the 1948 'truce' which was behind our loss of the war." "We'll come in here and guarantee nothing of the sort would happen," he said. "With Israel," I replied, "you can't guarantee anything! Besides, where are the tanks I asked for on the second day of the war? Your present air-bridge is only providing me with overdue equipment—things you should have sent us much earlier in 1973, long before the war."[123]

Exactly what Sadat understood by Kosygin's offer of a "guarantee" is not clear, since Kosygin claimed that he told Sadat that the Soviet Union would not become involved in the war, as he had been instructed to do. Sadat reportedly asked about the possibility of a joint U.S.-Soviet guarantee for a cease-fire, including a joint peace observation force, but Kosygin hedged, saying that the United States might not agree to the idea.[124] Kosygin met with Sadat each day until October 19, but returned home empty-handed, as the Egyptian president refused to agree to his call for a cease-fire.

Meanwhile, one of the most significant long-term consequences of the October War was set into motion on October 17, when the oil-exporting Arab states took the decision to cut oil production. This action and the subsequent Arab boycott of oil shipments to the United States received high praise in the Soviet media. Tomas Kolesnichenko predicted that the embargo would deeply effect the U.S. economy and attempted to place the blame for it on Israel's American supporters.[125] V. Osipov commented that the embargo had exacerbated the energy crisis in the United States and that increased competition for oil among America, Europe, and Japan could shatter the Western alliance.[126] B. Rachkov offered a similar analysis.[127] Not all of these dire predictions proved true, and any Soviet encouragement to use the "oil weapon" probably had little effect on the decision to impose the embargo, which was lead by the conservative Gulf states. Nevertheless, the ensuing rise in the price of oil probably did more damage to American economic strength, and thereby to American strategic power, than any aspect of Soviet policy toward the Third World.

In contrast to phase 5, during which some signs of increased U.S.-Soviet friction are visible, the crisis' sixth phase was a period of U.S.-Soviet collaboration in efforts to achieve a cease-fire. Kissinger traveled to Moscow on October 20 for talks with Brezhnev and Gromyko, which he claims resulted in Soviet acceptance of the American formula for a cease-fire along prewar lines.[128] The draft text they agreed upon, that would become U.N. Resolution 338, included the provision that "immediately and concurrently with the cease-fire, negotiations start between the parties concerned under appropriate auspices aimed at establishing a just and durable peace settlement in the Middle East."[129] An unpublished U.S.-Soviet "understanding" was also agreed upon, intended to clarify the superpowers' roles in the subsequent negotiations:

It is understood that the phrase "under appropriate auspices" in point 3 of the Security Council Resolution shall mean that the negotiations between the parties concerned will take place with the active participation of the United States and the Soviet Union at the beginning and thereafter in the course of negotiations when key issues of a settlement are dealt with.[130]

Moscow and Washington would later differ, however, about whose "auspices" would be most "appropriate" to broker a truce, and this difference would add to the tensions that escalated just a few days after Kissinger left Moscow.

Radio Moscow justified cooperation with the United States to its Arab listeners by saying that the cease-fire was a step aimed at "liquidating fully" the Arab-Israeli conflict and at securing an Israeli withdrawal from the occupied territories.[131] Other commentaries singled out "staunchness in the Arab nation" as the most important factor in resolution of the conflict, with Andrei Krushinskiy claiming that Arab unity, socialist aid, and the oil weapon would insure victory over Israel.[132]

Israel's leadership was still described as desperate and blamed for starting the war during this period. A TASS report said that Israel was offering $5,000 to American pilots with experience in Vietnam to replace Israeli pilots who had been shot down or executed for refusing to bomb civilians, and Agaryshev claimed that Israel began hostilities with a commando raid on Qantarah early in the morning of October 6.[133] Leontiev noted that Arab unity helped the military situation, but pointed also to foreign press reports that gave credit to Soviet weapons and training.[134] Leontiev joined other Soviet commentators in describing the war as "becoming protracted," but while Koriavin disparaged the United States for inflaming the conflict with military aid to Israel, A. Vasiliev and B. Orekhov concluded that the protracted nature of the conflict "dictates the need for a political settlement."[135]

The failure of the first cease-fire initiated the pivotal period of the crisis. Initial Soviet reports of the cease-fire said that it came into effect in the evening of October 22 but was soon violated by Israeli forces.[136] The Soviet government's official reaction to the failure of the first cease-fire called Israel's acceptance of it a "gross lie," decried subsequent Israeli military actions as a "flagrant flouting of the Security Council's resolution," and issued a stern demand for Israel's adherence to a new cease-fire:

> The Soviet Government, the entire Soviet people express an angry protest against these perfidious actions of the Israeli Government and demand that Israel should immediately cease fire and all the hostilities against the troops of the Arab States and pull back its troops to the line of cease-fire of 22 October, in accordance with the resolution of the Security Council of 22 October 1973. The Soviet Government warns the Government of Israel of the gravest consequences that the continuation of its aggressive actions against the Arab Republic of Egypt and the Syrian Arab Republic will entail.[137]

Israelyan recalls that the Soviet leadership felt betrayed when Israel failed to honor the cease-fire, blamed the United States for the crisis on the canal, and accused Kissinger of double-dealing. Brezhnev himself reportedly remarked, "Here in Moscow, Kissinger behaved in a cunning way. He vowed fidelity to the policy of détente, and then while in Tel Aviv he made a deal with Golda."[138]

Moscow also employed a variety of military measures to pressure Israel, directly and through the United States, to cease its operations against Egypt. Seven airborne divisions were placed on a higher state of alert on October 23.[139] Neutron emissions from a Soviet freighter that passed through the Bosporus on October 22 and arrived at Alexandria on October 25 may have indicated the presence of nuclear weapons on board.[140] Quandt notes, however, that since vessels of the Soviet Mediterranean squadron were equipped with nuclear weapons, the freighter may have supplied Soviet vessels with any warheads aboard before it reached Egypt. In any case, he concludes, there is "no reliable evidence" that Soviet nuclear weapons ever entered Egypt.[141]

Israelyan concludes that these military moves were not authorized by the Politburo, but were ordered by Defense Minister Grechko on his own authority.[142] Marshal Grechko also authorized the use of the most advanced Soviet weaponry in the Middle East without consulting with the Politburo. Vinogradov called the Foreign Ministry in Moscow on October 22 with an Egyptian request to fire a SCUD missile at a target in Israel. Because Gromyko was not immediately available, Vinogradov contacted Grechko, who reportedly answered, "Go the hell ahead and fire it!" Gromyko called Vinogradov a short time later and furiously countermanded Grechko's order, but the missile had already been fired.[143] The missile landed in the Sinai desert without effect, but it is disturbing to speculate what might have happened had the missile struck an Israeli city.

None of these measures persuaded Israel to comply with the USSR's demands. The Egyptian Third Army was completely encircled by midnight on October 23–24, and attacks on the cities of Suez and Ismailia continued after 0700 hours on October 24, when the second cease-fire was due to come into force.[144] The Soviet media reported both Syria's acceptance of the second U.N.-mandated cease-fire as well as Israel's violations of it throughout the Encirclement phase of the crisis.[145] Soviet responses to violations of the second cease-fire were likewise not limited to verbal threats. The airlift to the USSR's Arab allies stopped early on October 24, and Soviet transport aircraft involved in the airlift were stood down, indicating that they might have been readied to carry airborne troops.[146] Israelyan claims that this action was taken without explicit authorization from the Politburo.[147]

According to Kissinger, Sadat's call for joint Soviet-American intervention to enforce a cease-fire was received in Washington at about 1300 hours on October 24.[148] Israelyan's memoir gives us an unprecedented glimpse at

Soviet decision making at this point in the crisis. At a Politburo meeting on October 24, Brezhnev declared "the time for empty words has passed" and asked for opinions on how to respond to Sadat's desperate request. Simply endorsing Sadat's call for Soviet and American peacekeepers was dismissed as a waste of time, but unilateral Soviet intervention was also ruled out as too risky, and in any case it was quickly determined that substantial Soviet forces could not be deployed in time. With the range of Soviet options thus narrowing, Israelyan recalls that a thinly veiled threat was seen as the only way to save Sadat's regime:

> Therefore it was decided to hint to the Americans that in case the United States was not ready for joint action the Kremlin would not exclude the possibility of unilateral action in the Middle East. The participants were convinced that even a reference to such an eventuality would frighten Washington, and force it to take appropriate measures with Israel. However, no military measures in conjunction with such a Soviet statement were considered at the meeting.[149]

An appropriately threatening message was immediately drafted and presented for Politburo approval and Brezhnev's signature. About 2135 hours on October 24, Washington time, Dobrynin read Brezhnev's note over the phone to Kissinger.

> Let us together, the Soviet Union and the United States, urgently dispatch Soviet and American military contingents to Egypt, to ensure implementation of the Security Council decision of October 22 and 23 concerning the cessation of fire and all military activities, and also of our understanding with you on the guarantee of the implementation of the Security Council decisions. It is necessary to adhere without delay. I will say it straight, that if you find it impossible to act with U.S. in this matter, we should be faced with the necessity urgently to consider the question of taking appropriate steps unilaterally. Israel cannot be permitted to get away with the violation.[150]

Israelyan relates that this message was "drafted cautiously" in order "not to frighten the Americans too much."[151] This caution did not have the desired effect. Nixon recalled Brezhnev's note as having an "ominous sound to it," particularly because it warned that the USSR might act "unilaterally:"

> Now that to me was a code word. For the Soviet Union to move any kind of forces into the Mid-East would, first, tip the balance so that Israel would have been down the tube. But even more important, it would have established the precedent where the Soviets had a presence in the Mid-East. . . . And so it ran the risk of a great power confrontation.[152]

Nixon's response reveals that the United States took Brezhnev's threat seriously, although it appears to show selective memory regarding the "precedent" set by the stationing of Soviet forces in Egypt from 1970 to 1972. Kissinger recalls that he decided that an immediate and unequivocal response was required:

> There was no question in my mind that we would have to reject the Soviet proposal. And we would have to do so in a manner that shocked the Soviets into abandoning the unilateral move they were threatening—and, for all our information, planning. For we had tangible reasons to take the threat seriously. . . . And I could not avoid the conviction that Nixon's evident weakness over Watergate had not a little to do with the Politburo's willingness to dare so crass a challenge.[153]

After a meeting of the Washington Special Action group, with Nixon absent from the proceedings, a worldwide DEFCON 3 alert was ordered at 2341 hours (0641 on October 25 in Cairo). Subsequently, the U.S. 82nd Airborne Division was alerted, B-52s were ordered to stage to the United States from Guam, and the aircraft carriers *Franklin D. Roosevelt* and *John F. Kennedy* were ordered to join the *Independence* in the Mediterranean off Crete.[154] (The participation of ships named after U.S. presidents who achieved heroic stature by their actions in crises is an interesting irony.)

Kissinger freely admits that "The readiness measures were a signal to Moscow," intended as a gesture of firm resolve, and that while the National Security Council was concerned about public opinion over the apparent bellicosity of the alert, he felt that "the real charge is that we provoked this by being soft."[155] The key decision makers in both the United States and the Soviet Union were aware that the U.S. alert was intended for political signaling rather than military readiness, but it is clear that American leaders regarded Brezhnev's message as a coercive maneuver that required a response in kind.

There is some evidence that the Soviet threat and the American response to it had a significant effect on Israel's decision to accept the final cease-fire. Eban revealed in a postwar interview that the Israeli cabinet was persuaded that the Soviet threat was serious by the alert of Soviet airborne forces, the stand-down of transport aircraft, and other military measures.

> The feeling was that there could very will be a Soviet military intervention in the Middle East, unless the U.S. put up a very strong show. . . . In the Cabinet there was a consensus that the Soviets might intervene unless the Cabinet responded, it was that persuasive. There was physical evidence of Soviet strength. The Cabinet meeting of the 25th lasted until 4:00 in the morning. The entire meeting was devoted to the question, do we accept the second

cease-fire or do we not? The decision was unanimous The decisive factor was the Soviet threat, and the preparedness of the U.S. for a confrontation.[156]

The Soviet-American confrontation was hardly the only factor weighing upon the Israeli cabinet's decision to accept a second cease-fire. Defense Minister Moshe Dayan counts U.S. pressure as the deciding factor.[157] Nevertheless, it can be seen that Brezhnev's note was not regarded at the time as an empty face-saving gesture, and the threat of a Soviet-American confrontation it created added to the pressure on Israel to accept a second cease-fire.

The Politburo met on October 25 to formulate its response to the U.S. alert.[158] The Soviet leaders quickly reaffirmed their earlier decision not to become involved in a Middle East war, but felt that the U.S. alert required a response. Grechko reportedly recommended a partial mobilization of Soviet forces, and Andrei Kirilenko, Dmitri Ustinov, and Yuri Andropov seconded this idea. Grechko also suggested that Soviet troops in Syria could be sent to occupy the Golan Heights, but Kosygin and Gromyko adamantly opposed this notion and reasserted that Soviet forces must not become involved in the fighting. Israelyan gives credit for the course finally adopted to Brezhnev, who suddenly interjected, "What about not responding at all to the American nuclear alert? Nixon is too nervous—let's cool him down."[159] Podgorniy and Gromyko quickly agreed, and the rest of the Politburo soon came around to this viewpoint. Consequently, no additional military measures were adopted.[160] At 1440 hours on October 25 (Washington time), Dobrynin delivered Brezhnev's agreement that no U.S. or Soviet troops should be used to enforce the cease-fire, and the U.S. alert was called off at midnight.

The terminal phase of the crisis (October 26–28) was appropriately anticlimactic. TASS reported that Israel continued to violate the cease-fire on October 26, but that the situation on both fronts was calm on October 27.[161] Brezhnev said in his speech at the World Peace Congress on October 26 that "the risk of escalation of the conflict shows with absolute clarity how important it is to solve the problem in the name of strengthening general peace," but ignored the Soviet-American confrontation of the previous day as if it had never occurred:

> Urgent and resolute measures are needed to ensure the implementation of the decisions on a cease-fire and withdrawal of troops. The President of Egypt, As-Sadat, asked the Soviet Union and the United States of America to send to the region of military actions their own representatives to observe the fulfillment of the Security Council's cease-fire resolution. We expressed our readiness to satisfy Egypt's request, and have already sent representatives. We

hope that the Government of the United States of America will act in the same way.[162]

By 1230 hours on October 28, a final cease-fire was in effect and the crisis was over. *Pravda* commentator Yuriy Zhukhov, making no mention of the Soviet message that prompted the U.S. alert, delivered a particularly colorful criticism of the alert on Soviet television:

> [R]eports were received that the United States had placed its armed forces on alert in certain areas, including even in Europe. In justification a really absurd allegation was made asserting that the Soviet Union, imagine, the Soviet Union, had taken some kind of action, which allegedly gave cause for alarm. What in fact prompted this, to put it mildly, really clumsy act by Washington in placing U.S. forces on alert? As today's TASS statement notes, this step was taken with the clear object of scaring the Soviet Union. However, they chose the wrong address, they tried to attack the wrong people, as the saying goes.[163]

After the war, the Soviet press expended considerable energy to refute charges that insufficient support of Syria and Egypt had cost the USSR's Arab allies a victory.[164] One radio commentary held that the generous provision of Soviet aid during the war "dispelled and wiped out" the "myth" that détente undermined the USSR's commitment to the Arab cause.[165] Many of the USSR's allies in the Middle East, however, remained largely unconvinced and blamed the Soviet Union for the failure of the October War to reverse the consequences of the Six-Day War.[166]

Fifteen years later, Vinogradov acknowledged that the Politburo sent a warning to the United States in the conflict's final stages and claimed that the USSR deserved the lion's share of the credit for bringing the war to a close.

> Sadat appealed to the USSR and the U.S. to send their troops to Egypt (jointly or separately) to prevent the decimation of the 3rd Army. On October 26th, the Soviet Union approached the U.S. with the suggestion that Egypt's request be met. The Soviet leadership warned that if the United States refused, the USSR would go it alone. The Soviet move proved effective. The Israeli troops stopped their offensive the same day.[167]

Israelyan also believes that the Soviet actions achieved their intended result, at least in the short run.

> The Kremlin, by threatening to undertake unilateral action it never actually planned, had succeeded in dramatizing the situation, thus pushing the United States and Israel to speed up the actual end of war and saving Egypt from a humiliating surrender.[168]

The essential contradiction in Soviet goals remained, however, and the Politburo's actions in October 1973 did nothing to resolve them.

Soviet Risk-taking in the October War

The available evidence on Soviet communications and actions during the October War and the crisis that preceded it supports this study's hypotheses on Soviet risk-taking in phases 3 through 8. Soviet behavior in the Attack Preparations period (phase 2), however, does not support the hypotheses that the Politburo's tendency toward coercion increases with time pressure and risk of escalation. Although the value-conflict perspective cannot perfectly explain Soviet behavior in the early stages of the crisis, it still offers an explanation of Soviet risk-taking better than those offered by analyses that contend the USSR followed a predetermined strategy in 1973.

The Politburo took significant risks in issuing its coercive threat of unilateral Soviet intervention in the Encirclement phase, the peak of the crisis (phase 7, October 24–25). In this respect, Soviet behavior in the 1973 crisis closely parallels behavior in 1967, although in 1973 the Politburo had even more reason to fear that its most vulnerable ally would suffer a crushing defeat. The probability of Soviet military intervention into the region in October 1973 was clearly not very great, but new evidence shows that the Politburo seriously contemplated taking military action.[169] Brezhnev's threat of unilateral action, like the Soviet threat issued near the end of the 1967 war, came at a point where considerable danger still existed from the Soviet perspective. The Soviet threat of intervention was issued before the final Israeli decision to accept and observe a cease-fire had been taken and may have been an important factor in the Israeli cabinet's decision.[170] Moreover, the concurrent Soviet military moves, while not ordered by the entire Politburo, were authorized by Marshal Grechko, the Soviet decision maker who supported a coercive stance most strongly and advocated further military measures. In the light of this evidence, Soviet actions clearly cannot be regarded as postcrisis face-saving flourishes.

An eyewitness account also indicates that the Politburo believed that its threats would simultaneously advance both of its conflicting objectives. Israelyan's assessment of the Kremlin's mood after sending Brezhnev's note of October 24 offers a classic example of postdecisional bolstering and wishful thinking.

> Moscow . . . was confident that Washington now would do everything possible to stop Israel from defeating the Arabs totally. Thus the Soviet Union would meet Sadat's appeal, save its Arab friends, and demonstrate its solidarity with the "victims of aggression." At the same time, in urging Washington

to act jointly in accordance with the ideas shared by the superpower leaders, the Kremlin was fostering détente. Everything looked very nice, certainly from the Kremlin's point of view.[171]

The Kremlin's point of view would change after the U.S. nuclear alert, which dramatically demonstrated the impossibility of preserving détente while advancing Soviet interests in the Middle East.

As in 1967, the USSR's threat caused a sharp and probably needless escalation in Soviet-American tensions. Kissinger's decision to answer the Soviet threat with a deliberate gesture of firmness, in the form of a nuclear alert, contrasts markedly with Johnson's cautious response. The U.S. alert would have been very dangerous if the formal framework of détente had not been in place, but in an atmosphere of reduced global tensions, it was correctly perceived as a political signal rather than an increase of military readiness in anticipation of a possible war.

There was no guarantee, however, that the USSR's coercive maneuvers and the American responses to them would both be correctly perceived, especially since, unlike in 1967, they were backed by alerts of forces. With Israeli decision makers regarding the threat of Soviet intervention as quite serious, and with the president of the United States on the verge of a nervous breakdown, the superpowers should count themselves fortunate that misperception or accident did not touch off an escalatory spiral. The military moves ordered by Marshal Grechko, without the Politburo's explicit endorsement, were especially dangerous in this regard. Crisis control measures were in place in October 1973, but they might not have prevented a U.S.-Soviet confrontation over the Middle East similar to those that broke out over Berlin and Cuba. Fortunately, an acute crisis did not occur, and as Schlesinger said afterward in an effort to calm the American press and public, the two sides remained far from a confrontation.[172]

The Soviet threats of October 1973 in large measure succeeded in their purpose of persuading the United States to increase pressure on Israel to refrain from delivering a fatal blow to the USSR's regional allies. The coercive means chosen to pursue simultaneously global and regional interests entailed significant risks, however, and damaged the USSR's credibility as both champion of the Arab cause and partner in détente.[173] As Harold Saunders notes, the incident demonstrated the limits of the superpowers' tolerance of each other's behavior in the region. The USSR showed that it would not tolerate catastrophic harm to one of its Arab allies, while the United States communicated that it would not accept the reestablishment of a major Soviet military presence in the area.[174]

The duplicity employed by Soviet diplomats in attempting to get Sadat's acquiescence to an early cease-fire is reminiscent of Soviet efforts in 1967 to persuade Nasser to mobilize in support of Syria by passing false reports of Israeli preparations for an attack. This attempt to trick Sadat into calling for a cease-fire came during phase 3 of the crisis (Operation *Badr*, October 6–12), a period of high time pressure and autonomous risk analogous to mid-May 1967, when disingenuous reports of Israeli plans to attack Syria were transmitted to Egypt through a variety of channels. This time, however, the ploy did not work, partly because the information transmitted to Sadat about Syria's desire for a halt to the fighting was quickly proven to be false, and partly because the USSR's allies were firmly committed to their offensive. Sadat's account of his dialogue with Vinogradov, not quite four hours after the fighting commenced, illustrates this.

> "I doubt whether President al-Assad," I said, "had really demanded a cease-fire before the war started. I'd like to know, all the same, whether this new message you're conveying is an official message or just for information?"
>
> "This is," [Vinogradov] said, "an official message from the Soviet leaders; if you have any doubts you may get in touch with President al-Assad and talk it over with him."
>
> "I shall indeed get in touch with President al-Assad," I said, "to ascertain whether it is so. However, I'd like you to inform the Soviet leaders that, even if Syria did demand it, I won't have a cease-fire until the main targets of my battle have been achieved."[175]

Sadat himself, of course, was far from completely open and cooperative with his allies. Vinogradov and Soviet General Makhmut Gareev concur that Arab forces were poorly coordinated during the war and that the Egyptian president revealed his intentions to fight Israel to the last Syrian:

> In his talks with the Soviet advisors, he repeatedly said that all he needed was to gain "ten centimeters of land east of Suez" in order to draw the attention of the world public to the Middle East problem; whereupon, he said, "I will seek to end the war on terms acceptable to Egypt." Under any circumstances it was his duty to inform the Syrians of his plans. As it turned out, while calling the Syrians to act to great depth, Sadat was planning his own actions in a very different way.[176]

This lack of coordination, and the less than complete correspondence of Egyptian and Syrian war aims, hampered the effectiveness of a strategy of united action against Israel.

Nevertheless, just as an increase in Soviet coerciveness is observable at the peak of the crisis, an emphasis on Arab unity and superpower cooperation is more evident during the period of stability in the military situation in the Stalemate phase (phase 4, October 13–15). Kosygin's speech in Copenhagen, emphasizing détente and Arab unity, and the cool reception Algeria's President Boumedienne was given in Moscow underscore the Politburo's unwillingness to take risks during this period, when time pressure was moderate although significant autonomous risk remained.[177] In phase 6 (First Cease-Fire, October 19–24), when time pressure was again moderate but autonomous risk was high, the superpowers worked in concert in discussions in Moscow and at the United Nations to secure all parties' acceptance to a cease-fire. The cooperation achieved during this phase contrasts with Soviet accusations that American "volunteers" were preparing to fight for Israel during the Counteroffensive (October 16–19), when the success of Israel's Sinai offensive raised the time pressure acting upon the Politburo.

In the months leading up to the October War, the Soviet media published and broadcast frequent reports that Israel was preparing an offensive against its Arab neighbors, with Lebanon being the target mentioned most often. However, these accusations of an impending Israeli attack came only in the form of press reports, and not of intelligence passed through government and military channels, as was the case in 1967. The intended audience for these reports in 1973 was probably not the Arab states, but the Soviet public. As Galia Golan notes, the Soviet populace had to be prepared for a war that the Politburo was certain would come, but was uncertain as to exactly when.[178]

This study's hypotheses are not supported by Soviet actions in the second or Attack Preparations phase (October 1–6), when the probability of coercive action was rated moderately high. Here, Soviet decision makers followed a primarily accommodative strategy and acted to pursue global interests at the expense of regional objectives. Sadat recalls thinking that the evacuation of Soviet dependents on the eve of the Arab offensive was a "bad omen."[179] It may also have been a signal to the United States that fighting was about to erupt, an attempt to distance the USSR from the upcoming conflict, or both. Whatever the precise intentions of the evacuation, it evidences an acceptance by the Politburo of the trade-off between regional and global objectives and a decision to make an effort to preserve détente at the expense of relations with Egypt.

Alan Dowty concludes that U.S. leaders generally recognized the conflicts inherent in U.S. policy toward the USSR and the Middle East during 1973, but that coping with decisional stress by avoiding value trade-offs was more characteristic of the harder and riskier decisions made during the war.[180] It also indicates that the Politburo was resigned to its allies' determination to launch a new war and appreciated the risks inherent in the coming conflict.[181] This study's findings indicate that Soviet decision making followed a similar pattern before and during the October War. When time pressure was moderate and autonomous risk high (in phases 4 and 6, Stalemate and First

Cease-fire) or when both independent variables were moderately high (phase 2, Attack Preparations), the Politburo tended to lean toward cooperating with the United States and preserving détente. When both time pressure and autonomous risk were high, however, as in phases 3 (Operation *Badr*) and 7 (Encirclement), the Soviet leadership tended to act coercively in an attempt to simultaneously preserve the Soviet position in the Middle East while avoiding a direct confrontation with the United States.

Although Soviet behavior in the days immediately preceding the outbreak of the October War does not confirm perfectly to this study's expectations, the value-conflict perspective still presents a better explanation for Soviet risk-taking during the crisis and war than either variant of the chicken model. There is no evidence that the Politburo had a predetermined strategy of competing with the United States and exploiting the conflict for unilateral advantage. Soviet behavior in phases 2, 4, and 6 was generally cooperative, and the evacuation of dependents in phase 2 indicates a decision to place détente above expansion of regional influence, at least temporarily. Soviet statements and actions in phases 3, 5, and 7 were more competitive, but the proposal for joint intervention that accompanied the threat of unilateral action in the Encirclement period (phase 7) shows that some consideration was given to preserving détente even at the peak of the crisis.

The fact that the Soviet leadership acted most coercively at the point of highest tension, and during periods when the battle fronts were most unstable, refutes the arguments of the alternative form of the chicken model. The riskiest Soviet actions, including a verbal threat backed by military preparations, were taken when Israel had disregarded two cease-fires and was pressing its advantage against Egypt in a manner that threatened rapidly to inflict a major defeat on Sadat's army. The USSR did not step in after the crisis was essentially over to safeguard its beaten allies, as the protector game or a predetermined strategy of cooperation followed by bluffing would predict. Instead, Soviet leaders decided to issue a calculated threat of intervention at a point where their regional interests were still in great jeopardy. On October 24, 1973, the Politburo attempted to walk a tightrope between détente and support for the Arab cause, as the value-conflict perspective predicted they were likely to do. Their success in this balancing act was sufficient unto the moment, but the fact that they succeeded at all owes more to the framework of détente than their own poorly coordinated efforts to control risks.

Superpower Détente and Regional Conflict in the October War

By the time the Arab-Israeli conflict erupted once again into crisis and war in 1973, accords on U.S.-Soviet cooperation to moderate regional conflicts had been agreed upon at the May summit in Washington. The codification of the formal structure of détente clarified the need to make value trade-offs and may have made trade-offs in favor of the USSR's global interests more palatable for the Soviet leadership. At the same time, the pervasive view that détente meant a sellout of the USSR's regional allies and the consequent need to stand firm in the face of U.S. pressure impelled the Politburo toward a greater show of firmness in support of the embattled Arab countries.

The increased demands of Arab states, particularly Egypt, for more military aid may have had its greatest effect on Soviet arms transfer policies in the period prior to the crisis. Once the war had started, the USSR's worsening reputation in the Arab world may have complicated the value trade-offs Soviet leaders faced. The USSR's actions at the points where the Politburo was under high time pressure (just after the start of the war and the encirclement of the Third Army) prompt the conclusion that Soviet attempts to pursue simultaneously both regional and global goals met with little success and resulted in a loss of credibility with both the Arab allies and the United States.[182]

The means the Politburo chose to cope with value conflicts in 1973 also suggest an answer to the question of whether the USSR's actions during the war were primarily collaborative or competitive. Kohler et al. present the view that the USSR's regional interests overruled considerations of détente, and therefore the Politburo acted as would befit a competitor in a zero-sum game, exploiting the conflict for unilateral advantages over the United States.[183] Golan, on the other hand, concludes that concern for the preservation of détente predominated in Soviet decision making during most of the crisis and that the USSR acted as a partner in the moderation of the acute regional conflict.[184] A third view, expressed by Rubinstein and Breslauer, holds that the USSR acted in a pragmatic or opportunistic fashion, creating policies ad hoc and improvising to turn events to Soviet advantage.[185] The findings of this study indicate that the Politburo acted from mixed motives and thus support the third view of the nature of Soviet behavior in 1973. In general, when value trade-offs were made in favor of Soviet global interests (as in phases 2, 4, 6, and 8), the USSR acted in a collaborative manner, but when value trade-offs were made in favor of regional interests (in phases 1 and 5, Decision & Commitment and Counteroffensive) or avoided (in phases 3 and 7, Operation *Badr* and Encirclement), the Soviet Union acted competitively.

It must be said, however, that the debate over whether the USSR acted as competitor or collaborator with the United States is peripheral to the controversy over the determinants of Soviet behavior in regional crises. The debate seeks to infer the nature of the actor from its actions, which is not in itself an unreasonable or unproductive goal, but it assumes that the nature of the USSR as an actor on the international stage is the prime factor in its behavior. As both the game-theoretic and value-conflict perspectives on conflict resolution point out, the structure of the situation in which a state finds itself and the need for its leaders to resolve conflicting objectives are more important influences on its coercive and accommodative behavior than its aggressive or nonaggressive "inherent nature." During the era of détente, U.S.-Soviet interaction in Third World conflicts always included elements of both cooperation and competition. This ambivalent relationship was hardly unique to Washington and Moscow, as all great powers with opposing interests in developing areas frequently found themselves in similar positions. As finding the most useful balance of cooperation and competition in regional conflicts is a task very similar to, and inherently linked with, deciding upon the appropriate mix of coercion and accommodation in regional crises, the value conflict approach can help explain the balance that decision makers are likely to strike at specific points in a conflict.

In any event, it is clear that the October War did not provoke a severe conflict similar to the Cuban Missile Crisis, where conflict was directly driven by strategic concerns. In such crises, the challenger's actions immediately affect the strategic situation—this applied in the Cuban crisis even though the placement of missiles in Cuba did not alter the overall strategic balance.[186] Instead, the U.S.-Soviet crisis in 1973 resembled the Berlin crises or other more traditional great power crises, where the long-term effects of the challenger's actions may have changed the strategic situation, but the immediate effects did not. This is borne out by Kissinger's admission that the U.S. alert of October 24, 1973, was intended primarily for purely political reasons as a signal of American resolve, and not for strategic reasons, such as to decrease the vulnerability of U.S. forces to preemption.[187]

American military commanders knew that the alert was mainly intended as a political signal (many were directly informed of the reason for the alert by Joint Chiefs of Staff Chairman Moorer) and the danger of a Soviet attack was slight, and acted accordingly to reduce the risk of incidents and accidents.[188] This does not mean, however, that Soviet and American actions during the October War were not potentially dangerous George concludes that a tacit "rule of prudence" of U.S.-Soviet rivalry declared that each superpower should accept military intervention by the other if it becomes necessary to prevent a regional ally's overwhelming defeat.[189] This conclusion, while plausible, benefits too much from hindsight. Although American decision makers grasped the purpose of the Soviet threat of intervention in the war's final stages, the U.S. response to Brezhnev's threat could hardly be construed as an acceptance of the USSR's right to introduce military forces into the Middle East. If Soviet or American behavior had been misinterpreted by either side, as happened in other crises, the confrontation could have become very dangerous indeed.

From the Canal Front to Camp David

Although the Politburo prevented a disastrous defeat for its Arab allies in the October War, Soviet aspirations to become a broker of a settlement for the Arab-Israeli dispute were thwarted in the aftermath of the conflict. Sadat never forgave the Politburo for its restraint during the war, which he perceived as an abandonment of Egypt's fundamental interests as well as a personal betrayal:

> Everybody believed that the Soviet Union had backed us and established an air bridge to help us, but that wasn't the situation. I faced the United States and Israel; while the Soviet Union stood behind me, ready to stab me in the back if I lost 85 or 90 percent of my arms, just as in 1967.[190]

Not all of the USSR's regional allies shared Sadat's view, however. El Shazly refutes many of the charges Sadat levels at his erstwhile patrons, calling his former commander-in-chief's accusations "trivial and untrue" and contending that the USSR supplied generous quantities of modern equipment as well as information from satellite reconnaissance.[191] Heikal as well assesses the Soviet contribution to the Arab war effort more positively:

> It must be said that throughout the October War the Soviet attitude towards the Arabs was impeccable. They identified themselves wholeheartedly with the Arab cause, and did what they could to bring assistance to Egypt and Syria both at the local and at the international level; at the local level by the air-lift of arms and supplies, and at the international level by acting as the Arabs' advocate with the Americans and at the UN.[192]

Nevertheless, Soviet military and economic aid ultimately bought the Politburo little long-term influence in Egypt. The Soviet Union's attempts to balance its conflicting regional and global objectives by procrastination, evasion, and coercion earned it a reputation as an unreliable ally. This made it easier for Moscow's global rival to maneuver the USSR out of a leading role in the Arab-Israeli peace process within a few years. Despite all of its maneuvers on Egypt's behalf during the October War, the Israeli-Egyptian peace settlement, codified in the Camp David accords, was brokered by the United States.[193]

SIX

Summary of Findings

Two fixed ideas cannot exist together in moral nature, just as two bodies cannot occupy one and the same place in the physical world.

—Alexander Pushkin
"The Queen of Spades"

This study has examined a sufficient number of cases of Soviet behavior in Middle East crises to discern clear patterns in the Politburo's decisions to accept, avoid, or manipulate risks. There is substantial evidence that Soviet leaders did not follow a predetermined strategy during any of these Arab-Israeli clashes. Moreover, Soviet attempts to use coercive threats to escape the conflict between Moscow's regional and global objectives are consistent with the expectations of the value conflict approach.

This chapter's summary and discussion of the results of the studies of the 1967, 1969–70, and 1973 crises will be primarily qualitative rather than quantitative. Any statistical analysis of the support for the two hypotheses generated by the value-conflict perspective would be an attempt to lend a spurious mathematical rigor to this study's findings. By identifying and explaining the consistent patterns in Soviet actions during Middle East conflicts, we can learn much about how the Politburo—and other leaders caught in similar situations—attempt, and often fail, to manage regional crises. Finally, to provide closure for the discussion of Soviet actions in the Brezhnev era, the chapter shows how value conflict analysis can explain what many have characterized, wrongly, as a deliberate policy of maintaining a state of "no war, no peace" in the Middle East.

Value Conflict and Coercion in Three Middle East Crises

Comparison of Soviet communications and actions during the Six-Day War, the War of Attrition, and the Yom Kippur War with the predictions of Soviet behavior drawn from the hypotheses developed in Chapter Two yields strong but not totally unequivocal support for both hypotheses. Recall that both hypotheses shared the same dependent variable, Soviet coercive risk-taking, and that each proposed that a factor likely to intensify the pressures of value conflict would act to increase Soviet leaders' tendencies to take risks in support of a primarily coercive strategy, even though the balance of bargaining power in a Middle East crisis would call for a strategy based on accommodation.

Hypothesis One.   In regional crises, Soviet risk-taking tends to increase when time pressure is high and decrease when time pressure is low.

Hypothesis Two.   In regional crises, Soviet risk-taking tends to increase when autonomous risk is high and decrease when autonomous risk is low.

To study the effect of changes in the values of the two independent variables during the course of each conflict, the crises examined in this book were divided into a total of twenty phases. Expectations for Soviet risk-taking were then drawn from the two hypotheses, and these expectations were compared with actual Soviet behavior. The evidence from eighteen phases supports the two hypotheses being tested, while one phase yielded mixed evidence and in one phase Soviet decision makers acted in a manner contrary to the hypotheses' predictions. The results from all phases are collected in Table 5 on page 135. However, the simple fact that support for the hypotheses may be found in a majority of the phases means little in and of itself, as this study does not purport to make any numerical or mathematical argument. Instead, the results of this study show that at the points of highest tension in these three crises, Soviet behavior matched the predictions of hypotheses derived from the value-conflict perspective better than arguments that contend that the structure of the conflicts, or the Politburo's operational code, dictated a predetermined Soviet strategy.

The Six-Day War

Soviet leaders took risks in a dramatic fashion twice during the 1967 crisis. Throughout the Six-Day War and its antecedent events, autonomous risk remained at high levels. Time pressure alone varied significantly, but these variations sharply increased Soviet willingness to take risks. In the

Table 5 Summary of Results

Phase	Date	Time Pressure	Autonomous Risk	Predicted Likelihood of Risk-taking	Support for Hypotheses
Case 1. The Six-Day War, 1967					
1. Border Clashes	April 7–May 6	Low	Moderately High	Moderately Low	Good
2. Israeli Warnings	May 7–May 14	High	Very High	Very High	Good
3. Egyptian Mobilization	May 14–May 20	Moderate	Moderately High	Moderately High	Good
4. Tiran Blockade	May 20–June 4	High	High	High	Fair
5. Sinai Offensive	June 5–June 9	Low	High	Moderately Low	Good
6. Golan Offensive	June 9–June 10	High	Very High	Very High	Good
Case 2. The War of Attrition, 1969–1970					
1. Artillery Duels	March 9–July 19	Low	Low	Low	Good
2. Canal Raids	July 20–January 6	Moderately Low	Moderately High	Moderate	Good
3. Deep Penetration Raids	January 7–February 28	High	High	High	Good
4. Soviet Intervention	March 1–April 17	Moderate	Moderately High	Moderate	Good
5. SAM Extension	April 18–July 22	Moderately Low	Moderate	Moderately Low	Good
6. Disengagement	July 23–August 7	Low	Low	Low	Good
Case 3. The October War, 1973					
1. Decision & Commitment	August 26–September 30	Low	Moderately Low	Low	Good
2. Attack Preparations	October 1–October 6	Moderately High	Moderately High	Moderately High	Poor
3. Operation *Badr*	October 6–October 12	High	High	High	Good
4. Stalemate	October 13–October 15	Moderate	High	Moderate	Good
5. Counter-offensive	October 16–October 21	Moderately High	High	Moderately High	Good
6. First Cease-fire	October 21–October 24	Moderate	High	Moderate	Good
7. Encirclement	October 24–October 25	Very High	High	Very High	Good
8. Deescalation	October 26–October 28	Low	Moderately Low	Low	Good

Israeli Warnings phase (May 7–14), when political signals (and possibly intelligence information) indicated a high risk of an imminent Israeli attack, the Politburo took the ultimately disastrous step of encouraging an Egyptian mobilization. Its main intention during this phase was probably to use a firm stand by Egypt to deter a possible Israeli attack on Syria, but subsequent Egyptian provocations helped turn the expectation of an Israeli offensive into a self-fulfilling prophecy. In phase 6, near the end of the chain of events set in motion by the Israeli attack (the Golan Offensive phase, June 9–10), the Politburo created an unnecessary Soviet-American incident with a hot-line message on June 10, which hinted at the possibility of Soviet military action. This maneuver sparked off only a minor incident, and the vague Soviet threat did not provoke a strong American response, but by standing firm in the final minutes of the eleventh hour, the USSR alarmed its adversaries, while doing nothing to aid its allies at the nadir of their fortunes.

Soviet decision makers were clearly not pursuing a consistent strategy of either confrontation or conciliation throughout the crisis, and the actual pattern of Soviet risk-taking corresponds well with the predictions of the value-conflict perspective. The Soviet actions taken when time pressure was high and autonomous risk very high contrast markedly with the risk-aversion displayed in phases 1 (Border Clashes, April 7–May 6), 3 (Egyptian Mobilization, May 14–20), and 5 (Sinai Offensive, June 5–9) of the 1967 crisis, when autonomous risk remained high but time pressure varied from low to moderate levels. The Politburo attempted to manipulate or intimidate other parties into protecting its regional interests when time pressure was highest, but these attempts proved counterproductive. Skillful play of the game of chicken in 1967 would have involved a firm stand at first and damage control later, if necessary, but the Politburo twice delayed its attempts to influence events until junctures where autonomous risk lowered its ability to control the crisis. The Politburo thereby added too much coercive "leavening" to their strategy in 1967, and added it too late.

The War of Attrition

Both time pressure and autonomous risk changed noticeably during the War of Attrition. The crisis began with a period of increasing danger (phase 1, Artillery Duels, March 9–July 19, and phase 2, Canal Raids, July 20–January 6), built toward a clearly defined peak (phase 3, Deep-penetration Raids, January 7–February 28), and decreased in intensity gradually but steadily until a cease-fire was achieved (phase 4, March 1–April 17, phase 5, April 18–July 22, and phase 6, July 23–August 7). The riskiest Soviet action in this crisis, the intervention by Soviet air-defense forces, was undertaken at the peak of the crisis, when Israeli deep-penetration raids threatened to deal a mortal blow to Nasser's regime.

The Politburo made efforts in 1970 to limit the risks inherent in intervention by issuing vague warnings to the United States and its allies well in advance of the dispatch of Soviet troops. At least two factors could account for these efforts at risk-control during what was arguably the riskiest Soviet action in the three crises (as it led to combat between Soviet and Israeli forces). One is that the risks of introducing Soviet troops into combat were self-evident and the USSR's opponents could be less easily blamed for the dangers of direct Soviet military action. Although U.S. leaders might appreciate Soviet decision makers' perceptions that they had to take action in support of a collapsing ally, there could be little doubt that the dispatch of Soviet forces to the already overmilitarized Middle East would be interpreted as a significant challenge to American interests. If the possibility of Soviet intervention had been discussed openly, American pressure on Israel to accept the Rogers Plan might have increased after the initial shock had subsided, and the need to send Soviet troops might have abated. In the event, however, the vague warnings issued by the USSR were perceived as deceitful, and the secrecy of the operation was compromised almost from its inception, so these Soviet efforts at risk control accomplished nothing.

Another possible reason why the Politburo attempted to limit the risks of its action in 1970 is that the level of time pressure in the War of Attrition did not rise as high as it did during the other two crises. Soviet leaders had several days to deliberate and decide on a course of action during January 1970, and evidence disclosed in recent years indicates that they took advantage of it.[1] In June 1967 and October 1973, by contrast, they had only hours, barely enough time to arrive at and communicate a decision, let alone to carefully calculate its attendant risks and take steps to moderate them. The 1970 case, therefore, offers the highest probability that the decision to accept risks in support of the USSR's regional allies represents an effort to accept rather than deny the conflict between Soviet regional and global goals.

Nevertheless, the Kremlin's riskiest actions were taken at the point of highest tension, after the shipments of U.S. aircraft had signaled American resolve to support Israel's efforts to prosecute the war on its own terms. (Nixon's order to delay consideration of further arms supplies did not come until early March, after the decision to send Soviet forces had already been made.)[2] The best available evidence indicates that Soviet strategy was not premeditated and that Soviet decision makers did not adopt a plan for either coercion or accommodation early in the conflict and wait for the proper moment to execute it. Rather, Soviet strategy appears to have been formulated and its risks accepted at the peak of the crisis, when time pressure was greatest and the uncertainty produced by autonomous risk was highest.

The October War

The events immediately preceding the October War present an instance of disconfirmation of this study's hypotheses. In the Attack Preparations phase (phase 2, October 1–6), when the Politburo was finally informed that an Arab attack on Israel was imminent, Soviet decision makers disconcerted their allies (but did not sufficiently alert their adversaries) by ordering the evacuation of Soviet dependents in Egypt. This incident offers a clear example of a value trade-off, where Soviet leaders chose détente over support for regional allies, when the value conflict approach would expect the avoidance of such a trade-off.

Soviet acceptance of the need to choose between regional ambitions and détente on the eve of the war is probably best explained by their allies' firm determination to challenge the status quo. Sadat's attempt to reverse the results of the 1967 war presented a clear challenge to Western interests, in a manner entailing substantial risks the Politburo could not control. Unequivocal Soviet support for such a challenge could not have been viewed by the West as a defense of legitimate regional interests (although it might have been seen as such in the Arab world). Consequently, the "balance of resolve" between the United States and the USSR would have favored the United States. With this vital element of bargaining power tipped against them, the Politburo opted for a strategy of limiting damage to global interests, which still held some possibility of minimizing losses or realizing gains on regional interests. In this one instance where, in a situation of significant time pressure and autonomous risk, the USSR would have cast itself in the role of challenger had it acted forcefully, rather than issue an open challenge to the United States, the Politburo recognized and accepted the need to make value trade-offs, and decided to pursue a primarily accommodative strategy.

Once the fighting started, however, Soviet actions strongly support the hypotheses derived from the value-conflict perspective. During the period of stalemate (phase 4, October 13–15), the temporary lull in the fighting surrounding the first cease-fire (phase 6, October 21–24), and the anticlimactic period before the final cease-fire (the De-escalation phase, October 25–28), the USSR cooperated with the United States to bring about an end to the conflict. Both superpowers viewed a cease-fire as a common interest, which decreased the risks of cooperation for both parties and facilitated bargaining along the accommodative dimension. At the same time, both nations demonstrated their resolve to support their allies by resupplying them with military hardware. These phases of the October War, therefore, offer a rare example of both sides "playing the chicken game hard and well," striking an optimum balance between coercion and accommodation as dictated by relative bargaining power, just as Snyder concluded should occur during a stable equilibrium of power.[3] In the absence of high time pressure and/or autonomous risk, this cooperative behavior underpinned by determination fits well with the expectations of this study's hypotheses.

When events were moving rapidly and unpredictably, however, Soviet leaders tended to lean too far toward coercion. In phase 3 (Operation *Badr,* October 6–12) and phase 5 (Counteroffensive, October 16–21), the Politburo returned to reflexive attempts to blame the conflict on Israel and the United States. Most dramatically, in the Encirclement phase (phase 7, October 24–25), Brezhnev's letter, which threatened unilateral Soviet intervention in response to Sadat's request for forces to guarantee the cease-fire, escalated tensions unnecessarily and prompted a U.S. nuclear alert during the most dangerous period of the crisis. The Soviet note refused to concede either détente or Soviet interests in the Middle East. By seeking to justify threats of force by saying that the situation might require military action, which should be bilateral if possible but would be unilaterally Soviet if necessary, the Politburo attempted to convince itself that its threat was consistent both with détente and with Soviet regional objectives.[4] As the Politburo's main intention during this phase was to ensure that the Egyptian Third Army would not be destroyed, the threat may have made some contribution toward this aim, but whether this contribution was worth the risks inherent in this coercive endgame move seems questionable at best.

The contrast between the Brezhnev note's threat of unilateral Soviet intervention and the superpower cooperation visible during periods of de-escalation and stalemate during the October War shows how Soviet strategy was not uniform throughout the war. As recently disclosed evidence on the Politburo's decision making during the crisis indicates, Soviet strategy varied with the levels of time pressure and autonomous risk in a manner consistent with the two hypotheses on the effects of value conflict.

Alternative Explanations

There are two main reasons why the value-conflict perspective offers a better explanation for Soviet actions in these regional crises than either the confrontational or the conciliatory variants of the chicken model. The first is the inconstancy of Soviet policy in each conflict. Since Soviet strategy changed markedly and abruptly during each case, if Soviet decision makers did have a predetermined strategy in any of them, they did not stick to it. Additionally, there can no longer be any real question as to whether Soviet strategy was predetermined in 1969–70 or 1973, since there is evidence from a variety of sources, including eyewitnesses to the debates, that the decision to intervene was made ad hoc.[5] In all three cases, the timing of Soviet risk-taking is predicted reasonably well by the value-conflict approach, and Soviet behavior during the points of highest tension in each crisis matches its predictions very well.

The second and more theoretically interesting reason why the value-conflict perspective explains Soviet risk-taking in these Middle Eastern crises more thoroughly by this study's analytical framework than by the chicken model is the closer fit between this study's hypotheses and actual Soviet behavior at times of high time pressure and/or autonomous risk. Decision makers playing the chicken game when they are at a disadvantage in bargaining power can be expected to "lead" with coercive moves in order to ascertain the balance of forces, interests, and resolve through feedback from the opponent's moves. After relative bargaining power has been established, the chicken model expects concessions, possibly accompanied by face-saving gestures of firmness in an attempt to limit losses.[6]

Soviet behavior did not adhere to this pattern in any of the cases considered here. In 1967, the Politburo began by leaning toward accommodation, but did not follow through with an accommodative strategy after bargaining power had been established. Instead, the USSR acted most coercively when autonomous risk was highest—i.e., during periods when uncertainty was greatest and Soviet ability to control events was lowest, in phases 2 and 6 (Israeli Warnings, May 7–14, and Golan Offensive, June 9–10). In the War of Attrition, Soviet risk-taking in support of a coercive strategy started out low, peaked when time pressure and autonomous risk were highest (the Deep-penetration Raids phase, January 7–February 28) and then decreased steadily until the end of the conflict.

The October War might appear to offer the strongest case for the chicken model at first glance, because it could be argued that Soviet accommodative moves in the period of preparations for the joint Arab offensive (phase 2, October 1–6) should be discounted as precrisis attempts to limit possible losses that were followed by coercive risk-taking when Operation *Badr* began (in phase 3, October 6–12). Subsequent Soviet behavior, the chicken argument would continue, was balanced between coercion and accommodation, as befitted a case in which relative bargaining power was closest to being equivalent. Brezhnev's note of October 25 would then be interpreted as a final face-saving gesture.

As we have seen, however, this communication not only constituted the most serious Soviet attempt at coercive risk-taking during the crisis, but was made at a moment when considerable danger and uncertainty still existed from a Soviet perspective. As Chapter Five details, it is now clear that the threat of Soviet intervention was not merely a face-saving flourish made after the conflict had been safely resolved. A good chicken player would have made his or her most forceful move early in the crisis, not near its end. However, decision makers unwilling or unable to resolve a conflict between values and hampered in their efforts to do so by suddenly elevated time pressure and autonomous risk, might well make their riskiest move at a tense penultimate moment, coming after repeated violations of the cease-fire, when all could still be lost. The evidence now available fits best with this explanation.

Obviously, the approach adopted here has an inherent advantage over the chicken model, in that it attempts to explain Soviet behavior in each phase of the crises rather than treating each conflict as a single case. This does not invalidate the comparison between the two explanations, however, because the chicken model, like all approaches based on game theory, hypothesizes that the structure of a conflict is the primary determinant of the players' strategies. The conflicts considered here did not change enough during the course of the crises to change the game being played. The USSR's expected pattern of moves, therefore, would not change from the prescribed pattern of initial coercion followed by accommodation once relative bargaining power had been established. The optimum mix of coercion and accommodation would, therefore, not change significantly, unless events altered the balances of military forces or interests or unless the adversary's resolve changed markedly. While the balance of local forces did change in the three wars, it changed in each case in a manner that weakened the USSR's hand still further. According to the chicken model, this should have shifted Soviet strategy further toward accommodation, rather than toward the coercive moves the Politburo actually made.

The intention here in comparing the chicken model with the value-conflict approach is not to set up and knock down a straw man. Instead, the objective is to show how models of decision making and crisis interaction based on the assumption of rationality can be complemented by an approach that hypothesizes how leaders are likely to behave at times when that assumption becomes most suspect. A comparison with the chicken model in its pure form, and as it is embedded in empirical studies of Soviet crisis behavior, is made to show that one reason why this study's analytical framework is more thorough is that it is more sensitive to the rapidly changing conditions under which decision makers act during crises.

The Interaction of Time Pressure and Autonomous Risk

Overall, the support for both hypotheses from the three cases examined in this study strongly demonstrates the utility of the value-conflict perspective for analyzing Soviet decision making in regional crises. A few caveats are in order, however, regarding the covariation of the independent variables observable in all three cases. Covariation of time pressure and autonomous risk is a difficult problem for any study of crisis decision making, since even though the two factors vary independently, and one can remain at high levels while the other remains low (as discussed in Chapter One), an increase or decrease in one often leads to a corresponding rise or fall in the other. The two independent variables did not always vary directly with each other throughout the three cases selected here, but the scope of the present study is clearly not broad enough to thoroughly explore the effect of each variable while controlling for the other completely.

Nevertheless, the findings clearly suggest that high time pressure is a necessary but not sufficient condition for strong value-conflict effects. In four phases where autonomous risk was high and time pressure was moderate or lower, Soviet leaders did not exhibit pronounced tendencies to take risks. Two of these periods occurred during the 1967 war (phases 3, Egyptian Mobilization, May 14–20, and 5, Sinai Offensive, June 5–9) and two during the October War (phase 4, Stalemate, October 13–15, and phase 6, First Cease-fire, October 21–24). This would appear to indicate that a high degree of time pressure was a necessary condition for increased risk-taking due to the effects of value conflict, while high autonomous risk by itself did not suffice.

This finding should come as no surprise, as it is consistent with the observed effects of the "inverted 'U'" phenomenon on decision makers' performance. Time pressure exerts both psychological *and* physiological effects on decision makers, increasing fatigue as well as stress and anxiety while shortening the time available to search for and evaluate options.[7] Time pressure can be expected to degrade the performance of organizations as well as individuals. Autonomous risk, however, exerts only a psychological impact by increasing uncertainty and decreasing the hope that a better solution may be found. While the impact of these factors can be overwhelming if a decision must be made rapidly, it is reasonable to expect that both individuals and organizations may be able to overcome its effects and achieve some sort of compromise between threatened values if they are given enough time.

No instances were observed where time pressure was significantly higher than autonomous risk. (It is rated somewhat higher during the crucial Encirclement phase near the end of the 1973 war [phase 7, October 24–25], when the letter raising the possibility of unilateral Soviet intervention was transmitted, but the difference cannot be regarded as great enough to constitute an incidence of relatively low time pressure and relatively high autonomous risk.) Consequently, this study can draw no conclusions on the independent effect of time pressure in the absence of high levels of autonomous risk. Clearly, Soviet behavior in these Middle East crises indicates that time pressure is a necessary condition for increased coerciveness as a result of failure to resolve value conflicts, while more cases in which time pressure was high while autonomous risk remained low would have to be examined in order to determine if it is a sufficient condition in and of itself.

There are strong theoretical indications, however, that it is not. Janis and Mann's model of decision making suggests that in international conflicts, simultaneously high levels of both time pressure and autonomous risk are a necessary condition for defensive avoidance. Recall that it was pointed out in Chapter One, with reference to their model, that autonomous risk increases uncertainty, thus making any course of action appear less likely to improve the situation and facilitating a shift of responsibility onto factors beyond the decision makers' control.[8] Janis and Mann construct models of "hot cognitive processes," which by definition take place under conditions of high time pressure. Their formulation thus yields the expectation that autonomous risk and the uncertainty it creates will lead to defensive avoidance and its attendant greater likelihood of coercive risk-taking only when decision makers feel themselves to be under serious time constraints. The finding that the Politburo displayed marked tendencies toward coercive risk-taking only during periods of both high time pressure and autonomous risk suggests that this study's theoretical framework has successfully adapted Janis and Mann's model of decision making to the analysis of decisions in international crises.

Manipulation of Risk and Competition in Risk-taking

We have seen that the Politburo consistently undertook coercive maneuvers entailing substantial risks at points of high time pressure and autonomous risk in three Middle East crises. Did these actions represent deliberate attempts by Soviet leaders to manipulate autonomous risk, as Schelling's theories would expect, or were they incidents of avoidance of autonomous risk while warning the opponent of its dangers, as Snyder and Diesing found was more common?[9] A comparison of the four strongest examples of Soviet risk-taking in 1967, 1970, and 1973 suggests that while Soviet actions did raise autonomous risk significantly, manipulation of autonomous risk does not appear to have been a preferred Soviet strategy, and Soviet leaders seem to have accepted autonomous risk without deliberately manipulating it. Soviet decision makers attempted to control risks when this was possible, but when it was not, increased autonomous risk was accepted as an unavoidable consequence of coercive action. This acceptance of autonomous risk constitutes sufficient evidence that the Politburo engaged in a competition in risk-taking, although they may have been reluctant to do so at times. In the Middle East crises examined in this study, Soviet leaders stepped closer to the slippery slope, but did nothing to make it more slippery than it already was.

The first incidence of Soviet coercive risk-taking involved exaggerations of the possibility of an Israeli attack in May 1967. At least two political signals during the second phase of the crisis (Israeli Warnings, May 7–14) might have caused Soviet leaders to fear that a large-scale offensive against Syria was imminent. The first of these was the Israeli cabinet decision taken on May 7 for a contingency plan for possible offensive action. While this decision was made in secret, Soviet intelligence may have learned of it.[10] If this was the case, it is possible that Soviet intelligence did not discover all the details of this decision. For example, if the fact that it was only a contingency plan was not detected or transmitted, the decision may have seemed far more alarming to the Politburo than it would have if all of the details were known. The second signal of impending escalation was Eshkol's speech of May 11, in which the Israeli prime minister said that Israel would choose the time, place, and means of response to Syrian maneuvers.[11] If Soviet leaders, highly sensitive to political signals, came to believe that a large-scale Israeli attack was imminent in mid-May 1967, only the Soviet's regional allies would have been able to provide timely aid to Syria. Dispatch of Soviet forces at that point would have been regarded by the United States as recklessly provocative, and in any case was logistically impossible. Protection of Soviet interests in Syria would require Egyptian cooperation, but an Egyptian mobilization carried substantial risks of provocation or undesirable offensive action with it. (Offensive action at this point was undesirable from the Soviet viewpoint, but not necessarily from an Egyptian perspective.) Repeated Soviet warnings of Israeli preparations for an offensive convinced Nasser to order a mobilization, and as a result, the possibility of events getting out of Soviet and American control became a reality.

Because Soviet leaders had to rely on allied forces to defend their regional interests in May 1967, their ability to control risks in that crucial period was inherently limited. Destruction of the Syrian Ba'ath would have been a major blow to Soviet ambitions in the Middle East. If the Politburo perceived that the blow was about to fall unless something was done to deter it, the only option available could not avoid raising autonomous risk in a situation already fraught with it. There is no evidence to indicate that a strategy that involved raising autonomous risks was preferable to the Politburo, nor is it clear what the Soviet estimate of the probability of provocative action by Egypt actually was. Nevertheless, Soviet behavior in May 1967 indicates that increased autonomous risk was preferable to an increased probability of a crushing defeat to Syria. Soviet leaders were not actually faced with a situation of "no choice," as they were able to choose between coercion and accommodation. Making this choice, however, would have entailed concession of one of the Soviet Union's conflicting goals in favor of the other, in a situation of high time pressure. It is, therefore, easy to see how the limited options available for coercion and the potentially high cost of accommodation may have led to a perception of "no choice," or in terms of Janis and Mann's model, no realistic hope for finding a less risky solution to an acute value conflict.

In the second Soviet attempt at coercion, the hot-line message sent near the end of the Six-Day War (on June 10, during the Golan Offensive phase), Soviet leaders again had no recourse to coercive options that did not involve increased autonomous risk. Israeli troop movements before and after the hot-line message could easily have raised Soviet concerns that Israel would violate the cease-fire.[12] Kosygin's message to Johnson precipitated an American reaction (redeployment of elements of the Sixth Fleet), which increased the possibility of a Syrian-American incident. The possibility of accidental attacks on naval forces had already been demonstrated by the mistaken Israeli attack on USS *Liberty* on June 8.[13] The Soviet action near the end of the war did not increase autonomous risk as sharply as Soviet moves did before its beginning, and fortunately, the possibility of loss of control was not realized. Nevertheless, the incident demonstrates that when Soviet regional interests were subjected to a suddenly elevated threat, the Politburo preferred a coercive stance that involved acceptance of autonomous risk to an accommodative course that would have entailed a substantial risk of losses to Soviet regional interests.

Another eleventh-hour Soviet message provoked an American military response near the end of the October War. Unlike 1967, however, when Dobrynin read out Brezhnev's note on October 25, 1973 (during the Encirclement phase of the crisis), more realistic options for Soviet military intervention existed, and Grechko would later bring them before the Politburo.[14] Soviet airborne forces were on alert, and transport aircraft had stood down from participation in the airlift of military supplies to the USSR's allies.[15] Although Soviet forces almost certainly could not have arrived in substantial strength in time to halt a possible renewed Israeli attack into Egypt, there were still possibilities of coercive action directly involving Soviet forces. To be sure, such an action would have been an adventurous provocation, and Soviet decision makers did reject it, but it is mentioned here to show that a range of coercive options were available in 1973. Deployment of Soviet forces to Egypt would have entailed a far greater degree of autonomous risk than the option chosen, which itself prompted a U.S. nuclear alert. Brezhnev's letter in 1973 may then be viewed as a coercive action that increased autonomous risk but was selected over a course of action that would have raised the risk of loss of control to a frightening and potentially disastrous level. Soviet behavior in 1973 designed to enforce coercively the repeatedly violated cease-fire again demonstrated acceptance of autonomous risk, but did not indicate willingness to manipulate it deliberately.

The one instance of Soviet coercive risk-taking that directly involved Soviet forces also involved significant efforts to control autonomous risk. In 1970, the decision was taken at the peak of the crisis (phase 3, Deep-penetration raids, January 7–February 28) to dispatch Soviet troops to Egypt to shore up Cairo's collapsing air defenses and Nasser's crumbling regime. A number of measures were adopted with the intention of minimizing the probability of loss of control, but most failed to achieve their intended effects. The warnings issued to the United States were sufficiently strong to cause concern, but sufficiently vague to go unrecognized as statements of intent to deploy Soviet troops. On balance, they only served to raise American suspicions of Soviet duplicity.[16] Efforts at conducting the deployment in secret, perhaps designed to make the stationing of Soviet troops a *fait accompli* before the United States could react, failed from the outset. While these political means of limiting autonomous risk did not succeed, the caution used in the employment of Soviet forces minimized both Soviet casualties and the risk of loss of control. The "missile ambush" tactics offer a praiseworthy example of operational measures designed to limit autonomous risk, as they enabled Soviet SAM coverage to be extended from Cairo and the Nile delta to the Suez Canal while minimizing the probability of a major Soviet-Israeli military confrontation.

Although Soviet leaders operated under considerable time pressure at the height of the War of Attrition, the limited time available offered them an opportunity to take measures to limit autonomous risk. Adomeit observes that Soviet leaders tended to use allies or proxies to enable them to disavow coercive maneuvers if they encountered higher resistance than they anticipated.[17] In 1970, however, the use of Soviet forces in a defensive role may be seen as an effort to limit autonomous risk. Employing forces that would respond to direct orders from Moscow gave the Politburo a heightened ability to control events, which they would not have had if Soviet air-defense hardware had been supplied to poorly trained and less reliable Egyptian forces. If American forces had been directly involved in the fighting, of course, intervention by Soviet forces would have caused a dramatic jump in the probability of both inadvertent armed conflict and a major Soviet-American confrontation. As the events of the War of Attrition were played out, the deployment of Soviet forces, rather than provision of more sophisticated weapons to Egypt, represented the selection of a coercive option that entailed a lower level of autonomous risk.

However, the effort Soviet leaders expended in these three crises to limit autonomous risk does not prove that the Politburo shied away from a competition in risk-taking. Although increased autonomous risk may have been accepted by Soviet decision makers only reluctantly, it nevertheless was accepted on four separate occasions. In the one instance where Soviet troops actually intervened in the conflict, the manner of their employment suggests that the Politburo was attempting to make a Soviet military presence in Egypt a *fait accompli*. The secrecy in the initial deployments and the "missile ambushes" appear to have been designed to deploy Soviet forces before either the United States or Israel could react with sufficient force to dislodge them. However, although the Politburo attempted to reduce the likelihood of a forceful response by its adversaries, there was always a danger that a U.S. or Israeli response could move the conflict closer to a potentially disastrous confrontation. Schelling points out that engaging in a competition in risk-taking does not require a full commitment, but does require that the competitor's actions entail risks even if they work as intended.[18] Creation of a *fait accompli* in 1970 still left Soviet troops in a combat zone where they could be (and in fact were) subject to attack, either mistakenly or through the action of a third party neither superpower could control.

An attempt to shift the "last clear chance" to avoid disaster to an opponent may involve, or indeed require, efforts to reduce the risk of disaster until the adversary makes his move. If disaster occurs before the attempt to shift the "last clear chance" is completed, the attempt has failed. It is, therefore, in the best interests of decision makers who try to use such tactics to limit the autonomous risk entailed in the move *until the move is completed*. The strategy of *fait accompli* thus belongs in the repertoire of actions that leaders may take as part of a competition in risk-taking. Adomeit contends that careful preparations and calculations designed to limit risks were not inconsistent with, and indeed were integral components of, Soviet engagement in competitions in risk-taking during the Berlin crises of 1948 and 1961 and in the Middle East in 1967 and 1973.[19] This study finds a similar Soviet propensity to combine risk-limitation with coercion in all three Middle East conflicts.

Not all Soviet maneuvers in the crises studied here were examples of a *fait accompli* strategy, but all show how a competition in risk-taking does not require the making of the riskiest move possible. In 1973, Soviet forces could have been dispatched, but they were not. The threat of their employment prompted an American response that entailed a heightened degree of risk. The risks involved in the U.S. nuclear alert were downplayed by Schlesinger and Kissinger shortly after it was announced, but they nevertheless existed, particularly since Grechko was ordering concurrent military moves without Politburo authorization.[20]

Brezhnev's threat in 1973 also carried with it an implicit but rarely discussed risk of an escalatory response by Israel. Although the possibility would have been remote, the Soviet threat might have convinced Israeli decision makers to press the offensive against Egypt even more rapidly, in order to secure a more favorable position before Soviet and/or U.S. forces could arrive to enforce the cease-fire. In actual fact, the Israeli cabinet decision to accept the final cease-fire was unequivocal and unanimous, but unless Soviet leaders were in possession of uncannily accurate intelligence, they could not and should not have entirely discounted this potential source of autonomous risk.[21] In any case, the Soviet intervention threat in 1973 involved a calculated and intentionally limited, but nonetheless significant, element of risk.

The capability of the USSR to carry out the threat alluded to in Kosygin's hot-line message near the end of the June 1967 war was markedly lower, but the message still carried some risk (of an American reaction leading to a U.S.-Soviet or U.S.-Syrian incident) even if it succeeded, which it arguably did. An earlier Soviet move made in an electric atmosphere of tension in the region, the pressure for an Egyptian mobilization in support of Syria between May 7 and 14, entailed far greater risks. Nasser ordered a mobilization against the possibility of war between Israel and Syria, and Egyptian forces subsequently undertook actions intended to provoke a war.[22]

The ability of both the United States and the USSR to control events in the crisis was always low, and Soviet exaggeration of the possibility of an Israeli attack in May raised the probability that events would get out of control. The crisis erupted into a full-scale war in the region because of decisions taken by local actors, not the superpowers, and as a result, Soviet interests in the Middle East suffered damage that could only be repaired by massive military aid and that was never completely mended. Soviet strategy in the crucial period between the Israeli cabinet decision on a contingency plan for a limited offensive and the Egyptian mobilization showed the least effort to control autonomous risks of any Soviet move in the three crises. At a point where autonomous risk was already dangerously high, Soviet leaders deliberately if reluctantly raised it, and the risk of escalation inherent in their actions was realized. Essentially, the operation was successful, but the patient died.

Conflicting Objectives and Soviet Risk-taking in the Middle East

Soviet behavior when autonomous risk and time pressure was at its highest in the three crises examined here indicates, therefore, that while Soviet leaders did not manipulate risks by creating a danger of loss of control where none was present, their decisions enhanced and exploited the autonomous risk that already existed. There was no need for Soviet decision makers to introduce uncertainty into the situations they and their opponents faced in order to issue "threats that leave something to chance," because uncertainty and unpredictability were inherent features of the crises. The threats made by the Politburo in 1967 and 1973 were simultaneously deterrent and compellent, as they sought both to deter Israel from further offensive action and compel the United States to put additional pressure on Israel to stop attacking. An element of coercion was present in both of these objectives. Soviet leaders attempted to impress upon their adversaries that their actions could have unpredictable and potentially disastrous consequences and raised the possibility that Soviet forces could become involved in order to drive home the impression.

The heightened autonomous risk introduced by Soviet maneuvers in the three crises cut both ways, however. Soviet regional and global interests could have suffered serious damage if a major U.S.-Soviet confrontation had erupted from any of the conflicts. Why would Soviet leaders enter into a competition in risk-taking? In situations where high uncertainty already existed, and time pressure imposed stringent constraints on the ability to formulate and evaluate a variety of options, it became all too easy for the Politburo to shift the blame for negative consequences onto the USSR's adversaries.

When decision makers convince themselves that they are not responsible for what follows, or that circumstances give them no choice but to act forcefully, the additional risks of loss of control introduced by their own actions may appear more acceptable along with the other risks of compellence.[23] The findings of this study strongly suggest that during periods of high time pressure and autonomous risk, the psychological coping mechanism of defensive avoidance prompted Soviet leaders to take greater risks rather than face up to the conflict between their regional and global objectives. Their failure to recognize this conflict cost them dear, and their allies dearer still, but accident or misperception could easily have driven the costs even higher.

No War, No Peace, No Decision

The Politiburo's desire to ignore the inherent contradictions in its Middle East policy was hardly unique. Throughout the 1960s and 1970s, in the Middle East and other regions, each superpower acted to defend its interests against threats and challenges from the other. The intense antagonism and strategic volatility of Middle East conflicts, and the vulnerability of both powers' regional allies, made the defense of regional interests frequently necessary and always dangerous Both powers also attempted to exploit regional conflicts and resolve them on favorable terms to gain advantages in their global political competition. For both Moscow and Washington, therefore, regional interests often conflicted with global interests, and leaders frequently had difficulty managing the contradictions.[24]

As we might expect from politicians with conflicting goals, avoidance of such a choice was usually the preferred option. In day-to-day policymaking, the Politburo avoided this choice through procrastination, while in crises, it sought to avoid it by coercion. Value-conflict analysis shows us that although specific features of Soviet decision making shaped the way in which Moscow tried to balance its regional and global interests, neither the problem the Politburo faced nor the solution it attempted was uniquely Soviet.

Characteristic organizational features of the Soviet decision-making process probably exerted their greatest impact in the crisis preceding the Six-Day War. Between May 7 and 14, 1967 (phase 2 of the crisis), both time pressure and autonomous risk were high before a conventional war had actually begun. This distinguishes this critical period from other points where the value-conflict perspective expects a high or very high probability of Soviet coercive risk-taking. In early May 1967, war was thought to be imminent; in January 1970 and October 1973, war was already in progress, and an allied defeat was believed to be imminent. This distinction is important, because in wartime, decision makers must be alert to tactical warning of escalation, while in a potential prewar situation, strategic warning of impending hostilities is vital. While war was highly probable in the Israeli Warnings phase of the 1967 crisis, it was not yet inevitable, although Soviet actions at that crucial point helped to make it so.

These actions, specifically the encouragement of an Egyptian mobilization to deter a suspected Israeli attack on Syria, may have been prompted by Soviet leaders' particular sensitivity to political signals of risk. Israeli forces were not yet in an offensive posture, and a final decision for military action against Syria had not been made, but several Israeli leaders made speeches on May 12 that raised the possibility of a military response to ongoing border incidents.[25] At that point in the crisis, when a sudden escalation of armed conflict seemed likely, these political signals may have convinced Soviet leaders that an Israeli attack was coming. Decision makers who gave less weight to political indicators of strategic warning might have been less likely to conclude that war was imminent. For whatever reasons, the Politburo came to that conclusion and warned Egyptian officials that Israel was about to launch an offensive. According to one report, Podgorniy personally informed Sadat the following day that Israel was massing its troops for an attack on Syria.[26] By encouraging an Egyptian mobilization in response to an attack that had not yet been ordered, Soviet decision makers adopted a fateful course of action in May 1967 that leaders less sensitive to political signals would have delayed or refrained from altogether.

During other periods characterized by high time pressure and autonomous risk, the Politburo acted much as any leaders intent on protecting their clients might have. In so doing, they may have stretched the tacit "rules of the game" of U.S.-Soviet superpower competition without openly breaking them. As Alexander George observes, both the United States and the

USSR adhered to an implicit "rule" stating that neither superpower should initiate military action against the forces of another.[27] He further observes that the Middle Eastern crises of 1967, 1970, and 1973 created acute policy dilemmas when the USSR was required to support its allies while restraining them from actions that could have drawn the Soviet Union into a dangerous confrontation with the United States. The high frequency of regional conflicts in the détente era encouraged a pattern of restraint that George formulates as a corollary to the basic rule: each superpower shall accept military intervention by the other in a regional conflict, if intervention becomes necessary to prevent a regional ally from suffering an overwhelming defeat, and shall pressure its own allies to stop short of inflicting a defeat on the other's allies that could require such intervention.

If, as George argues, these uncodified "rules" comprised part of a U.S.-Soviet regime for managing regional conflicts, the Politburo may have been within its "rights" to threaten intervention in 1973, when Israel seemed on the verge of dealing Egypt a potentially fatal blow. In 1967 and 1970, however, while Soviet leaders had good reason to believe that the domestic regimes of their regional allies were in immediate danger, value-conflict effects probably helped exaggerate both the danger perceived by the Politburo and the forcefulness of its response to it.

The acceptance of "rules of the game" by both the United States, the status-quo power, and the Soviet Union, a challenging power, highlights that both superpowers faced dilemmas of value conflict in their Middle East policy. America's dilemma in the Arab-Israeli conflict, before the Camp David accords, was the need to protect Israel while simultaneously ensuring a continued ample supply of Arab oil. American decision makers, accepting the necessity for a trade-off between these goals, chose to support Israel in 1973, and the American economy suffered serious consequences in the form of an oil embargo. Conflicts between regional and global interests have historically led nations with global ambitions into many similar dilemmas, that were often resolved by taking assertive or aggressive measures in the hope of avoiding losses. British imperial expansion in Asia and Africa in the nineteenth century, some of which was driven by the need to defend India, offers a classic example. Without asserting that the objectives of Soviet Middle East policy were identical to those of Victorian Britain or Wilhelmine Germany, we can see that while many of the motivations that drove Soviet regional and global policy in the 1960s and 1970s were certainly unique, the USSR's need to resolve conflicts between regional and global interests was not. The behavior patterns engendered by this need are likewise similar to those exhibited by other expansionist or imperial powers.[28]

The far from unprecedented nature of the Soviet Union's policy dilemmas in the Middle East and the attempted solutions to them shed light on the question of whether the USSR pursued a strategy of "no war, no peace." Value-conflict analysis cannot completely resolve the debate between analysts who conclude that the Soviet leadership deliberately attempted to maintain a state of unresolved tension in the Middle East and those who contend that the USSR actually sought a resolution to the region's seemingly intractable conflicts.[29] It does, however, lend weight to the argument that the prevailing situation of "no war, no peace" was a consequence rather than a goal of Soviet strategy. The case studies in this book show that avoidance of losses was the Politburo's prime motivation for coercive risk-taking in regional crises. Compromising regional goals in favor of global objectives, or vice versa, would have entailed acceptance of losses on the compromised goal.

Put simply, Soviet leaders favored loss-avoidance over settlement of the conflicts they became involved in. The conflicts indigenous to the Middle East offered opportunities for Soviet foreign policy, but fulfilling commitments to parties to those conflicts entailed dangers. While the Politburo's first preference would have been a regional settlement on Soviet terms, its failures to resolve the conflict between Soviet values contributed to the perpetuation of regional conflict, which they deemed preferable to a solution brokered by the United States. Reluctance to accept an unfavorable resolution of regional conflicts does not imply reluctance to accept any resolution at all. "No war, no peace" thus appears not as a favored Soviet solution, but as a default option, and a course eminently compatible with procrastination.

The alleged Soviet policy of "no war, no peace" is, therefore, best understood as the result of repeated avoidance of a persistent value conflict. Whenever possible, the Politburo adopted incremental decisions designed to minimize the losses to both regional and global policy objectives. When conflicts erupted into crises, and crises led to wars, Soviet decision makers used coercive diplomacy to avoid losses to regional interests. On several occasions, actions that were more coercive than the balance of interests would have dictated risked losses to the global objective of keeping the U.S.-Soviet rivalry a peaceful one. Even during regional crises, however, this global objective was never subordinated to regional interests, just as the regional objective of expanding Soviet influence was never abandoned during routine policy formulation. Since resolution of the Arab-Israeli conflict would have required trade-offs between deeply held values for both superpowers, it should come as no great surprise that neither the United States nor the USSR was willing to make the sacrifices necessary to impose or broker a durable settlement.

Continued avoidance of value trade-offs combined with the intransigence of the local actors to create a regional equilibrium of "no war, no peace" in the Middle East, punctuated by recurrent crisis and war. As the Camp David process demonstrated, the value calculus of the principal parties would have to change before a more stable equilibrium could be established. Moscow's exclusion from that process speaks volumes about how, by using procrastination and coercion to avoid defeat in the Middle East, the Brezhnev Politburo also did a masterful job of avoiding victory.[30]

SEVEN

Conclusions: Value Conflict and Crisis Management

So far from regarding the foreign policy of Russia as consistent, or remorseless, or profound, I believe it to be a hand-to-mouth policy, a policy of waiting upon events, of profiting by the blunders of others, and as often committing the like herself.

—George N. Curzon
Russia in Central Asia

The conflicts studied in this book and the Cold War that helped to generate them are history, but international crises are all-too-current events. Indeed, the type of crisis considered here—an explosive regional conflict that demands a response from the global powers—has become an even more salient feature of the post–Cold War international environment, exemplified in the 1990s by conflicts in the former Yugoslavia, the Persian Gulf, the Caucasus, and elsewhere. The danger of nuclear war has abated; the danger now is that those who are capable of deterring aggression, use of weapons of mass destruction, or genocide will misuse their capabilities or shirk their responsibilities. The former superpowers and their close allies may breathe a little easier, but the rest of the world has not become a more peaceful place.

Just as crises have not vanished in the wake of the Cold War, the crisis manager's basic tool kit remains little changed. Coercion, accommodation, deterrence, and reassurance are still fundamental instruments for crisis bargaining and resolution and as such remain important subjects within the study of international relations.[1] The value-conflict approach used in this book cannot help resolve all future crises, but it can inform the theory and practice of crisis management by explaining the behavior of leaders forced to choose between conflicting goals in crisis situations.

To this end, this chapter will examine the implications of value conflict for contending conceptions of deterrence, discuss some further lessons for crisis management, and suggest how future research into the effects of value conflict can enhance our understanding of the still mysterious process of crisis decision making. Finally, it will return to the Kremlin to consider whether democratization can help future Russian leaders avoid or escape the traps their Soviet forebears fell into in regional conflicts, or whether those who remember Moscow's past mistakes may still be condemned to repeat them.

Contending Approaches to Deterrence

Contemporary thinking on deterrence divides into two contending schools of thought, which will be referred to here as the rationalist and the psychological. The references to works on deterrence in this section are by no means exhaustive, but are meant to point the reader toward representative recent examples of the contending schools.[2]

As one might expect, authors belonging to the rationalist school typically proceed from the assumption of rationality to either formal modeling or quantitative studies with a large number of cases to explore the conditions under which deterrence is more or less likely to succeed.[3] Adherents of this school do not claim that decision makers always act rationally, even in crisis situations. Their main contention is, rather, that states may be treated as if their leaders behaved rationally in international conflicts in order to use formal theory and comparative case studies to identify the conditions that contribute to or detract from the success of deterrence.

The psychological school is less sanguine that decision makers will act rationally when the need to do so is strongest. Analyses from this perspective tend to focus on the external pressures and internal motivations weighing on decision makers and are not reassured by what they find. Richard Ned Lebow and Janice Gross Stein, prominent members of this school, argue that empirical evidence throws the core assumptions of rational deterrence theory into question. They contend that the assumptions that leaders are instrumentally rational, risk-prone gain maximizers, free of domestic constraints and able to identify themselves as challenger and defender, are idealizations that lack sufficient empirical referents. They further argue that rational deterrence theory does not offer adequate definitions of success and failure, usually relying on counterfactual arguments, and assumes that challengers respond to opportunities, although empirical evidence shows that many are driven instead by needs.[4]

Proponents of the rationalist school respond that deterrence theory can accommodate the concerns raised by psychological arguments without abandoning the assumption of rationality. Defending this school, Paul Huth finds that the probability of successful deterrence is enhanced if the defender's strategy addresses the challenger's defensive concerns as well as offensive motivations.[5]

A second line of defense of the rational approach to nuclear deterrence questions the validity of evidence derived from nonnuclear cases. According to this line of thinking, because the tremendous destructive power of nuclear weapons imposes lower rationality requirements for nuclear deterrence than conventional deterrence, runs this line of thinking, examples of deterrence failure in prenuclear crises have little probative value.[6] The psychological school counters with evidence from U.S.-Soviet crisis that, in their view, casts doubt on the central assumptions of rational deterrence.[7]

Though the Cold War has melted away, the debate between the rationalist and psychological perspectives continues to rage. However, as some neutral observers have noted, the two approaches are actually complementary rather than antagonistic, because if psychological studies succeed in convincing decision makers to reduce cognitive and motivated biases, they will succeed in making actual decision making more closely resemble the analytical ideal described by the rational theorists whom they attack.[8]

In a similar vein, some late Soviet-era work on deterrence suggests a novel way of combining the two approaches, using cognitive mapping to model American situation assessments during the Cuban Missile Crisis.[9] And as we will see, decision studies grounded in prospect theory can make important contributions to both lines of argument. In any case, the story of Politburo decision making in Arab-Israeli crises has a moral for both schools of thought on deterrence and crisis management.

Implications for the Rational Approach

Alexander George and Richard Smoke pointed out some time ago that while rational deterrence theory was developed as an abstract, deductive model, it has been employed as a normative and prescriptive model to inform policy, and this has always entailed a risk of oversimplification.[10] The value-conflict approach suggests a means for guarding against oversimplification by specifying the manner in which key situational variables can affect the decision calculus of challengers and defenders. Finding that time pressure and autonomous risk will affect decision making is not exactly a startling new revelation, but incorporating value-conflict effects into rational models can yield new insight into the likely strength and direction of the influence of these factors.

The operation of defensive avoidance, for example, could be incorporated into rational deterrence theory as a discount on the costs of coercion in situations in which decision makers face strict time constraints and high uncertainty. This would not mean that deterrence will always fail in such circumstances, but it does suggest that high time pressure and autonomous risk could result in lower perceived costs of acting forcefully, for both challenger and defender. In other words, decision makers seeking to avoid the need to balance conflicting values may be more likely to resort to force than they would if they were seeking to maximize a single value. Rational-choice theories would be unlikely to predict the existence of such an "irrational" decision dynamic, but its operation could be incorporated into formal models of deterrence.

Additionally, a "bonus for solving value conflict" could be added to the expected utility of options that offer genuine prospects of fulfilling two conflicting objectives, even if each were to be only partially fulfilled. The added value of reducing stress and cognitive dissonance could make the total value of such options significantly greater than the sum of gains on each individual goal.

The value-conflict approach also encourages rationalist modelers to recognize that decision makers often pursue multiple objectives. Consequently, strategies of deterrence and reassurance must take all of the opponent's major objectives into account. It is curious that both schools of thought on deterrence did not explicitly deal with the possibility of multiple motivations until fairly recently, even though bargaining in many international crises has long been recognized as a mixed-motive game. This may reflect the origins of deterrence theory in the political context of the Cold War, in which one superpower was typically cast in the role of "defender" and the other as "challenger," although many case studies recognized that both sides possessed both offensive and defensive motivations in specific conflicts.[11]

Analysis of the cognitive and motivated biases created by value conflict suggests that shifting responsibility onto the opponent at times of acute crisis could result in an increased willingness to accept the risks, regardless of whether decision makers are motivated by opportunities or dangers. Clearly, deterrence is most likely to succeed when defenders address the challenger's defensive concerns as well as offensive motivations. Decision makers who fail to make value trade-offs may be more likely to accept the risks of an offensive challenge if no effort is made to assuage their defensive concerns. Additionally, like the Politburo in 1973, leaders may blame their adversaries for creating a conflict between these two motivations, when the conflict actually stems from their own contradictory goals.

Recognition of the challenger's need to deal with value conflict can also help defenders successfully combine coercion with reassurance. Recognition of the cognitive and motivated biases introduced by failure to resolve value conflicts should make defenders bear in mind that a challenger who is forced to choose between opposing objectives always has the option of refusing to make the choice. This option is likely to seem especially attractive to decision makers who set high values on loss-avoidance, particularly when the risk of losses can be conveniently blamed on the adversary.

As we have seen, events can rapidly change the relative weight decision makers give to offensive and defensive motivations during a crisis. Soviet actions in Middle East crises help illustrate that while they are crucial for decision makers, perceptions of offense and defense and the roles of challenger and defender are too broad to have much analytical utility in formal models.

Prospect theory emphasizes that the point around which decision makers frame losses and gains is crucially important to their decision process. Leaders challenging the status quo are especially likely to experience an "instant endowment effect" whereby they quickly consider the gains resulting from a recent challenge to be part of the status quo, and thus take greater risks to protect their newly realized gains.[12] Iraq's attempt to absorb Kuwait in 1990–1991 is a perfect illustration of this pattern: the "offensive" goal of taking Kuwait, from which Baghdad might have been deterred, was immediately transformed into the "defensive" goal of holding on to Iraq's Nineteenth Province, for which Saddam Hussein was willing to risk a devastating war. Though it is not clear that any deterrence strategy would have avoided conflict in the gulf, better recognition of the "instant endowment effect" and of value conflict might have helped lower the costs and risks of extricating Iraqi forces from Kuwait.[13]

Implications for Psychological Theories

The discussion of framing and perception of roles provides a useful starting point for considering the implications of this study's findings for the psychological perspective on deterrence. Soviet leaders saw themselves as defenders and framed their problem as one of loss-avoidance in all three crises, while American policy makers perceived Soviet actions as challenges. This highlights an important distinction between the psychological and the rationalist conceptions of the informational value of bargaining. In rational models of crisis bargaining, states initially estimate the "balance of interests" and the "balance of resolve" independently, but the process of comparing these estimates with demonstrated resolve changes both relative bargaining power and both sides' appreciation of it. Theoretically, inaccurate estimates of resolve will be corrected during negotiations, with the result that near the end of the bargaining process, perceived bargaining power will approximate inherent bargaining power.[14]

From the psychological perspective, however, there is no guarantee that perceptions of bargaining power will approach inherent resolve during the course of a crisis. Instead, there is every reason to expect that perceptions will become more rather than less biased. This study's hypotheses suggest that especially under conditions of high time pressure and autonomous risk, *both sides* will come to view themselves as defenders and shift responsibility for negative consequences of their own actions onto their adversaries. This mutual abdication of responsibility can easily result in more coercive risk-taking by both parties, which in turn can increase the likelihood of deterrence failure. The findings of this study thus suggest that, in regional crises at least, the psychological school's lack of faith in deterrence is well founded.

The value-conflict approach also illustrates how successful deterrence must take need-driven challenges into account. Explicit recognition of the conflict between decision makers' goals can help identify when defensive avoidance is most likely to push leaders toward issuing a need-driven challenge. Moreover, it should be remembered that coping with value conflict is itself a need. As we have seen, when time pressure and autonomous risk are greatest, decision makers are most likely to meet this need by coercing their opponents.

Since both sides in a crisis will probably perceive themselves as defenders, either initially or as a result of the "instant endowment effect," it is necessary to look at the influence of value conflicts on defenders as well as challengers. Attention to defenders' needs to reconcile opposing goals can help identify the conditions under which they are most likely to issue a coercive deterrent threat or preempt a challenge, as Soviet leaders tried to do in May 1967.

The likelihood that both challengers and defenders are likely to react to value conflict with defensive avoidance points out the main limitation on policy prescriptions derived from psychological theories of decision making. Like many other analyses, the present study identifies and suggests avoiding a specific psychological trap that decision makers are likely to fall into under identifiable conditions during crises. The most useful prescription that can be drawn from this conclusion is one commonly offered by many rational and psychological studies of deterrence: avoid situations of high time pressure and autonomous risk.[15] Given the inherent fallibility of decision makers and the persistence of many regional conflicts, this is equivalent to a doctor telling a chronically ill patient not to get sick. To be really useful for policy makers, psychological approaches to crisis management must offer better preventive medicine.

Happily, more practical recommendations are possible. Lebow and Stein, champions of the psychological approach, contend that "psychological explanations that predict denial or wishful thinking . . . do not tell us which option leaders are likely to choose."[16] However, hopefully as this book has shown, value conflict can warn us of specific circumstances when decision makers are most likely to choose coercion over concession, even when their relative bargaining power indicates that they should back down. Therefore, while value conflict analysis certainly cannot cure all decision pathologies, it can be used to diagnose some of them, identify their warning signals, and suggest prophylaxis and treatment for defensive avoidance.

Managing Future Crises

While deterrence of a major war in Europe is not the vital issue it once was, deterrence generally has taken on a new urgency in the post–Cold War world. If states such as Iran and North Korea continue their nuclear programs, the United States could easily find itself deterring nuclear-armed regional powers from aggression against regional allies. Though banned by international conventions, chemical and biological weapons provide relatively cheap and more easily obtainable tools of mass destruction for aggressive or paranoid regimes.[17] Moreover, as the tragedies in Bosnia, Rwanda, and elsewhere illustrate all too graphically, mass murder does not require weapons of mass destruction; mass brutality suffices. The field of application for deterrence and crisis management remains, therefore, discouragingly broad.

Fortunately, the study of value conflict can help refine the use of the two key tools for crisis management, deterrence and reassurance. These concepts are linked to, but by no means synonymous with, the bargaining elements of coercion and accommodation. Although deterrence and compellence are both forms of coercion, accommodation refers to concessions made to offensive interests. Reassurance, on the other hand, appeals to defensive motivations.[18]

The Middle East crises discussed in this study show that the difference between accommodation and reassurance is far more than semantic, as a coercive move can contain elements of reassurance without implying accommodation. In 1970, for example, Soviet forces deployed to Egypt were intended to coerce Israel into cessation of deep-penetration raids, but the preponderance of SAMs rather than fighter aircraft in this force served as reassurance that Soviet forces would not participate in offensive action. This element of reassurance was a major reason behind the comparative lack of American alarm at the deployment.[19] In 1973, by contrast, the alert status of Soviet airborne divisions indicated that the possible Soviet intervention mentioned in Brezhnev's letter would most likely involve forces with significant offensive capability. The Politburo failed to include reassurance measures in this coercive maneuver, and the United States reacted with a nuclear alert.

Reassurance can appeal to an adversary's domestic concerns as well as its foreign policy objectives. To give an example particularly relevant in the Middle Eastern context, measures intended to show that an opposing state's regime is not under threat of destabilization could help induce concessions on expansionist goals. In the crises considered in this study, reassurance of this sort was conspicuously and deliberately absent. In particular, the perceived weakness of Nasser's regime made the 1969–1970 war seem extremely dangerous in Moscow and was a major factor in the Politburo's unprecedented decision to send Soviet troops into the conflict.

The effectiveness of deterrent threats can be enhanced by combining them with statements and actions that show that one side does not intend to exploit the crisis to undermine the other's domestic stability. These reassurance measures can also indicate that the opponent has only limited goals in the conflict and may be open to compromise, without indicating weakness of resolve. The same would apply to compellence situations as well. Conversely, the intention of one side actively to destabilize the other, as in the Persian Gulf War, makes both deterrence and compellence less likely to succeed.

Attention to the effects of value conflict may also help make reassurance more effective in other ways. For example, decision makers seeking to defend their interests might profit by taking steps to convince their adversaries that autonomous risk is low. The United States was careful to do this in 1973, by taking special safety precautions with nuclear weapons that were not standard operating procedure for DEFCON 3 alerts.[20]

That said, it must be recognized that reassurance measures can involve risks of their own, as an adversary will mistake reassurance for concession and a sign of weakening resolve. Although the psychological perspective emphasizes the need for reassurance as part of a successful strategy of deterrence, the tension between reassurance and demonstrating resolve will not always be an easy problem to overcome. Resolving the conflicts between these objectives might well require the same sort of creative solution necessary for resolving other value conflicts.

While reconciling their own opposing values will never be easy, prospect theory points out one form of cognitive bias that can make crisis managers' jobs easier. Many experimental studies have found that individuals give excessive weight to outcomes that are certain, as opposed to those that are merely probable.[21] In other words, decision makers like to bet on "sure things" even though other options may afford greater expected utility. This suggests that the proper mix of deterrence and reassurance could offer decision makers a guaranteed outcome that may be less attractive in terms of expected utility, but which offers the advantage of certainty. Presented as a package deal with an admonition to take it or leave it (with the costs of leaving it made abundantly clear), the offer of a certain outcome may allow leaders to shift the blame for setbacks or compromise onto an adversary of demonstrably superior strength without resorting to force.

This kind of solution requires that those attempting to deter or reverse aggression display credible commitment and firm resolve. These have proven notoriously difficult to achieve in multinational responses to crises in the Persian Gulf, Bosnia, and elsewhere in the post–Cold War world. If the United States and other leading states hope to rely on "assertive multilateralism" to manage future crises, they must prove beyond a reasonable doubt that the term is not an oxymoron.[22]

Future Research on Value Conflict

The value-conflict perspective has succeeded fairly well in explaining how decision makers are likely to act at points in international conflicts where the assumption of rationality is least plausible. This study does not offer sufficient evidence to prove that the assumption of rationality should be discarded during periods of high time pressure and autonomous risk, but that was never its intention. By using a structured, focused comparison of case studies to test its hypotheses, this study's analytical framework has been able to specify the conditions under which decision makers are more or less likely to accept or resolve contradictions between objectives.[23]

Although new evidence sporadically comes to light, no study may ever be able to pry completely open the "black box" of Soviet decision making in the Brezhnev era. This analysis has nevertheless tested its hypotheses on Soviet crisis decision making in order to pursue two (hopefully noncontradictory) goals. First, this book shows how new theories, supported by new evidence, can refute the contention that Soviet strategy in Middle East conflicts was straightforward, premeditated, and cunningly duplicitous While many Soviet moves involved duplicity and deception (including self-deception), the value-conflict approach contends that the Politburo reacted to events rather than follow an opportunistic master plan. Second, Politburo decisions were examined to demonstrate how psychological theories of decision making could be usefully applied even to the state that Churchill described as "a riddle wrapped in a mystery inside an enigma."[24] The leadership of the USSR during the "period of stagnation" was chosen as a test subject to show how studies of even such an impenetrable entity can help us better understand how cognitive and motivated biases influence crisis decisions.

As this book was only able to consider a limited number of cases in order to keep the number of potential intervening variables (such as major changes in the Soviet leadership and differences between various conflict-prone regions) to a minimum, further research will clearly be required in order to determine how well the value conflict approach explains Soviet behavior in other conflicts. Fortunately, at least for the researcher, Soviet policy objectives in many regions between the death of Stalin and the rise of Gorbachev frequently contradicted the goal of improvement of relations with the West, so the range of applications of value conflict analysis is quite broad.

Appropriate care must be taken to account, however, for changes in leadership or official ideology when designing comparative case studies. Although the longevity of the Brezhnev Politburo facilitated this objective in the present study, it was impossible to hold ideology completely constant even during the relatively brief time period considered here, as the line on the nature of relations between the socialist and capitalist spheres changed with the development of détente. Caution should also be exercised in attempting to apply the value-conflict perspective to decisions made outside of crisis situations, as the comparatively long time available for making difficult decisions gives policy makers ample room to avoid value conflict through procrastination.

While domestic concerns indubitably play a crucial role in everyday foreign policymaking, it is less certain that they exert a major impact on the life-or-death decisions made during acute crises, particularly in nondemocratic states. In the absence of evidence that domestic considerations were uppermost on decision makers' minds during international crises, therefore, it is not unreasonable to leave domestic politics in the background. However, this does not mean that the value conflict approach has no value for explaining economic or domestic political decisions, as the theories underlying this analytical framework were designed to apply to a wide variety of decisions dominated by conflicting objectives. (Economic decisions, of course, rarely involve autonomous risk, and the ability to set monetary values on potential gains and losses facilitates acceptance of value trade-offs.)[25]

Just as analysis of value conflicts may be usefully extended to Soviet behavior in other time periods or regions, it should prove easily adaptable to American and other non-Soviet decision makers. Indeed, the analytical framework presented here is likely to be even more useful for the study of American crisis behavior than for Soviet actions. Studies that apply the value conflict approach to American decision making will additionally enjoy a comparatively data-rich environment in most cases, although as has been previously mentioned, all governments tend to guard information about crisis decisions quite jealously.

The greatest difficulty in applying this study's analytical framework to American crisis decisions may be case selection, as it will not be easy to find many conflicts after 1945 in which the United States acted more coercively than its bargaining power would dictate. This is not meant to imply that American leaders have not engaged in coercive diplomacy; they have done so explicitly on many occasions.[26] It merely illustrates the fact that few postwar crises found the United States in an inferior position with regard to the balance of interests and the balance of forces in areas where it had explicit defensive commitments. This winning record is evidence of the successful application of containment as the overall goal of U.S. foreign policy during the Cold War. Nevertheless, the United States was caught in situations of high time pressure and inferiority of local American or allied conventional forces, with serious consequences. The outbreak of the Korean War stands out in this regard, while the Tonkin Gulf incident is a less clear-cut example.

The potential for cross-national comparison also appears high, so long as the design of the study accounts for the fact that the values of situational variables will often be different for each nation or party to a conflict. These variations will sometimes be created by asymmetries in forces or the fortunes of war. At other times, they will be created deliberately, as adversaries vie to give each other the "last clear chance" to avoid mutual disaster. Jack Snyder has already argued in a cursory analysis that avoidance of value trade-offs played an important role in the origins of the First World War, although his more comprehensive study of the events of 1914 focuses on other factors.[27] Analysis of the Suez Crisis from the viewpoints of Britain and France might offer a more modern example of increased coerciveness as a result of defensive avoidance under conditions of high time pressure and autonomous risk.

Of course, the behavior of Israel and the Arab states in the conflicts covered in this study could be examined for evidence of value-conflict effects on decision making. Israeli actions in 1967 and Egyptian decisions in 1969–1970, in particular, would very likely support the two hypotheses on value-conflict effects more strongly than Soviet behavior in those wars and their antecedent crises.

Future research should also seek to refine the independent variables used in hypotheses on value conflict. In particular, studies should explore whether the *value* of each independent variable, or the *rate of change* in its value, has more influence on value conflict. Is it the degree of time pressure or the perception that the pace of events is accelerating that impels decision makers to react with defensive avoidance? Does some threshold level of autonomous risk result in increased coerciveness, or does the impression that events are more rapidly running out of control have greater effect? Future studies should be constructed to examine these questions, using cases in which sufficient data on leaders' perceptions are available, such as the extensively researched Cuban Missile Crisis.

Toward a General Theory of Crisis Decisions?

As noted in its introduction, this book seeks to supplement rather than supplant existing theories of decision making. Though it can shed light on many crisis decisions, value-conflict analysis cannot purport to explain them all. The analytical framework advanced in this study cannot even claim the status of an incomplete theory. Despite its complexities, the avoidance and resolution of value conflict is too narrow a basis for a true causal theory and should properly remain a subsection of a general cognitive theory of decision making.

A comprehensive set of hypotheses on the role of value conflict in decision making would not be a grand theory of international politics, but it would be no mean achievement. As many leaders have demonstrated the ability to accept or resolve value conflicts, this set of hypotheses must explicate the conditions under which value integration is most likely and, if possible, the criteria that decision makers are likely to use in choosing between mutually exclusive alternatives of equal expected utility.

Bitter experience tells us that temporizing, procrastination, and attempts to avoid responsibility remain characteristic features of government decision making. At the same time, the ability to prioritize goals, skill in resolving conflicts, and the courage to accept responsibility for consequences are essential qualities of leadership. For these reasons, an analytical framework that can explain how, why, and when governments accept value conflicts or attempt to avoid them would help us understand how seemingly typical decision makers become exceptional leaders.

Russia and the New Arc of Crisis

Will history repeat itself yet again? Conflicting Russian priorities in the Caucasus and Central Asia, and the potential for conflict in those regions, suggest that it may. The risk that many of the same factors that made the Middle East prone to crises (oil, arbitrary borders, ethnic conflicts, Islamic radicalism, weak regimes, and competition by external powers) also may draw Russia into future regional conflicts cannot be ignored.[28] The bloody fighting in Chechnya illustrates the explosive potential of conflicts along Russia's southern borders and the weakness of Russian capabilities to manage them.[29]

Will a more democratic Russia play the Great Game by different rules and be better able to reconcile its contradictory objectives in future regional crises? Probably not, for three main reasons.

First, the conflict between Russian global objectives and regional interests in Central Asia and the Caucasus will remain, regardless of the type of regime in power in Moscow. Russia's interests in establishing hegemony, maintaining stability (on its own terms), and consolidating strategic and economic relationships in these regions cut across the lines of domestic political competition.[30] At the same time, even an extreme nationalist government would have strong incentives to keep relations with the West on an even keel, as an authoritarian Russia would still need access to Western capital, technology, and markets, particularly for oil and gas.

Continued democratization could soften the contradictions between Western and Russian interests, as a democratic Russia is likely to set a higher value on developing relations with Europe and the United States. Paradoxically, however, this may actually intensify the conflict between Russia's regional and global interests, as a government oriented toward cooperation with the West may find it more difficult to compromise global objectives in pursuit of regional goals and thus be more likely to temporize when the two come into conflict.

Second, democratization of domestic politics may matter little if decisions are still made undemocratically in crisis situations. Even in the United States, the most democratic global power with one of the most open political systems in the world, crisis decisions have been made by a small group consisting of the chief executive and close presidential advisors (such as Ex-Comm during the Cuban Missile Crisis). The need for speed and secrecy in acute crises often overpowers the requirements for open, democratic debate and search for alternative options. As discussed in Chapter Two, under these conditions, any small group of decision makers can fall victim to groupthink or resort to defensive avoidance and act forcefully to resolve conflicting values.

The Suez Crisis, in which Britain and France reacted to Egypt's nationalization of the Suez Canal in 1956 with military intervention in secret collusion with Israel, offers a cautionary example of how insular decision making by democratic leaders during a Middle East crisis can lead to a foreign policy disaster.[31] With all due respect to the new occupants of the Kremlin, there is no reason to expect that Russian decision makers will prove more adept at balancing conflicting values than their British, French, or American counterparts.

Finally, as our examination of Middle East crises has shown, even the actions of superpowers are strongly shaped by situational factors in regional crises. If Russian leaders face great time pressure and high autonomous risk in Central Asian or Caucasian conflicts, they may very well fail to resolve contradictions in their objectives and resort to military force, much like their predecessors.

Most speculations on post-Soviet foreign policy conclude that democratization, or the lack thereof, will be the most important influence on Russia's international relations. Some observers contend that this will be true for the other former Soviet states of Central Asia as well, and that the pattern of regional relations will be determined by the success of democratization.[32] In crises, however, democratic leaders and authoritarians alike often succumb to decision pathologies, including inadequate search for options, groupthink, and defensive avoidance. There is thus good reason to doubt that democratization will automatically equal regional stability, as leaders of all ideological stripes can fail to resolve the inherent conflicts in their objectives, at great cost to their own interests and the security of their regional allies.

Extensive research has found that democracies never (or hardly ever) go to war with each other, and a number of hypotheses have been advanced to explain why this is so.[33] It is certainly clear that democracies are almost always able to resolve direct conflicts peaceably *with each other*. When democracies find themselves on opposite sides in regional crises, however, especially when unpredictable, nondemocratic, subnational actors are involved, the complexity of the conflict increases geometrically, and the mechanisms that maintain peace among democracies may well fail to operate. In these instances, democratic leaders may still fail to resolve value conflicts, refuse to compromise regional objectives in favor of the norm of cooperation with other democracies, and therefore act forcefully. Democratic global powers may not actually go to war in such cases, but their regional allies, democratic or not, may suffer from the great powers' coercion and indecision.

Even if future Russian leaders display the skill and creativity needed to pursue both their regional interests and global goals simultaneously in the new arc of crisis, they will probably lack the resources. If Russia attempts to attain unchallenged dominance before it builds the requisite economic strength, any efforts to establish hegemony in the Caucasus and Central Asia will be worse than useless, and may very well increase regional instability.[34] Moreover, even after a spectacular economic recovery, Moscow's expansive policy will be in constant danger of the overcommitment and overextension that have undone many other great powers.[35] If Russia tries to satisfy the many conflicting economic and security needs of its regional allies, it will probably satisfy none of them, and both Russia and the vulnerable new states will pay the price of Moscow's failure.

All bids for mastery eventually collapse, so Russia will find itself in good company if its hegemonic enterprise fails. Perhaps the best we may hope for in any regional crisis, managed from any set of capitals, is that when decision makers have sufficient time, adequate advice, and reasonable confidence that the situation will not get out of hand, they will successfully prioritize their goals and make compromises among their contradictory objectives. The crises examined in this book reinforce the conclusion that small groups of leaders, isolated and insulated from the public, are least likely to integrate their values and most likely to resort to force. Decisions made by Soviet oligarchs, U.S. presidents, and a long line of so-called world leaders show us that democratization of the decision making process—not just the political system—offers the best chance to avoid disaster in future crises. As Machiavelli observed in his discourse on the best and worst aspects of leadership, "The people are wiser and more constant than princes."[36]

Notes

Chapter One

1. Michael Brecher with Benjamin Geist, *Decisions in Crisis: Israel, 1967 and 1973* (Berkeley: University of California Press, 1980), p. 4.

2. Distinctive characteristics of Soviet decision-making will be discussed Chapter Two. For comprehensive treatments of the effects of crisis situations on the decision process, the reader is referred to Ole R. Holsti, *Crisis, Escalation, War* (Montreal: McGill-Queen's University Press, 1972); Charles F. Hermann, ed., *International Crises: Insights from Behavioral Research* (New York: Free Press, 1972), pp. 259–81; Zeev Maoz, *National Choices and International Processes* (Cambridge: Cambridge University Press, 1990); and James L. Richardson, *Crisis Diplomacy: The Great Powers Since the Mid-Nineteenth Century* (Cambridge: Cambridge University Press, 1994).

3. John D. Steinbruner, *The Cybernetic Theory of Decision: New Dimensions of Political Analysis* (Princeton: Princeton University Press, 1974), p. 28.

4. Graham T. Allison, *Essence of Decision: Explaining the Cuban Missile Crisis* (Boston: Little, Brown, 1971), pp. 28–35.

5. Thomas C. Schelling, *The Strategy of Conflict* (Cambridge: Harvard University Press, 1960) and *Arms and Influence* (New Haven: Yale University Press, 1966); Glenn H. Snyder and Paul Diesing, *Conflict Among Nations: Bargaining, Decision Making, and System Structure in International Crises* (Princeton: Princeton University Press, 1977); Robert Powell, *Deterrence Theory: The Search for Credibility* (Cambridge: Cambridge University Press, 1990. Glenn H. Snyder, "'Prisoner's Dilemma' and 'Chicken' Models in International Politics," *International Studies Quarterly* 15, no. 1 (March 1971), pp. 66–103, and Snyder and Diesing, 1977, offer a comprehensive treatment of the use of game matrices for the analysis of international conflicts. Maoz attempts to combine game models of strategic interaction with individual- and group-level models of decision making in his 1990 volume.

6. Snyder and Diesing, pp. 189–92.

7. Eric Herring, *Danger and Opportunity: Explaining International Crisis Outcomes* (Manchester: Manchester University Press, 1995).

8. See, for example, Arnold L. Horelick and Myron Rush, *Strategic Power and Soviet Foreign Policy* (Chicago: University of Chicago Press, 1966); Francis Fukuyama, "Soviet Threats to Intervene in the Middle East 1956–1973" (Santa Monica: RAND Note N-1577-FF, June 1980); Uri Ra'anan, "Soviet Decision

Making in the Middle East, 1969–1973," in Michael MccGwire et al., eds., *Soviet Naval Policy: Objectives and Constraints* (New York: Praeger, 1975), pp. 182–210; Stephen S. Kaplan et al., *The Diplomacy of Power* (Washington: Brookings, 1981); Jonathan R. Adelman, "The Soviet Use of Force: Four Cases of Soviet Crisis Decision Making," *Crossroads* 16 (Winter-Spring 1985), pp. 47–81; and T. Clifton Morgan, *Untying the Knot of War: A Bargaining Theory of International Crises* (Ann Arbor: University of Michigan Press, 1994).

9. On the development and application of prospect theory, see Amos Tversky and Daniel Kahneman, "The Framing of Decisions and the Psychology of Choice," *Science* 2, no. 11 (1981), pp. 453–58; Tversky and Kahneman, "Advances in Prospect Theory: Cumulative Representation of Uncertainty," *Journal of Risk and Uncertainty* 5 (1992), pp. 297–323; Jack S. Levy, "An Introduction to Prospect Theory" and "Prospect Theory and International Relations: Theoretical Applications and Analytical Problems" *Political Psychology* 13, no. 2 (June 1992), pp. 171–86, 283–310, and his "Loss Aversion, Framing, and Bargaining: The Implications of Prospect Theory for International Conflict," *International Political Science Review* 17 (1996), pp. 177–93.

10. For overviews of the contending perspectives on this issue, see John Steinbruner, "Beyond Rational Deterrence: The Struggle for New Conceptions," *World Politics* 28, no. 2 (January 1976), pp. 223–45; Donald R. Kinder and Janet Weiss, "In Lieu of Rationality: Psychological Perspectives on Foreign Policy Decision Making," *Journal of Conflict Resolution* 22, no. 4 (December 1978), pp. 707–35; Robert Jervis, "Deterrence Theory Revisited," *World Politics* 31, no. 2 (July 1979), pp. 289–324; George W. Downs, "The Rational Deterrence Debate," *World Politics* 41, no. 2 (January 1989), pp. 225–37, and Richard Ned Lebow and Janice Gross Stein, *We All Lost the Cold War* (Princeton: Princeton University Press, 1994).

11. Alexander L. George, "The Operational Code: A Neglected Approach to the Study of Political Leaders and Decision-Making," *International Studies Quarterly* 13, no. 2 (June 1969), pp. 190–222.

12. Nathan Leites, *The Operational Code of the Politburo* (New York: McGraw-Hill, 1951), *A Study of Bolshevism* (Glencoe, IL: Free Press, 1953), and "Kremlin Moods" (Santa Monica: RAND Memorandum RM-3535-ISA, 1964).

13. Hannes Adomeit, *Soviet Risk-Taking and Crisis Behavior: A Theoretical and Empirical Analysis* (London: Allen and Unwin, 1982), pp. 315–25.

14. Richard K. Herrmann, *Perceptions and Behavior in Soviet Foreign Policy* (Pittsburgh: University of Pittsburgh Press, 1985).

15. James M. Goldgeier, *Leadership Style and Soviet Foreign Policy: Stalin, Khrushchev, Brezhnev, Gorbachev* (Baltimore: Johns Hopkins University Press, 1994).

16. See, for example, Douglas W. Blum, "The Soviet Foreign Policy Belief System: Beliefs, Politics, and Foreign Policy Outcomes," *International Studies Quarterly* 37, no. 4 (1993), pp. 373–95, and Celeste A. Wallander, "International Institutions and Modern Security Strategies," *Problems of Communism* 41, nos. 1–2 (1992), pp. 44–63.

17. See, for example, Jack Snyder, "Rigor, Richness, and Relevance in the Study of Soviet Foreign Policy," *International Security* 9, no. 3 (Winter 1985), pp. 89–109.

18. This approach is adopted in H. Gordon Skilling and Franklyn Griffiths, *Interest Groups in Soviet Politics* (Princeton: Princeton University Press, 1971), pp.

19–46; James G. Richter, *Khrushchev's Double Bind: International Pressures and Domestic Coalition Politics* (Baltimore: Johns Hopkins University Press, 1994); Robert M. Slusser, *The Berlin Crisis of 1961* (Baltimore: Johns Hopkins University Press, 1973); Ilana Kass, *Soviet Involvement in the Middle East: Policy Formulation, 1966–1973* (Boulder: Westview, 1978); Dina Rome Spechler, *Domestic Influences on Soviet Foreign Policy* (Washington: University Press of America, 1978); and Jiri Valenta, *Soviet Intervention in Czechoslovakia, 1968* (Baltimore: Johns Hopkins University Press, 1979).

19. Adomeit, *Soviet Risk-Taking*, (pp. 340–45), for example, subscribes to this view, as do Paul Jabber and Roman Kolkowicz, "The Arab-Israeli Wars of 1967 and 1973," in Kaplan et al., pp. 412–67.

20. See for example Oleg Troyanovski, "The Cuban Crisis: A Viewpoint from the Kremlin," *International Affairs* (Moscow) 4–5 (April–May 1992); Anatoliy Dobrinyn, "The Caribbean Crisis: An Eyewitness Account," *International Affairs* (Moscow) 8 (August 1992); James G. Blight, Bruce J. Allyn, and David A. Welch, *Cuba on the Brink: Castro, the Missile Crisis, and the Soviet Collapse* (New York: Pantheon, 1993); and Viktor Israelyan, *Inside the Kremlin During the Yom Kippur War* (University Park: Pennsylvania State University Press, 1995).

21. On the extent and problems of access to Soviet archives, see Mark Kramer, "Archival Research in Moscow: Progress and Pitfalls," *Cold War International History Project Bulletin,* no. 3 (Fall 1993), pp. 1, 18–39.

22. Philip D. Stewart, Margaret G. Hermann, and Charles F. Hermann, "Modeling the 1973 Decision to Support Egypt," *American Political Science Review* 83, no. 1 (March 1989), pp. 35–60, and Richard D. Anderson, Margaret G. Hermann, and Charles Hermann, "Explaining Self-Defeating Foreign Policy Decisions: Interpreting Soviet Arms for Egypt in 1973 Through Process or Domestic Bargaining Models," *American Political Science Review* 86, no. 3 (September 1992), pp. 759–66.

23. Foreword to Theodore Sorenson, *Decision-Making in the White House* (New York: Columbia University Press, 1963), p. xi.

24. America's classic Middle East dilemma is described from various perspectives in: Alan Dowty, *Middle East Crisis: U.S. Decision-Making in 1958, 1970, and 1973* (Berkeley: University of California Press, 1984); Henry A. Kissinger, *Years of Upheaval* (Boston: Little, Brown, 1982), William B. Quandt, *Decade of Decisions: American Policy Toward the Arab-Israeli Conflict, 1967–1976* (Berkeley: University of California Press, 1977), and *Peace Process: American Diplomacy and the Arab-Israeli Conflict since 1967* (Washington and Berkeley: Brookings / University of California Press, 1993).

25. For differing perspectives on the regional and global motivations of imperial powers, see Michael Doyle, *Empires* (Ithaca, NY: Cornell University Press, 1986); Benjamin Miller, *When Opponents Cooperate: Great Power Conflict and Collaboration in World Politics* (Ann Arbor: University of Michigan Press, 1995); and Jack Snyder, *Myths of Empire: Domestic Politics and International Ambition* (Ithaca: Cornell University Press, 1991).

26. For detailed analyses of Soviet policies toward the Middle East in this period, see George W. Breslauer, "Soviet Policy in the Middle East, 1967–1972: Unalterable

Antagonism or Collaborative Competition?" in Alexander L. George et al., *Managing U.S.-Soviet Rivalry: Problems of Crisis Prevention* (Boulder: Westview, 1983), pp. 139–54; Karen Dawisha, *Soviet Policy Towards Egypt* (New York: St. Martin's Press, 1979), Robert O. Freedman, *Soviet Policy Toward the Middle East Since 1970,* 3rd ed. (New York: Praeger, 1982); Jon D. Glassman, *Arms for the Arabs: The Soviet Union and War in the Middle East* (Baltimore: Johns Hopkins University Press, 1975); and Galia Golan, *Soviet Policies in the Middle East from World War II to Gorbachev* (Cambridge: Cambridge University Press, 1990).

27. For discussions of cognitive dissonance theory, see Leon Festinger, *A Theory of Cognitive Dissonance* (Stanford: Stanford University Press, 1957); Jack W. Brehm and Arthur R. Cohen, *Explorations in Cognitive Dissonance* (New York: John Wiley & Sons, 1962); Festinger, ed., *Conflict, Decision, and Dissonance* (Stanford: Stanford University Press, 1964); Arnold Lewis Glass and Keith James Holyoak, *Cognition,* 2nd ed. (New York: Random House, 1986); John D. Jecker, "Conflict and Dissonance: A Time of Decision," in Robert P. Abelson, et al., eds., *Theories of Cognitive Consistency: A Sourcebook* (Chicago: Rand McNally, 1968), pp. 571–76; Robert A. Wicklund and Jack W. Brehm, *Perspectives on Cognitive Dissonance* (New York: John Wiley & Sons, 1976); and Susan T. Fiske and Shelley E. Taylor, *Social Cognition,* 2nd ed. (New York: McGraw-Hill, 1991).

28. Robert Jervis, *Perception and Misperception in International Politics* (Princeton: Princeton University Press, 1976), pp. 132–41.

29. Jervis, *Perception and Misperception,* p. 142.

30. Irving L. Janis and Leon Mann, *Decision Making: A Psychological Analysis of Conflict, Choice, and Commitment* (New York: Free Press, 1977), pp. 81–91.

31. Janis and Mann, *Decision Making,* pp. 88–95.

32. See for example Ole R. Holsti, "The 1914 Case," *American Political Science Review* 59, no. 2 (June 1965), pp. 365–78; Paul Rosenfeld, John G. Kennedy, and Robert A. Giacalone, "Decision Making: A Demonstration of the Postdecision Dissonance Effect," *Journal of Social Psychology* 126, no. 5 (October 1986), pp. 663–65; Robert Jervis, Richard Ned Lebow, and Janice Gross Stein, *Psychology and Deterrence* (Baltimore: Johns Hopkins University Press, 1985); Alexander L. George, "The Impact of Crisis-Induced Stress on Decision Making," in National Academy of Sciences, Institute of Medicine, *The Medical Implications of Nuclear War* (Washington: National Academy Press, 1986), pp. 529–52; and Gregory M. Herek, Irving L. Janis, and Paul Huth, "Decision Making During International Crises: Is Quality of Process Related to Outcome?" *Journal of Conflict Resolution* 31, no. 2 (June 1987) pp. 203–26.

33. Alexander George, *Presidential Decisionmaking in Foreign Policy: The Effective Use of Information and Advice* (Boulder: Westview, 1980), pp. 25–34.

34. George, *Presidential Decisionmaking,* pp. 25–32.

35. Richard Ned Lebow, *Between Peace and War: The Nature of International Crisis* (Baltimore: Johns Hopkins University Press, 1981), p. 305.

36. Jack Snyder, "Rationality at the Brink: The Role of Cognitive Processes in Failure of Deterrence" (Santa Monica: RAND Paper P-5740, October 1976).

37. Jack Snyder, *The Ideology of the Offensive: Military Decision Making and the Disasters of 1914* (Ithaca: Cornell University Press, 1984), pp. 212–13.

38. This phenomenon is discussed in Holsti, *Crisis;* Thomas W. Milburn, "The Management of Crises," in Charles F. Hermann, ed., *International Crisis: Insights from Behavioral Research* (Ann Arbor: University of Michigan Press, 1972), pp. 259–81; George, *Presidential Decisionmaking,* p. 48; and George, "The Impact of Crisis-Induced Stress," p. 534.

39. Janis and Mann, pp. 57–62.

40. See H. C. Foushee, "Dyads and Triads at 35,000 Feet: Factors Affecting Group Process and Aircrew Performance," *American Psychologist* 39 (1984), pp. 885–93; Rosenfeld, Kennedy, and Giacalone, "Decision Making"; H. C. Foushee and R. L. Hemrech, "Group Interaction and Flight Crew Performance," in E. L. Warner and D. C. Nagel, eds., *Human Factors in Aviation* (San Diego: Academic Press, 1988); and James E. Duskell and Eduardo Salas, "Group Decision Making Under Stress," *Journal of Applied Psychology* 76, no. 3 (June 1991), pp. 473–78.

41. Snyder and Diesing, pp. 210–11.

42. These risks, and the Politburo's partially successful tactics for managing them, are detailed in Israelyan, *Inside the Kremlin.*

43. Holsti, "The 1914 Case," and *Crisis,* p. 18.

44. Quoted in Max Montgelas and Walther Schucking, eds., *Outbreak of the World War: German Documents Collected by Karl Kautsky* (New York: Oxford University Press, 1924), p. 321. Emphasis in original.

45. Holsti, "The 1914 Case," p. 372.

46. Snyder, "Rationality at the Brink," pp. 9–11, 32–36.

47. See, for example, Jabber and Kolkowicz, pp. 415–25.

48. Kass, *Soviet Involvement,* Spechler, *Domestic Influences,* Stewart, Hermann, and Hermann, "Modeling the 1973 Decisions," and Anderson, Hermann, and Hermann, "Explaining Soviet Foreign Policy Decisions: Interpreting Soviet Arms to Egypt in 1973 Through Process or Domestic Bargaining Models," *American Political Science Review* 86, no. 3 (September 1992), pp. 759–66, are entirely devoted to this topic, as is Spechler, "The USSR and Third-World Conflicts: Domestic Debate and Soviet Policy in the Middle East, 1967–1973," *World Politics* 38, no. 3 (April 1986), pp. 435–61. See also Goldgeier, *Leadership Style and Soviet Foreign Policy.*

49. Horelick, Johnson, and Steinbruner, "The Study of Soviet Foreign Policy"; Stephen Meyer, "Soviet National Security Decisionmaking: What Do We Know and What Do We Understand?" in Jiri Valenta and William C. Potter, eds., *Soviet Decisionmaking for National Security* (London: Allen and Unwin, 1984), pp. 255–98; and William C. Potter, "The Study of Soviet Decisionmaking for National Security: What Is to Be Done?," in Valenta and Potter, eds., pp. 299–307.

50. Roy D. Laird, *The Politburo: Demographic Trends, Gorbachev, and The Future* (Boulder: Westview, 1986), pp. 168–85.

51. Arthur J. Alexander, "Decision Making in Soviet Weapons Procurement," Adelphi Papers, nos. 147 & 148 (London: IISS, 1978), pp. 14–16; Ellen Jones, "The Defense Council in Soviet Leadership Decisionmaking," Occasional Paper, no. 188 (Washington: Kennan Institute for Advanced Russian Studies, 1984).

52. Irving L. Janis, *Groupthink: Psychological Studies of Policy Decisions and Fiascoes,* 2nd ed. (Boston: Houghton Mifflin, 1983).

53. Jones, "The Defense Council"; Stephen Meyer, "Soviet Perspectives on the Paths to Nuclear War," in Graham Allison, Albert Carnesale, and Joseph S. Nye, eds., *Hawks, Doves, and Owls: An Agenda for Avoiding Nuclear War* (New York: Norton, 1985), pp. 167–205; Condoleezza Rice, "The Party, the Military, and Decision Authority in the Soviet Union," *World Politics* 40, no. 1 (October 1987), pp. 55–81; and Stephen Shenfeld, "Crisis Management: The Soviet Approach," in Carl G. Jacobsen, ed., *Strategic Power USA / USSR* (London: Macmillan, 1990), pp. 198–205.

54. Douglas M. Hart, "Soviet Approaches to Crisis Management: The Military Dimension," *Survival* 26, no. 5 (September–October 1984), pp. 214–23.

55. Stephen M. Meyer, "Soviet Nuclear Operations," in Ashton B. Carter, John D. Steinbruner, and Charles A. Zraket, eds., *Managing Nuclear Operations* (Washington: Brookings, 1987), pp. 470–534.

56. Meyer, "Soviet Perspectives," p. 198.

57. For discussions of preemption in Soviet military-technical doctrine, see Meyer, "Soviet Perspectives," pp. 195–200, and Raymond L. Garthoff, *Deterrence and the Revolution in Soviet Military Doctrine* (Washington: Brookings, 1990), pp. 29–48.

58. Janis and Mann, pp. 129–33.

Chapter Two

1. For representative examples of conventional analyses of Soviet behavior in Middle East crises, see Fukuyama, pp. 4–25, and Snyder and Diesing, pp. 145–48.

2. Note that the table specifically describes Soviet policy options in a Middle East conflict. If the crisis being considered originated in an area of vital interest to the USSR, such as Eastern Europe, the Soviet value structure would tend to be weighted toward competition with the United States, because both sides recognized the legitimacy of Soviet interests in that region, and any significant political losses there would have immediately and directly harmed Soviet economic and security interests. In an Eastern European crisis, therefore, where relative bargaining power was asymmetric in the Soviet Union's favor, standing firm against the United States would most likely avoid serious losses, and the risks inherent in a Soviet-American confrontation would have been more acceptable. By the same token, a very different matrix would be needed to model Soviet decisions in a direct U.S.-Soviet confrontation, such as the Berlin or Cuban crises.

3. Alvin Z. Rubinstein, *Red Star on the Nile: The Soviet-Egyptian Influence Relationship Since the June War* (Princeton: Princeton University Press, 1977), pp. 32–37.

4. Henry A. Kissinger, *White House Years* (Boston: Little, Brown, 1979), p. 564.

5. Snyder and Diesing, pp. 145–48.

6. George, *Presidential Decisionmaking*, pp. 25–32.

7. Ibid., pp. 26–28.

8. Janis and Mann, *Decision Making*, p. 46.

9. George, *Presidential Decisionmaking*, pp. 32–34.

10. Adomeit, *Soviet Risk-Taking*, passim; Richard K. Betts, *Nuclear Blackmail and Nuclear Balance* (Washington: Brookings, 1987), pp. 23–31.

11. George C. Herring, *America's Longest War: The United States and Vietnam, 1950–1975* (New York: Wiley & Sons, 1979), pp. 260–62.

12. Snyder and Diesing, p. 210.

13. Adomeit, *Soviet Risk-Taking*, pp. 9–17.

14. Snyder, "Rigor, Richness, and Relevance," pp. 89–109.

15. Adomeit, *Soviet Risk-Taking*, pp. 101–2; Betts, pp. 27–28.

16. Herring, *America's Longest War*, pp. 260–62.

17. Brecher, *Decisions in Crisis*, pp. 18–19.

18. George, "The Operational Code," p. 212–16.

19. Adomeit, *Soviet Risk-Taking*, pp. 316–27, and "Soviet Crisis Prevention and Management: Why and When Do Soviet Leaders Take Risks?" (Santa Monica: RAND / UCLA Center for the Study of Soviet International Behavior Occasional Paper OPS-008, October 1986), pp. 17–19.

20. Fukuyama, pp. 17–25.

21. Snyder, *The Ideology of the Offensive*, p. 212.

22. George, "The Operational Code," pp. 214–15; Adomeit, *Soviet Risk-Taking*, pp. 317–19.

23. George, "The Operational Code," p. 214; Hart, pp. 214–23; Adomeit, "Soviet Crisis Prevention," pp. 17–19.

24. Snyder, "'Prisoner's Dilemma' and 'Chicken' Models," pp. 87–90; Snyder and Diesing, pp. 191–93.

25. Snyder and Diesing, p. 122.

26. For a comprehensive discussion of these issues, see Kaplan, *The Diplomacy of Power;* Stephen T. Hosmer and Thomas W. Wolfe; *Soviet Power and Practice Toward Third World Conflicts* (Lexington, MA: Lexington Books, 1983), and Alvin Z. Rubinstein, *Moscow's Third World Strategy* (Princeton: Princeton University Press, 1990).

27. Soviet and American interests at stake in the conflicts considered in this analysis will be considered in greater depth in the chapters devoted to them. For an overview of the balance of interests in the region, see Walter Laqueur, *The Struggle for the Middle East: The Soviet Union in the Mediterranean, 1958–1968* (New York: Macmillan, 1969); Freedman, *Soviet Policy;* and Golan, *Soviet Policies.*

28. Fukuyama, pp. 5–25.

29. Snyder and Diesing, p. 147.

30. Fukuyama, pp. 8–9.

31. The Politburo's membership did not, of course, remain totally constant between April 1967 and October 1973. Out of a maximum of sixteen voting members during this period, however, nine were full members for the entire period, including the paramount leaders Brezhnev, Kosygin, Podgorniy, Shelepin, and Suslov. Additionally, two individuals who headed important government institutions, Grechko and Gromyko, were appointed as full members near the end of the period. See Laird, *The Politburo*, pp. 168–85.

32. Kass, *Soviet Involvement,* and Spechler, *Domestic Influences,* and "The USSR and Third-World Conflicts," passim.

33. Lilita Dzirkals, Thane Gustafson, and A. Ross Johnson, "The Media and Intra-Elite Communication in the USSR" (Santa Monica: RAND Report R-2869, September 1982), pp. 76–87.

34. For more discussion of the use of press sources, see Kass, *Soviet Involvement;* Spechler, *Domestic Influences* and "The USSR and Third-World Conflicts"; Dzirkals, Gustafson, and Johnson, "The Media and Intra-Elite"; Horelick, Johnson, and Steinbruner, "The Study of Soviet Foreign Policy," pp. 55–57; Galia Golan, "Soviet Decisionmaking in the Yom Kippur War, 1973," in Valenta and Potter, *Soviet Decisionmaking,* pp. 185–236; and Snyder, "Rigor, Richness, and Relevance," pp. 89–108.

35. Quoted in Mohamed Heikal, *The Sphinx and the Commissar: The Rise and Fall of Soviet Influence in the Arab World* (London: Collins, 1978), pp. 70–71. Fukuyama, p. 43, note 3, reports that Anthony Love and Kennett Nutting confirmed this account in separate interviews with Nasser.

36. Fukuyama, pp. 17–25; Adomeit, *Soviet Risk-Taking,* pp. 17–19.

37. For a discussion of this method, see Alexander George, "Case Studies and Theory Development: The Method of Structured, Focused Comparison," in Paul Gordon Lauren, ed., *Diplomacy: New Approaches in History, Theory, and Policy* (New York: Free Press, 1979), pp. 43–68.

38. George, "The Operational Code," pp. 214–15; Adomeit, *Soviet Risk-Taking,* pp. 317–24, and "Soviet Crisis Prevention," pp. 17–19.

Chapter Three

1. Nikita Khrushchev, *Khrushchev Remembers: The Last Testament,* trans. Strobe Talbot (Boston: Little, Brown, 1974), p. 345.

2. For detailed analyses of Soviet policy toward the Middle East before and during the war, see Laqueur, *The Struggle for the Middle East;* Arnold Horelick, "Soviet Policy in the Middle East, Part I: Policy from 1955 to 1969," in Paul Y. Hammond and Sidney S. Alexander, *Political Dynamics in the Middle East* (New York: American Elsevier, 1972), pp. 553–604; Glassman, *Arms for the Arabs;* Kass, *Soviet Involvement in the Middle East;* Dawisha, *Soviet Policy Towards Egypt;* and Golan, *Soviet Policies in the Middle East.*

3. Laqueur, *The Struggle for the Middle East,* pp. 68–79; Hosmer and Wolfe, *Soviet Policy,* pp. 12–28.

4. Jabber and Kolkowicz, p. 414; Mohammed H. Heikal, *The Road to Ramadan* (New York: Ballantine, 1975), pp. 39–40.

5. Mohammed H. Heikal's account of Nasser's relations with Soviet leaders are very colorful, although they may also be slightly colored by the author's closeness to his subject. See *The Cairo Documents: The Inside Story of Nasser and His Friendship with World Leaders, Rebels, and Statesmen* (Garden City, NY: Doubleday, 1973), pp. 1–30, 121–58, and *The Sphinx and the Commissar.*

6. Laqueur, *The Struggle for the Middle East,* pp. 85–89; Horelick, "Soviet Policy in the Middle East," pp. 581–91.

7. Text of the communiqué published in *Pravda,* 12 February 1967, pp. 1, 4. The delay in publication may indicate some difficulty in arriving at an appropriate formula for concealing the two parties' disagreements.

8. For additional evidence of Soviet perceptions of the weaknesses of the Syrian regime, see Audrey McInerney, "Prospect Theory and Soviet Policy Towards Syria, 1966–1967," *Political Psychology* 13, no. 2 (1992), pp. 265–82.

9. Glassman, *Arms for the Arabs,* pp. 25–35; L. Koriavin, *Izvestiia,* 8 January 1967, p. 4, and 10 May 1967, p. 1.; Igor Beliaev, *Pravda,* 18 January 1967, p. 3; Radio Moscow Domestic Service broadcast 14 June 1967, transcribed in *FBIS USSR* 115 (14 June 1967), p. BB7.

10. For discussions of this dependency relationship, see Ronald D. McLaurin, *The Middle East and Soviet Policy* (Lexington, MA: Lexington Books, 1975), pp. 20–25, and Golan, "The Soviet Union in the Middle East after Thirty Years," in Andrzej Korbonski and Francis Fukuyama, eds., *The Soviet Union and The Third World: The Last Three Decades* (Ithaca: Cornell University Press, 1987), pp. 187–88.

11. See for example K. Vishnevetskiy, *Izvestiia,* 23 May 1967, p. 3; unsigned editorial, *Krasnaia zvezda,* 4 July 1967, p. 1; and Mark N. Katz, *The Third World in Soviet Military Thought* (London: Croom Helm, 1982), pp. 37–43.

12. Lyndon Baines Johnson, *The Vantage Point: Perspectives on the Presidency, 1963–1969* (New York: Holt, Rinehart, and Winston, 1971), p. 291.

13. See for example the interchange between Nasser and Podgorniy on 23 June 1967, as recorded by 'Abd-al-Majid Farid, trans. in "'Abd-al-Nasir's Secret Papers" (Arlington: U.S. Joint Publications Research Service Translations on Near East and North Africa no. 1865 (14 November 1978), pp. 11–12.

14. On perceptions of relative U.S. and Soviet power during this period, see William C. Wohlforth, *The Elusive Balance: Power and Perceptions During the Cold War* (Ithaca: Cornell University Press, 1993).

15. Snyder and Diesing, pp. 145–48.

16. Fukuyama, pp. 5–25.

17. Johnson, p. 302.

18. Brecher, *Decisions in Crisis,* pp. 282–85.

19. Ibid., pp. 44–46.

20. There are many historical accounts of the Six-Day War and the events surrounding it. The following were most helpful to the author: Daniel Dishon, et al., eds., *Middle East Record 1967,* vol. 2 (Jerusalem: Israel Universities Press, 1971); Trevor N. Dupuy, *Elusive Victory: The Arab-Israeli Wars, 1947–1974* (New York: Harper & Row, 1978); Chaim Herzog, *The Arab-Israeli Wars: War and Peace in the Middle East* (New York: Random House, 1982); Walter Laqueur, *The Road to Jerusalem: The Origins of the Arab-Israeli Conflict 1967* (New York: Macmillan, 1968), and Edgar O'Ballance, *The Third Arab-Israeli War* (London: Faber & Faber, 1972).

21. It was possible, of course, that American actions could have precipitated turning points in the crises, and U.S. actions did serve to heighten and lessen tension on several occasions. As the conflicts actually unfolded, however, most American maneuvers were made as immediate responses to Soviet, Israeli, or Arab initiatives. So as far as can be determined, U.S. actions did not directly produce changes in the type or level of tensions acting upon Soviet decision makers.

22. Robert Jervis, "Cooperation Under the Security Dilemma," *World Politics* 30, no. 2 (July 1978), pp. 187–94.

23. Stephen Van Evera, "The Cult of the Offensive and the Origins of the First World War," *International Security* 9, no. 1 (Summer 1984), pp. 64–65.

24. *Middle East Record 1967* (hereafter *MER 1967*), pp. 176- 79.

25. The text of this protest was published in *Izvestiia,* 26 April 1967, p. 1.

26. Brecher, *Decisions in Crisis,* pp. 35–36.

27. Nadav Safran, *From War to War: The Arab-Israeli Confrontation, 1948–1967* (New York: Pegasus, 1969), pp. 277–78.

28. *Qol Yisra'el* broadcast, 11 May 1967, trans. in *MER 1967,* p. 179.

29. *Jerusalem Post,* 14 May 1967, p. 1.

30. Text of this speech published in *Pravda,* 20 June 1967, p. 1.

31. *MER 1967,* pp. 185–86.

32. Koriavin, *Izvestiia,* 17 May 1967, p.1; Yevgeniy Primakov, *Pravda,* 18 May 1967, p. 1; O. Ivanov, *Krasnaia zvezda,* 19 May 1967, p. 3; V. Rogov, *Trud,* 19 May 1967, p.1.

33. *MER 1967,* p. 194.

34. Viktor Maevskiy, *Pravda,* 22 May 1967, p. 1; Koriavin, *Izvestiia,* 25 May 1967, p. 3; Ivanov, *Krasnaia zvezda,* 25 May 1967, p. 3; D. Volskiy, *Krasnaia zvezda,* 28 May 1967, p. 3.

35. Soviet government statement, 5 June 1967, published in *Pravda,* 6 June 1967, p. 1; Soviet government communiqué to Israel, 7 June 1967, published in *Pravda,* 8 June 1967, p. 1; statement of the Communist and Workers' parties and governments of Bulgaria, Hungary, the GDR, Poland, the USSR, Czechoslovakia, and Yugoslavia, issued 9 May 1967, published in *Pravda,* 10 June 1967, p. 1. The last statement, often referred to as the Moscow Declaration, was prepared by a formal multilateral meeting and is highly unlikely to reflect decisions made in response to Israeli actions on the day of its issue.

36. *MER 1967,* p. 229.

37. Text of this note published in *Pravda,* 11 June 1967, p.1.

38. *Pravda,* 11 June 1967, p. 4.

39. Quoted in Johnson, pp. 301–2.

40. *Izvestiia,* 26 April 1967, p. 1.

41. Avigdor Dagan, *Moscow and Jerusalem: Twenty Years of Relations Between Israel and the Soviet Union.* (New York: Abelard-Schuman, 1970), pp. 202–3.

42. Dagan, pp. 203–4.

43. Ivanov, *Krasnaia zvezda,* 12 April 1967, p.1; Vishnevetskiy, *Izvestiia,* 16 April 1967, p. 3; Primakov, *Pravda,* 12 April 1967, p.5, and 19 April 1967, p. 5.

44. Vishnevetskiy, *Izvestiia,* 16 April 1967, p. 5.

45. David Kimche and Dan Bawly, *The Sandstorm: The Arab-Israeli War of June 1967: Prelude and Aftermath* (New York: Stein and Day, 1968), p. 88.

46. Safran, p. 277.

47. *Qol Yisra'el* broadcast, 11 May 1967, trans. in *MER 1967,* p. 179

48. Kimche and Bawly, 1968, p. 88.

49. Anwar el-Sadat, *In Search of Identity: An Autobiography* (New York: Harper & Row, 1977), pp. 171–72. Sadat was at that time the vice president of the UAR. Although it is hardly unusual for aircraft departures to be delayed, especially in Russia, one

cannot help but wonder whether Sadat's plane was detained to ensure that Semenov would have ample time to convince him of the "seriousness" of the danger to Syria.

50. Laqueur, *The Road to Jerusalem*, p. 71.

51. O'Ballance, *The Third Arab-Israeli War*, p. 23; Jabber and Kolkowicz, p. 425.

52. *Pravda*, 20 June 1967, p. 3.

53. Brecher, *Decisions in Crisis*, p. 36; Safran, p. 277.

54. Richard B. Parker, *The Politics of Miscalculation in the Middle East* (Bloomington: Indiana University Press, 1993), pp. 9–14.

55. Abba Eban, *Abba Eban: An Autobiography*, p. 318.

56. Parker, pp. 17–34.

57. Heikal, *The Sphinx and the Commissar*, pp. 174–75. Mobilization of the UAR armed forces was actually ordered on May 14 (*MER 1967*, p. 185).

58. Interview with Georgii Mirskii by author, Santa Monica, 15 August 1991.

59. Koriavin, *Izvestiia*, 10 May 1967, p. 1.

60. Primakov, *Pravda*, 16 May 1967; *Izvestiia*, 16 May 1967, p. 1.

61. Quoted in Dagan, p. 213.

62. E. Tuma, *Izvestiia*, 18 May 1967, p. 2;

63. Primakov, *Pravda*, 18 May 1967, p. 1, and 20 May 1967, p. 1; Koriavin, *Izvestiia*, 17 May 1967, p.1, 19 May 1967, p. 1, and 20 May 1967, p. 2.

64. V. Pustov, *Krasnaia zvezda*, 17 May 1967, p. 2; Ivanov, *Krasnaia zvezda*, 19 May 1967, p. 3; V. Rogov, *Trud*, 19 May 1967, p. 1.

65. Dagan, p. 218; Kass, pp. 28–29; Jabber and Kolkowicz, pp. 430–31.

66. V. Vashedchenko, *Krasnaia zvezda*, 26 May 1967, p. 4.

67. *Izvestiia*, 27 May 1967, p. 4; G. Vasil'ev, *Pravda*, 27 May 1967, p. 5; Primakov, *Pravda* 27 May 1967, p. 5. Koriavin later chastised the United States and Britain for sending "dreadnoughts instead of diplomats" to resolve the conflict in the region. (*Izvestiia*, 4 June 1967, p. 1).

68. *MER 1967*, p. 223. While the possibility that U.S. naval forces might act to break the blockade could not be ruled out, Soviet reports of preparations for intervention appeared before the U.S. began to assemble its naval forces. Although Johnson discussed the formation of an Anglo-American joint task force as early as May 24, the multinational force intended to be sent to the Red Sea was still in the planning stages on June 4.

69. Text published in *Pravda*, 24 May 1967, p. 1.

70. Heikal, *The Sphinx and the Commissar*, pp. 178–79.

71. Sadat, p. 173.

72. Heikal, *The Cairo Documents*, p. 244. The tortuous route described for this information cannot be confirmed.

73. Quoted in Heikal, *The Sphinx and the Commissar*, p. 179.

74. Heikal, *The Sphinx and the Commissar*, p. 180.

75. For an account of the USSR's activities at the U.N., see *MER 1967*, pp. 236–41, and Eban, pp. 365–413.

76. Text published in *Pravda*, 6 June 1967, p. 1.

77. Ibid., 7 June 1967, p. 1.

78. Ibid., 10 June 1967, p. 1.

79. Ibid., 10 June 1961, p. 1.

80. Quoted in Heikal, *The Sphinx and the Commissar,* p. 182.

81. For reports of Soviet naval operations, see *The New York Times,* 8 June 1968, p. 1, and 9 June 1969, p. 1.

82. Outstanding examples of this theme are offered by Polianov, *Izvestiia,* 8 June 1967, p. 5, V. Nekrasov, *Pravda,* 9 June 1967, p. 5, and the pseudonymous "V. Petrov," *Izvestiia,* 10 June 1967, p. 2.

83. *Pravda,* 6 June 1967, p. 3. See also *Izvestiia,* 7 June 1967, p. 2; *Pravda,* 8 June 1967, p. 3; and Y. Dymov, *Krasnaia zvezda,* 8 June 1967, p. 1.

84. A. Leontiev and Y. Dymov, *Krasnaia zvezda,* 9 June 1967, p. 3.

85. Unsigned editorial, "Inspirers of Aggression," *Izvestiia,* 6 June 1967, p. 1; Polianov, *Izvestiia,* 8 June 1967, p. 5; V. Kurdriavtsev, Izvestiia, 9 June 1967, p. 2; Beliaev, *Pravda,* 10 June 1967, p. 3.

86. Beliaev, *Pravda,* 6 June 1967, p. 3; Vishnevetskiy, *Izvestiia,* 7 June 1967, p. 2.

87. Y. Dymov, *Krasnaia zvezda,* 8 June 1967, p. 1.

88. Report of the Soviet Committee in Solidarity with the Countries of Asia and Africa, *Pravda,* 7 June 1967, p. 5; Koriavin, *Izvestiia,* 9 June 1967, p. 1.

89. "V. Petrov," *Izvestiia,* 10 June 1967, p. 1.

90. Eban, pp. 422–23; *MER 1967,* p. 240.

91. Text published in *Pravda,* 11 June 1967, p. 1. Czechoslovakia, Bulgaria, Hungary, Yugoslavia, and Poland all followed suit by June 12. The GDR did not have diplomatic relations with Israel, and Rumania, which had not signed the June 9 joint communiqué, maintained relations.

92. Eban, p. 423.

93. *MER 1967,* pp. 229–30.

94. Text quoted in Johnson, p. 302.

95. Johnson, p. 302.

96. Fukuyama, pp. 8–9.

97. Odd Bull, *War and Peace in the Middle East: The Experiences and Views of a U.N. Observer* (London: Leo Cooper, 1976), p. 120.

98. Johnson, p. 302.

99. *MER 1967,* p. 230.

100. V. Matveev, *Izvestiia,* 11 June 1967, p. 3. (This commentary was quoted in a Radio TASS broadcast on 10 June, trans. in *FBIS USSR* 113, 12 June 1967, p. BB23); unsigned editorial, *Pravda,* 11 June 1967, p. 1.

101. *Krasnaia zvezda,* 11 June 1967, p. 3.

102. CPSU Plenum Resolution, *Pravda,* 22 June 1967, p. 1.

103. *Izvestiia,* 13 June 1967, p. 5.

104. Text of speech in *Izvestiia,* 6 July 1967, p. 1.

105. For a discussion of these personnel changes, see Kass, *Soviet Involvement in the Middle East.*

106. Dagan, p. 202–3.

107. According to Heikal (*The Sphinx and the Commissar,* p. 183), Yugoslavia showed more willingness to materially aid the Arab cause than the USSR at this meeting.

108. Primakov, *Pravda,* 18 May 1967, p. 1; Koriavin, *Izvestiia,* 17 May 1967, p. 1, 19 May 1967, p. 1; TASS, *Pravda,* 19 May 1967, p.1.

109. *Pravda,* 10 June 1967, p. 1.

110. Koriavin, *Izvestiia,* 9 June 1967, p. 1; "V. Petrov," *Izvestiia,* 10 June 1967, p. 1

111. Outstanding examples of these themes are offered by Primakov, *Pravda,* 12 April 1967, p. 5; by Ivanov, *Krasnaia zvezda,* 19 May 1967, p. 2; and by Vishnevetskiy, *Pravda,* 6 June 1967, p. 3.

112. Heikal, *The Cairo Documents,* p. 244, and *The Sphinx and the Commissar,* p. 179.

113. Heikal, *The Sphinx and the Commissar,* pp. 178–80.

114. Vashedchenko, *Krasnaia zvezda,* 16 May 1967, p. 4; Vasil'ev, *Pravda,* 27 May 1967, p. 5; Koriavin, *Izvestiia,* 4 June 1967, p. 1.

115. Sadat, pp. 171–72; Laqueur, *The Road to Jerusalem,* p. 71.

116. Kimche and Bawly, p. 88; Jabber and Kolkowicz, p. 425.

117. Sadat, p. 172.

118. *MER 1967,* pp. 558–61.

119. Johnson, p. 302; Bull, p. 120.

120. Snyder and Diesing, p. 147.

121. Text of this draft resolution published in *Pravda,* 20 June 1967, p. 3.

122. Fukuyama, pp. 8–9.

Chapter Four

1. The television program quoted at the beginning of this chapter presents this viewpoint, as does D. Makarov, "'Neizvestnaia voina na Vostoke," *Argumenty i fakty* 34 (August 25–31, 1990), p. 5. The editors of *Argumenty i Fakty* note that the Ministry of Defense refused to disclose casualty figures for the Egyptian operation, saying that the figures were still secret. Public discussion of Soviet forces' participation in the conflict began in the late 1980s and accelerated when veterans of the "secret" operation complained in the military press that they had received no recognition for their combat experience. See Ekaterina Dobrynina, "Znoinoe leto 70-go," *Sobesednik* 47 (November 1988), pp. 12–13; letter to *Krasnaia zvezda* from I. Probylov, 8 March 1989, p. 2; and A. Dokuchaev, "Tot egipetskii god," *Krasnaia zvezda,* 25 March 1989, p. 2.

2. Ra'anan, "Soviet Decision Making in the Middle East," and Fukuyama, "Soviet Threats," present this argument, that will be discussed in detail later in this chapter.

3. While other Arab nations and the Palestine Liberation Organization were involved in the War of Attrition, the great majority of engagements took place between Egyptian and Israeli forces, and the struggle between those two countries was of the greatest immediate concern to both the United States and the USSR. This chapter will therefore concentrate on Soviet decisions regarding the Israeli-Egyptian conflict

4. Text of the resolution published in *Pravda,* 22 June 1967, p. 1.

5. *Pravda,* 9 August 1967, p. 1.

6. Quoted in Farid, pp. 11–12.

7. Ibid., p. 7.

8. Ibid., p. 86. The translation gives the date of this meeting as April 7, 1967, but this must be regarded as a typographical error.

9. For details on Soviet arms deliveries after the June War, see Rubinstein, *Red Star on the Nile*, pp. 17–30, and Glassman, pp. 65–68.

10. Institute for Strategic Studies, *Strategic Survey 1970* (London: Institute for Strategic Studies, 1971), p. 46.

11. Edgar O'Ballance, *The Electronic War in the Middle East, 1968–1970* (London: Faber & Faber, 1974), pp. 32–33. Heikal also comments on the friction between Soviet advisors and Egyptian officers (*The Sphinx and the Commissar*, pp. 212–14).

12. O'Ballance, *The Electronic War*, p. 34; Glassman, pp. 66–69.

13. *Al-Ahram*, 25 August 1967, trans. in William B. Quandt, "Soviet Policy in the October 1973 War," (Santa Monica: RAND Report R-1864-ISA, May 1976), p. 24.

14. Ra'anan, pp. 190–91.

15. Sadat, pp. 185–86.

16. Georgii Mirskii, "Ob"edinenaia Arabskaia Respublika v god tiazhelykh ispytanii," *Mezhdunarodniy Ezhegodnik 1968* (Moscow: Politicheskaia Literatura, 1968), pp. 219–24.

17. Igor Beliaev and Yevgeniy Primakov, "Izrail'skaia agressiia i Arabskii mir," *Mezhdunarodnaia zhizn'* 3(March 1968), pp. 56–65; Mirskii, "Vnutrenni front v OAR," *Novoe vremia* 50(13 December 1968), pp. 8–11.

18. Sadat, pp. 183–90.

19. For more on Soviet concern with and involvement in Egyptian internal politics, see Rubinstein, *Red Star on the Nile*, and Freedman, *Soviet Policy Toward the Middle East*.

20. Kurdriavtsev, *Izvestiia*, 24 November 1967, p. 2.

21. Examples of this argument may be found in Rubinstein, *Red Star on the Nile*, and Robert O. Freedman, "Détente and U.S.-Soviet Relations in the Middle East During the Nixon Years (1969–74)," in Della W. Sheldon, ed., *Dimensions of Détente* (New York: Praeger, 1978), pp. 84–121.

22. George Breslauer, "Soviet Policy in the Middle East;" Oded Eran, "Soviet Policy Between the 1967 and 1973 Wars," in Itamar Rabinovich and Haim Shaked, eds., *From June to October: The Middle East Between 1967 and 1973* (New Brunswick: Transaction, 1978), pp. 25–52.

23. Beliaev, "Aziatskii bumerang Vashingtona," *Mezhdunarodnaia Zhizn* 5(May 1969), pp. 83–89. For more on the beginning of détente, see Robin Edmonds, *Soviet Foreign Policy, 1962–1973: The Paradox of Superpower* (New York: Oxford University Press, 1975), Kissinger, *White House Years;* John Newhouse, *Cold Dawn: The Story of SALT* (New York: Holt, Rinehart & Winston, 1973); and Richard W. Stevenson, *The Rise and Fall of Détente: Relaxations of Tension in U.S.-Soviet Relations* (New York: Macmillan, 1985).

24. Eran, pp. 33–34.

25. Kissinger, *White House Years*, p. 347. Many of Kissinger's comments suggest that he also felt that the U.S. Department of State equaled or surpassed the USSR as an obstacle to American policy in the region during this period.

26. For more on this dynamic, see David A. Korn, *Stalemate: The War of Attrition and Great Power Diplomacy in the Middle East, 1967–1970* (Boulder: Westview, 1992).

27. Kissinger, *White House Years,* p. 559.

28. Farid, p. 8.

29. Harry Gelman, *The Brezhnev Politburo and the Decline of Détente* (Ithaca: Cornell University Press, 1984), pp. 100–3.

30. Fukuyama, pp. 9–11.

31. G. U. Dolnikov, commander of the Soviet group of forces, recalls (*7 Dnia* television program, 25 February 1990, trans. in FBIS USSR 41 [1 March 1990], pp. 32–33) that he arrived in Cairo on March 3, 1970; reports of Soviet combat forces in Egypt began appearing in the Western press on March 19. See *The New York Times* 19 March 1970, and Daniel Dishon, ed., *Middle East Record,* Vol. 5 *1969–1970* (Jerusalem: Israel Universities Press, 1977) pt. 1, p. 147 (hereafter *MER 1969–1970*).

32. Ra'anan, pp. 190–99.

33. Ibid., pp. 198–99.

34. Rubinstein, *Red Star on the Nile,* p. 105.

35. Heikal, *The Road to Ramadan,* pp. 78–85, and *The Sphinx and the Commissar,* pp. 194–98.

36. Sadat, p. 197.

37. Glassman, p. 74; Eran, p. 36; Freedman, "Détente and U.S.-Soviet Relations," pp. 87–92.

38. For more detailed accounts of the War of Attrition, see Korn, *Stalemate;* O'Ballance, *The Electronic War;* Lawrence L. Whetten, *The Canal War: Four-Power Conflict in the Middle East* (Cambridge: MIT Press, 1974); *MER 1969–70;* and Yaacov Bar-Siman-Tov, *The Israeli-Egyptian War of Attrition, 1969–70: A Case Study of Limited Local War* (New York: Columbia University Press, 1980).

39. Primakov, *Pravda,* 10 March 1969, p. 5; Koriavin, *Izvestiia* 12 March 1969, p. 2; Beliaev, TASS radio international service, 18 March 1969, trans. in *FBIS USSR* 53 (19 March 1969), pp. A61–62.

40. Koriavin, *Izvestiia,* 16 April 1969, p. 2. An unnamed *Izvestiia* correspondent reported on April 19 that the "situation was fraught with serious danger of an explosion" (p. 4), and the *Izvestiia* press service noted on April 25 that "the situation is becoming increasingly explosive," (p. 4), but similar anonymous, nonspecific warnings of the possibility of escalation appear frequently in Soviet coverage of all periods of the Arab-Israeli conflict.

41. Vladimir Yermakov, *Pravda,* 27 July 1969, pp. 1–4.

42. See *MER 1969–70,* p. 137.

43. *Krasnaia zvezda,* 3 December 1969, p. 1.

44. Text of the communiqué published in *Vneshnaia politika Sovietskogo Soiuza 1969* (Moscow: Mezhdunarodnye otnosheniia, 1970), pp. 261–63.

45. *MER 1969–70,* p. 141.

46. Bar-Siman-Tov, pp. 118–44.

47. Piotor Demchenko, *Izvestiia,* 10 January 1970, p. 2.

48. *Izvestiia,* 15 January 1970, p. 1.

49. Rubinstein, *Red Star on the Nile,* pp. 110–12; *MER 1969–70,* p. 122, 147.

50. R. Vasiliev and Yu. Belenko, *Krasnaia zvezda,* 15 March 1970, p. 3.

51. *MER 1969–70,* p. 147.

52. *Pravda,* 3 March 1970, p. 3.

53. *MER 1969–1970,* pp. 156–57.

54. TASS Radio international service in English, 9 July 1970, trans. in *FBIS USSR 133* (10 July 1970), p. A1.

55. Aleksei Basenko, "V nebe nad Egiptom," *Krasnaia zvezda,* 20 September 1990, p. 3.

56. Sadat, pp. 198–99.

57. *MER 1969–70,* p. 160.

58. *Pravda,* 30 April 1969, p. 4.

59. Rumiantsev, *Pravda,* 6 June 1969, p. 4.

60. Primakov, *Pravda,* 9 May 1969, p. 5; Demchenko, *Izvestiia,* 11 May 1969, p. 1; Koriavin, *Izvestiia,* 20 June 1969, p. 2; Radio Peace and Progress broadcast in English to Africa, 13 May 1969, trans. in *FBIS USSR 93* (14 May 1969), pp. A28–29. Israel is widely believed to have been developing nuclear weapons in this period, but without U.S. assistance.

61. Radio Peace and Progress broadcast in English to Africa, 23 April 1969, trans. in *FBIS USSR 79* (24 April 1969), pp. A11–12.

62. S. Astakhov, *Krasnaia zvezda,* 16 April 1969, p. 3; A. Markov and R. Vasiliev, *Krasnaia zvezda,* 16 May 1969, p. 3; Aleksei Gurkov, Radio Moscow broadcast in English to North America, 25 June 1969, trans. in *FBIS USSR 123* (26 June 1969), pp. A4–5.

63. Dmitri Ugolkov, *Pravda,* 18 March 1969, p. 5; Primakov, *Pravda,* 18 March 1969, p. 5.

64. Text published in *Pravda,* 14 June 1969, p. 5.

65. Heikal, *The Sphinx and the Commissar,* p. 193–95.

66. Beliaev, *Pravda,* 23 July 1969, p. 4; Yermakov, *Pravda,* 27 July 1969, p. 4.

67. *Pravda,* 30 July 1969, p. 5.

68. A. Agaryshev, *Komsomolskaia pravda,* 10 September 1969, p. 3.

69. *Pravda,* 27 August 1969, p. 4.

70. G. Shishkin, *Sel'skaia zhizn',* 30 August 1969, p. 5; German Ryzhikov, Radio Moscow domestic service broadcast, 31 July 1969, trans. in *FBIS USSR 148* (1 August 1969), p. A16.

71. Demchenko, *Izvestiia,* 6 January 1970, p. 2.

72. *Pravda,* 27 August 1969, p. 5.

73. Nikolai Kupenko, *Krasnaia zvezda,* 24 September 1969, p. 3.

74. Georgii Ratiani, *Pravda,* 7 September 1969, p. 5.

75. *Izvestiia,* 28 October 1969, p. 5.

76. *Krasnaia zvezda,* 4 September 1969, p. 1.

77. *Pravda,* 2 October 1969, p. 5.

78. Sofia BTA international service broadcast in English, 18 September 1969, trans. in *FBIS USSR 181* (19 September 1969), p. E1.

79. Reported by TASS, 31 October 1969.

80. *Krasnaia zvezda,* 3 December 1969, p. 1.

81. *Vneshnaia politika Sovetskogo Soiuza 1969,* pp. 261–63.

82. *Izvestiia,* 10 January 1970, p. 2.

83. V. Shmarov, *Izvestiia,* 10 January 1970, p. 2; Radio Moscow broadcast in Turkish, 21 January 1970, trans. in *FBIS USSR* 15 (22 January 1970), p. A46.

84. Beliaev, *Pravda,* 9 January 1970, p. 5.

85. Sadat, p. 197. Sadat mistakenly claims that Nasser's request was prompted by the bombing of a factory at Abu Zabal; the Abu Zabal bombing actually took place on February 12 (*MER 1969–70,* p. 145).

86. Heikal, *The Road to Ramadan,* p. 80.

87. Heikal, *The Sphinx and the Commissar,* p. 197.

88. Heikal, 1975, pp. 81–82.

89. Heikal, *The Road to Ramadan,* p. 83. A 1990 Soviet article cites Heikal as its source of information on Nasser's secret visit.

90. Sadat, p. 197. Sadat also says that Nasser's request for Tu–16 bombers was denied at this meeting (p. 198).

91. Igor Timofeev, "War on the Day of Atonement," *New Times* 45 (November 1988), pp. 18–22.

92. Timofeev, p. 20.

93. Koriavin, *Izvestiia,* 25 January 1970, p. 3; Yevgeniy Maksimov, *Pravda,* 27 January 1970, p. 4.

94. Beliaev, *Pravda,* 31 January 1970, p. 5; Glukhov, *Pravda,* 29 January 1970, p. 5.

95. Quoted in Kissinger, *White House Years,* p. 560.

96. Richard M. Nixon, *RN: The Memoirs of Richard Nixon* (New York: Grosset & Dunlap, 1978), p. 479; see also Kissinger, p. 561.

97. Parker, pp. 145–46.

98. Kissinger, *White House Years,* pp. 561–62.

99. Kurdriavtsev, *Izvestiia,* 17 February 1970, p. 1.

100. Interview with Nasser by James Reston, *The New York Times,* 15 February 1970, p. 18.

101. Aleksei Vasiliev, *Pravda,* 9 March 1970, p. 3.

102. Volskiy, *Krasnaia zvezda,* 24 March 1970, p. 3; Primakov, *Pravda,* 31 March 1970, p. 5.

103. Tsoppi, Radio Moscow broadcast in Rumanian to Rumania, 13 April 1970, trans. in *FBIS USSR* 72 (14 April 1970), pp. A1–2.

104. Kissinger, p. 570.

105. Ibid., p. 569–70.

106. Text published in *Pravda,* 15 April 1970, pp. 1–2.

107. *MER 1969–70,* pp. 151–52.

108. *Pravda,* 1 May 1970, p. 5.

109. Radio Moscow domestic service, 4 May 1970, trans. in *FBIS USSR* 87 (5 May 1970), pp. A10–11.

110. Yurii Tyssovskiy, TASS Radio international service broadcast in English, 31 May 1970, trans. in *FBIS USSR* 99 (21 May 1970), pp. A27–28.

111. Evelyn Mathes and Karl Yegorov, Radio Moscow broadcast in English to Africa, 16 July 1970, transcr. in *FBIS USSR* 138 (17 July 1970), p. A2; Beliaev, Radio Moscow domestic service broadcast, 20 July 1970, trans. in *FBIS USSR* 140

(21 July 1970), pp. A4–6; *Pravda,* 21 July 1970, p. 5; and *Novoe vremia* 29 (17 July 1970), p. 11.

112. A. Kislov, TASS Radio international service broadcast in English, 30 May 1970, trans. in *FBIS USSR* 106 (2 June 1970), p. A41; Aleksandr Dmitriev, Radio Moscow broadcast in Arabic, 5 June 1970, trans. in *FBIS USSR* 110 (8 June 1970), pp. A13–15.

113. Radio Moscow domestic service broadcast, 13 June 1970, trans. in *FBIS USSR* 115 (15 June 1970), pp. A5–6.

114. *Pravda,* 24 June 1970, p. 5.

115. Heikal, *The Sphinx and the Commissar,* p. 200.

116. Sadat, pp. 198–99. Sadat also claims that Nasser had asked the Politburo for a "deterrent weapon" on this visit, though he does not specifically mention nuclear weapons, and no independent confirmation of this request can be found.

117. Heikal, *The Road to Ramadan,* p. 91.

118. Examples of these arguments are presented by Beliaev in "Blizhnovostochniy krizis i manevri Vashingtona," *Mezhdunarodnaia zhizn'* 3 (March 1970), pp. 28–35, and *Pravda,* 3 July 1970, p. 2, and by S. Bychkov, *Novoe vremia* 27 (3 July 1970), p. 7.

119. Volskiy, *Novoe vremia* 30 (24 July 1970), pp. 4–5.

120. *Pravda,* 30 July 1970, p. 5.

121. Broadcast of 30 July 1970, transcr. in *FBIS USSR* 148 (31 July 1970), pp. A2–3; Vishnevetskiy, *Pravda,* 2 August 1970, p. 1.

122. *Pravda,* 9 August 1970, p. 5.

123. *Izvestiia,* 11 August 1970, p. 2.

124. *Novoe vremia* 32 (7 August 1970), pp. 4–5.

125. See, for example, *Izvestiia,* 15 January 1970, p. 2; Demchenko, *Izvestiia,* 10 January 1970, p. 2; and Beliaev, *Pravda,* 7 February 1970, p. 5.

126. Heikal, *The Road to Ramadan,* p. 79.

127. Kissinger, *White House Years,* p. 561.

128. Alexander L. George, "Missed Opportunities for Crisis Prevention: The War of Attrition and Angola," in Alexander L. George, Philip J. Farley, and Alexander Dallin, eds., *U.S.-Soviet Security Cooperation: Achievements, Failures, Lessons* (New York: Oxford University Press, 1988, pp. 192–199.

129. Timofeev (p. 20) reports that the first shipment of new arms and group of accompanying personnel began moving to their (undisclosed) port of embarkation in January 1970; Kosygin's note was received in Washington on January 31.

130. Timofeev, p. 20.

131. Heikal, *The Road to Ramadan,* pp. 80–83; Sadat, p. 197.

132. Fukuyama, pp. 10–11, 18.

133. Bar-Siman-Tov, pp. 159–66.

134. Sadat, pp. 185–99; Heikal, *The Road to Ramadan,* pp. 80–91, and *The Sphinx and the Commissar,* pp. 193–214.

135. Adomeit, *Soviet Risk-Taking,* pp. 317–24.

136. For discussions of the role of détente in Soviet politics, see Kenneth Jowitt, "Images of Détente and the Soviet Political Order" (Berkeley: University of California Institute of International Studies Policy Papers in International Affairs No. 1,

1977); Adam B. Ulam, *Dangerous Relations: The Soviet Union in World Politics* (New York: Oxford University Press, 1983); Stevenson, *The Rise and Fall of Détente;* and Herrmann, *Perceptions and Behavior.*

137. For examples of contending viewpoints on this issue, see Freedman, *Soviet Policy Toward the Middle East;* Andrzei Korbonski and Francis Fukuyama, eds., *The Soviet Union and the Third World: The Last Three Decades* (Ithaca: Cornell University Press, 1987); Galia Golan, *The Soviet Union and National Liberation Movements in the Third World* (Boston: Unwin Hyman, 1988); and Rubinstein, *Moscow's Third World Strategy.*

138. Kissinger, *White House Years,* pp. 561–89.

Chapter Five

1. Victor Israelyan, p. 16.

2. Richard K. Betts considers the Yom Kippur War a higher-risk example of a nuclear crisis in *Nuclear Blackmail and Nuclear Deterrence,* pp. 123–29.

3. For more on Soviet-Egyptian friction during this period, see Freedman, *Soviet Policy Toward the Middle East,* pp. 49–91.

4. Quoted in Saad el Shazly, *The Crossing of the Suez* (San Francisco: American Mideast Research, 1980), pp. 175–76.

5. Broadcast version of interview in *Al-Ahram,* 29 March 1974, trans. in *FBIS Middle East and North Africa Daily Report* 63 (1 April 1974), p. D4.

6. Sadat, p. 231.

7. Ibid., p. 231.

8. Kissinger, *White House Years,* pp. 1292–97.

9. Freedman, *Soviet Policy Toward the Middle East,* pp. 100–1; Glassman, pp. 93–96.

10. Shazly, p. 273.

11. For estimates of Soviet arms deliveries before and after the rapprochement, see Glassman, pp. 99–116, and U.S. Central Intelligence Agency, "Soviet Military Posture and Policies in the Third World," Vol. 1 (Washington: National Intelligence Estimate 11–10–73, 2 August 1973), pp. 32–34.

12. Sadat interview with Arnaud de Borchgrave, *Newsweek,* 9 April 1973.

13. Heikal, *The Road to Ramadan,* p. 183.

14. Freedman, *Soviet Policy Toward the Middle East,* pp. 50, 105–15.

15. Ibid., pp. 78–82.

16. For examples of Soviet appeals for the use of the "oil weapon," see Radio Moscow broadcast in Arabic, 20 August 1973, trans. in *FBIS USSR* 162 (21 August 1973), pp. F3–4; Radio Moscow Arabic broadcast of Kurdriavtsev commentary, 29 August 1973, trans. in *FBIS USSR* 169 (30 August 1973), pp. F3–4; and Radio Moscow Arabic broadcast of Glukhov commentary, 5 September 1973, trans. in *FBIS USSR* 174 (7 September 1973), pp. F1–2.

17. Israelyan, p. 98.

18. Heikal, *The Road to Ramadan,* 208–10; el Shazly, p. 18.

19. Shazly, pp. 27–39.

20. Broadcast version of Sadat interview in *Al-Ahram,* 29 March 1974, trans. in *FBIS Middle East and North Africa Daily Report* 63 (1 April 1974), p. D3.

21. Sadat, pp. 241–42.

22. Ibid., p. 242.

23. Garthoff, pp. 290–91.

24. Ibid., pp. 334–50.

25. Quoted in Bernard Kalb and Marvin L. Kalb, *Kissinger* (Boston: Little, Brown, 1974), p. 466.

26. Israelyan, p. 215.

27. Foy D. Kohler, Leon Goure, and Mose L. Harvey, "The Soviet Union and the October 1973 Middle East War: The Implications for Détente" (Miami: Center for Advanced International Studies, 1974), pp. 124–26.

28. Rubinstein, *Red Star on the Nile,* pp. 253–54.

29. Fukuyama, pp. 14–16.

30. Snyder and Diesing, pp. 145–48.

31. Rubinstein, *Red Star on the Nile,* p. 279.

32. Stuart Britton, "Competition or Collaboration? The Soviet Union, Détente, and the October 1973 War," *Comparative Strategy* 9, no. 3 (July 1990), pp. 287–306.

33. See Israelyan, *passim,* especially pp. 211–19.

34. Helpful histories of the October War and the events surrounding it include International Institute for Strategic Studies, *Strategic Survey 1973* (London: International Institute for Strategic Studies, 1974); Chaim Herzog, *The War of Atonement: October 1973* (Boston: Little, Brown, 1975); Quandt, *Decade of Decisions;* and Edgar O'Ballance, *No Victor, No Vanquished* (San Rafael: Presidio, 1978).

35. Sadat interview in *Al Ahram,* in *FBIS Middle East and North Africa* 63 (1 April 1974), p. D3.

36. Galia Golan, *Yom Kippur and After: The Soviet Union and the Middle East Crisis* (Cambridge: Cambridge University Press, 1977), pp. 66–69.

37. Radio Moscow broadcast in Arabic, 11 September 1973, trans. in *FBIS USSR* 177 (12 September 1973), p. F1.

38. Glukhov, *Pravda,* 15 September 1973, p. 5.

39. The text of Sadat's order to senior Egyptian commanders is reprinted in Sadat, pp. 325–27.

40. Sadat, p. 246.

41. Golan, *Yom Kippur and After,* p. 69.

42. Israelyan, p. 2.

43. Jabber and Kolkowicz, pp. 442–49; Quandt, "Soviet Policy," pp. 19–20.

44. Matveev, *Izvestiia,* 11 October 1973, p. 2.

45. O'Ballance, *No Victor, No Vanquished,* p. 195; Herzog, *The War of Atonement,* pp. 132–36. Pustov admitted in *Krasnaia zvezda* that the Israeli counterattack had achieved "some success" on the Golan front (13 October 1973, p. 3.)

46. Brecher, *Decisions in Crisis,* p. 173.

47. Israelyan, p. 43.

48. Both incidents were naturally condemned resoundingly in the Soviet media; see TASS International Service broadcast, 12 October 1973, transcribed in *FBIS USSR* 199 (15 October 1973), pp. F1–2.

49. Israelyan, pp. 56–60.

50. Quandt, "Soviet Policy," pp. 19, 23n.

51. There are reports that the Israeli cabinet discussed using nuclear weapons during this phase of the crisis (see O'Ballance, *No Victor, No Vanquished,* pp. 174–75), but evidence sufficient to determine whether the Politburo had any knowledge of the possibility of an Israeli nuclear strike, or how this possibility this may have affected Soviet decision making, is not available from open sources.

52. O'Ballance, *No Victor, No Vanquished,* pp. 199–203.

53. A. Vasiliev and B. Orekhov, *Pravda,* 13 October 1973, p. 5.

54. Glukhov, *Pravda,* 15 October 1973, p. 3.

55. TASS International Service broadcast, 15 October 1973, transcr. in *FBIS USSR* 200 (16 October 1973), pp. F1–2.

56. O'Ballance, *No Victor, No Vanquished,* p. 226.

57. Israelyan, p. 115.

58. Kissinger, *Years of Upheaval,* pp. 545–59. For a detailed account of Kissinger's visit, see Israelyan, pp. 115–49.

59. Koriavin, *Izvestiia,* 17 October 1973, p. 2.

60. Israelyan, pp. 110–11. Sadat himself reports that he informed Vinogradov of his decision on 19 October (Sadat, pp. 261–64), but no Soviet accounts collaborate this.

61. Herzog, *The War of Atonement,* p. 247.

62. O'Ballance, *No Victor, No Vanquished,* p. 255.

63. Israelyan, p. 151, outlines Soviet anxieties at this point in the crisis.

64. Herzog, *The War of Atonement,* p. 248.

65. O'Ballance, *No Victor, No Vanquished,* pp. 258–66.

66. Golan, *Yom Kippur and After,* p. 120.

67. Kissinger, *Years of Upheaval,* p. 579; Sadat, pp. 266–67.

68. Israelyan, p. 160.

69. Kissinger, *Years of Upheaval,* p. 583.

70. Ibid., *Years of Upheaval,* pp. 585–88.

71. O'Ballance, *No Victor, No Vanquished,* pp. 261–62.

72. Kissinger, *Years of Upheaval,* pp. 587–89.

73. Ibid., *Years of Upheaval,* p. 597.

74. O'Ballance, *No Victor, No Vanquished,* p. 269.

75. *Pravda,* 27 October 1973, p. 5.

76. TASS International Service broadcast, 27 October 1973, transcr. in *FBIS USSR* 208 (28 October 1973), pp. B2–3.

77. Kissinger, *Years of Upheaval,* p. 585.

78. Quoted in Israelyan, p. 180

79. O. Orlov, *Pravda,* 28 August 1973, p. 5.

80. Radio Moscow broadcast in Arabic, 12 September 1973, trans. in *FBIS USSR* 178 (13 September 1973), p. F1

81. Vitaliy Korionov, *Pravda,* 16 September 1973, p. 4.

82. Koriavin, *Izvestiia,* 29 September 1973, p. 2; Yurii Potomov, *Pravda,* 28 September 1973, p. 4.

83. Yassir Arafat, *Za rubezhem* 22 (20–26 September 1973), p. 14.

84. Reported by TASS, 21 September 1973.

85. Radio Moscow broadcast in Arabic, 15 September 1973, trans. in *FBIS USSR* 181 (18 September 1973), p. F3.

86. TASS International Service broadcasts, 16 September 1973, trans. in *FBIS USSR* 180 (16 September 1973), p. F3, and 21 September 1973, trans. in *FBIS USSR* 185 (24 September 1973), pp. F6–7; Koriavin, *Izvestiia,* 18 September 1973, p. 3.

87. See for example TASS International Service broadcast, 16 August 1973, transcr. in *FBIS USSR* 160 (17 August) 1973, p. B1; Koriavin, *Izvestiia,* 14 August 1973, p. 2; and M. Ponomarev and V. Vinogradov, *Krasnaia zvezda,* 19 August 1973, p. 3.

88. A. Kurov, Radio Moscow Domestic Service broadcast, 15 September 1973, trans. in *FBIS USSR* 180 (17 September 1973), p. F2.

89. Golan, *Yom Kippur and After,* pp. 66–69.

90. Sadat, p. 246. Sadat's choice of words here—"I and Syria," rather than "Egypt and Syria" or "Assad and I"—is interesting.

91. Jabber and Kolkowicz, pp. 442.

92. George, "The Arab-Israeli War of 1973," pp. 139–54.

93. TASS International Service broadcast, 4 October 1973, and Radio Moscow broadcast in Arabic, 4 October 1973, trans. in *FBIS USSR* 194 (5 October 1973), pp. F1–2.

94. Glukhov, *Pravda,* 6 October 1967, p. 5.

95. Text published in *Pravda,* 7 October 1967, p. 1.

96. Primakov commentary, Radio Moscow broadcast in English to Africa, 7 October 1973, transcr. in *FBIS USSR* 195 (9 October 1973), pp. F11–12.

97. Koriavin, *Izvestiia,* 9 October 1973, p. 4.

98. Radio Moscow broadcast in Arabic, 9 October 1973, trans. in *FBIS USSR* 196 (10 October 1973), p. F3.

99. *Pravda,* 12 October 1973, p. 1.

100. Sadat, pp. 252–53.

101. Ibid., p. 253.

102. Israelyan, p. 57.

103. Quandt, "Soviet Policy," pp. 19–26.

104. Quandt, *Decade of Decisions,* p. 179.

105. Robert G. Weinland, "Superpower Naval Diplomacy in the October 1973 Arab-Israeli War" (Alexandria, VA: Center for Naval Analyses, 1978), pp. 47–51.

106. TASS International Service broadcast, 15 October 1973, transcr. in *FBIS USSR* 200 (16 October 1973), pp. F1–2.

107. Sadat, p. 264.

108. Quandt, "Soviet Policy," p. 26.

109. Radio Moscow Broadcast in Arabic, 15 October 1973, trans. in *FBIS USSR* 200 (16 October 1973), pp. F11–12.

110. Golan, *Yom Kippur and After,* p. 105.

111. *Pravda,* 14 October 1973, p. 4.

112. Excerpt from 15 October 1973 speech, trans. in *FBIS USSR* 200 (16 October 1973), p. E2.

113. Israelyan, pp. 92–98.

114. TASS International Service broadcast, 16 October 1973, transcr. in *FBIS USSR* 201 (17 October 1973), p. B1.

115. *Izvestiia,* 18 October 1973, p. 2.

116. Mikhail Sagatelian, *Literaturnaia gazeta,* 17 October 1973, p. 9.

117. Leonid Latyshev, TASS International Service broadcast, 17 October 1973, transcr. in *FBIS USSR* 202 (18 October 1973), p. F11.

118. Radio Moscow Domestic Service, 17 October 1973, trans. in *FBIS USSR* 202 (18 October 1973), p. F8.

119. A. Urazov, *Trud,* 18 October 1973, p. 5.

120. Quandt, "Soviet Policy," p. 25.

121. Ibid., p. 24.

122. *The New York Times,* 19 October 1973, p. 1; interview with Adm. Worth H. Bagley, *U.S. News and World Report,* 24 December 1973, pp. 27–28.

123. Sadat, p. 258.

124. Israelyan, pp. 103–14.

125. T. Kolesnichenko, Radio Moscow broadcast in English to North America, 20 October 1973, transcr. in *FBIS USSR* 204 (23 October 1973), pp. F6–7.

126. V. Osipov, *Izvestiia,* 20 October 1973, p. 4.

127. B. Rachkov, *Ekonomicheskaia gazeta* 43 (22 October 1973), p. 21.

128. Kissinger, *Years of Upheaval,* pp. 545–52.

129. United Nations Security Council, Resolution 338.

130. Quoted in Israelyan, p. 137.

131. Radio Moscow broadcast in Arabic, 22 October 1973, trans. in *FBIS USSR* 204 (23 October 1973), pp. F2–3.

132. TASS International Service broadcast, 22 October 1973, transcr. in *FBIS USSR* 204 (23 October 1973), pp. F1–2; Andrei Krushinskiy, *Komsomolskaia pravda,* 21 October 1973, p. 3.

133. Ibid., 20 October 1973, transcr. in *FBIS USSR* 207 (26 October 1973), pp. F4–5; Agaryshev, *Komsomolskaia pravda,* 21 October 1973, p. 3.

134. Leontiev, *Krasnaia zvezda,* 20 October 1973, p. 3.

135. Koriavin, *Izvestiia,* 20 October 1973, p. 1; A Vasiliev and B. Orekhov, *Pravda,* 22 October 1973, p. 3.

136. TASS International Service broadcast, 23 October 1973, transcr. in *FBIS USSR* 205 (24 October 1973), p. F1.

137. Text of this statement published in *Pravda,* 23 October 1973, p. 1.

138. Israelyan, p. 160.

139. Quandt, "Soviet Policy," p. 30.

140. Reported by U.S. Secretary of Defense James Schlesinger at a press conference on 27 October 1973, text published in *The New York Times,* 27 October 1973, p. 10.

141. Quandt, "Soviet Policy," p. 31.

142. Israelyan, pp. 191–93.

143. Ibid., p. 143–44. For Sadat's version of this incident, see Sadat, p. 265.

144. Herzog, *The War of Atonement*, p. 248; O'Ballance, *No Victor, No Vanquished*, pp. 258–66.

145. TASS International Service broadcast, 24 October 1973, transcr. in *FBIS USSR* 206 (25 October 1973), p. F1; V. Kurdriavtsev and Yu. Tsinkov, Radio Moscow broadcast in Arabic, 24 October 1973, trans. in *FBIS USSR* 206, pp. F6–7; Sagatelian, *Izvestiia*, 24 October 1973, p. 2.

146. Schlesinger, press conference of 26 October 1973; text published in *The New York Times*, 26 October 1973, p. 20.

147. Israelyan, p. 192

148. Kissinger, *Years of Upheaval*, p. 579.

149. Israelyan, pp. 168–69.

150. Text quoted in *The New York Times*, 10 April 1974, p. 9.

151. Israelyan, p. 169.

152. Interview with David Frost, 12 May 1977, quoted in Brecher, *Decisions in Crisis*, p. 225.

153. Kissinger, *Years of Upheaval*, p. 584.

154. Ibid., pp. 588–89.

155. Ibid., p. 589.

156. Interview with Abba Eban by Michael Brecher, 15 July 1974, in Brecher, *Decisions in Crisis*, pp. 227–28.

157. Moshe Dayan, *The Story of My Life* (Jerusalem and Tel Aviv: Steimatzky's Agency, 1976), pp. 447–48.

158. The account of this meeting is taken from Israelyan, pp. 179–84.

159. Israelyan, p. 182. The Politburo was apparently unaware that Nixon had not been involved in the decision to put U.S. forces on alert.

160. A small group of Soviet warships (including two landing craft) began moving toward Egypt on October 25 but they turned away before noon Washington time. See Quandt, "Soviet Policies," p. 33.

161. TASS International Service broadcasts, 27 and 28 October 1973, transcr. in *FBIS USSR* 208 (29 October 1973), p. F3.

162. Broadcast of Brezhnev's speech on Radio Moscow, 26 October 1973, trans. in *FBIS USSR* 207 (26 October 1973), pp. CC9–10. In fact, a small contingent of Soviet troops was detailed on October 25 to participate in a U.N. observer force; see Quandt, "Soviet Policies," p. 33.

163. Moscow Central Television broadcast, 27 October 1973, trans. in *FBIS USSR* 208 (29 October 1973), p. F6.

164. TASS International Service broadcast, 30 October 1973, transcr. in *FBIS USSR* 210 (31 October 1973), p. F1, and *Pravda*, 29 October 1973, p. 4.

165. Radio Moscow broadcast in Arabic, 30 October 1973, trans. in *FBIS USSR* 210 (31 October 1973), pp. F3–4.

166. See, for example, Sadat, p. 263.

167. Interview with Vinogradov in Timofeev, "War on the Day of Atonement," p. 22.

168. Israelyan, p. 206.

169. A number of former Soviet officials, including Vadim Zagladin, Aleksandr Kislov, and Anatoliy Gromyko, verify that contingency plans for sending Soviet forces to Egypt were drawn up during the crisis; see Richard Ned Lebow and Janice Gross Stein, *We All Lost the Cold War* (Princeton: Princeton University Press, 1994), p. 237.

170. Dayan, pp. 447–48.

171. Israelyan, p. 170.

172. Schlesinger press conference, 26 October 1973; text in *The New York Times*, 26 October 1973, p. 20.

173. For more on this issue, see Golan, "Soviet Decisionmaking," pp. 213–16.

174. Harold H. Saunders, "Regulating Soviet-U.S. Competition in the Arab-Israeli Arena, 1967–86," in Alexander L. George, Philip J. Farley, and Alexander Dallin, eds., *U.S.-Soviet Security Cooperation: Achievements, Failures, Lessons* (New York: Oxford University Press, 1988), p. 562.

175. Sadat, pp. 252–53.

176. Interview with Makhmut Gareev in Timofeev, "War on the Day of Atonement," p. 22.

177. For excerpts from Kosygin's speech, see *FBIS USSR* 200 (16 October 1973), pp. E2–3.

178. Golan, *Yom Kippur and After*, p. 66.

179. Sadat, p. 247.

180. Dowty, pp. 564–70.

181. See Israelyan, pp. 6–12.

182. Golan reaches a similar conclusion in "Soviet Decisionmaking," pp. 213–16.

183. Kohler et al., pp. 124–26. Britton, "Competition or Collaboration," p. 303, argues that the USSR continued to be a competitor with the United States despite détente, but moderated its actions and took an indirect approach to achieving unilateral advantage, and that the United States followed a similar strategy.

184. Golan, *Yom Kippur and After*, p. 13.

185. Rubinstein, *Red Star on the Nile*, p. 279; Breslauer, "Soviet Policy," p. 96.

186. The opinions of U.S. decision makers on this issue are documented in Marc Trachtenberg, ed., "White House Tapes and Minutes of the Cuban Missile Crisis," *International Security* 10, no. 1 (Summer 1985), pp. 164–203. For further discussion from American and Soviet viewpoints, see Blight et al., *On the Brink*.

187. Kissinger, *Years of Upheaval*, pp. 587–91.

188. Scott D. Sagan, "Nuclear Alerts and Crisis Management," *International Security* 9, no. 4 (Spring 1985), pp. 99–139.

189. George et al., "U.S.-Soviet Security Cooperation," p. 584.

190. Sadat, p. 263.

191. Shazly, pp. 273–75.

192. Heikal, *The Sphinx and the Commissar*, p. 259.

193. For a thorough account of the Camp David process, see William B. Quandt, *Camp David: Peacemaking and Politics* (Washington: Brookings, 1986), and *Peace Process*.

Chapter Six

1. See especially Timofeev, p. 20.
2. Kissinger, *White House Years,* pp. 565–66.
3. Snyder, "'Prisoner's Dilemma' and 'Chicken' Models," p. 102.
4. Israelyan, p. 170.
5. Heikal, *The Road to Ramadan,* pp. 80–83; Sadat, pp. 197–98; Timofeev, p. 20; Vladimir Makarov, *Argumenty i fakty* 34 (25–31 August 1990), p. 5; and Israelyan, *passim.*
6. Snyder and Diesing, pp. 118–22.
7. George, "The Impact of Crisis-Induced Stress," *passim.*
8. Janis and Mann, pp. 81–91.
9. Schelling, *Arms and Influence,* pp. 92–125; Snyder and Diesing, pp. 489–90.
10. Brecher, *Decisions in Crisis,* p. 36; Safran, p. 277.
11. Charles W. Yost, "The Arab-Israeli War: How It Began," *Foreign Affairs* 46, no. 5 (Winter 1968), p. 308.
12. *MER 1967,* p. 230; Bull, p. 120.
13. Johnson, 1971, pp. 300–2. This action, the Tonkin Gulf incident and the Pueblo incident seem to reveal that the Johnson administration was curiously plagued with autonomous risk involving naval forces.
14. Israelyan, pp. 180–81.
15. Schlesinger press conference, October 26, 1973, in *Department of State Bulletin,* (19 November 1973), p. 620ff.
16. Nixon, 1978, p. 479; Kissinger, *White House Years,* pp. 561–62.
17. Adomeit, "Soviet Crisis Prevention and Management," p. 18.
18. Schelling, "Arms and Influence," p. 105n.
19. Adomeit, *Soviet Risk-Taking,* pp. 317–19.
20. Schlesinger, *Department of State Bulletin,* 19 November 1973, p. 622; Kissinger, *Years of Upheaval,* pp. 594–97; Israelyan, pp. 170, 192.
21. Eban, pp. 528–30.
22. Sadat, p. 172; *MER 1967,* pp. 185–94.
23. Snyder, "Rationality at the Brink," pp. 8–11.
24. Parker, *The Politics of Miscalculation in the Middle East,* gives a number of examples of how these contradictions led many actors in the Middle East to make faulty decisions.
25. Many of these are excerpted in *MER 1967,* pp. 179–80, 186–92.
26. Heikal, *Sunday Telegraph,* 21 October 1973.
27. George, "U.S. Efforts to Cooperate," pp. 583–84.
28. For differing perspectives on the regional and global motivations of imperial powers, see Michael Doyle, *Empires,* and Snyder, *Myths of Empire.*
29. For examples of the "no war, no peace" thesis, see Rubinstein, *Red Star on the Nile,* and Freedman, "Détente and U.S.-Soviet Relations." For the opposing viewpoint, see Breslauer, "Soviet Policy in the Middle East."
30. For detailed analysis of subsequent Soviet and recent Russian policies in the Middle East, see Freedman, *Soviet Policy Toward the Middle East Under Gor-*

bachev, The Washington Papers, no. 150, (New York: Praeger, 1991); Alexei Vasiliev, *Russian Policy in the Middle East: From Messianism to Pragmatism* (Reading, UK: Ithaca Press, 1993), Rosemary Hollis, ed., *The Soviets, Their Successors, and the Middle East: Turning Point* (New York: St. Martin's Press, 1993); David H. Goldberg and Paul Marantz, eds., *The Decline of the Soviet Union and the Transformation of the Middle East* (Boulder: Westview, 1994); Fred Wehling, "Three Scenarios for Russia's Middle East Policy," *Communist and Post-Communist Studies* 26, no. 2 (June 1993), pp. 182–204; and Wehling, "Prospects for US-Russian Cooperation in the Middle East," in Sharyl Cross and Marina A. Oborotova, eds., *The New Chapter in United States-Russian Relations: Opportunities and Challenges* (Westport: Praeger, 1994), pp. 169–92.

Chapter Seven

1. For discussions of the relevance of deterrence theory to international conflicts after the Cold War, see George H. Quester, "The Future of Nuclear Deterrence," *Survival* 34, no. 1 (Spring 1992), pp. 75–88, and "No–1st-Use and Nonproliferation: Redefining Extended Deterrence," *Washington Quarterly* 17, no. 2 (Spring 1994), pp. 103–14; G. H. Canavan, "Traditional Notions of Deterrence: Stability in a Multipolar, Proliferated Environment," *Comparative Strategy* 13, no. 1 (January-March 1994), pp. 147–54; Scott D. Sagan, "The Perils of Proliferation: Organization Theory, Deterrence Theory, and the Spread of Nuclear Weapons," *International Security* 18, no. 4 (Spring 1994), pp. 66–107; and Herring, *Danger and Opportunity: Explaining International Crisis Outcomes* (Manchester: Manchester University Press, 1995), pp. 227–54.

2. The forum in *World Politics* 41, no. 2 (January 1989), pp. 143–237, which includes contributions from Christopher H. Duncan Snidal, George and Smoke, Jervis, Lebow and Stein, and George W. Downs, offers an outstanding example of the debate between these two positions.

3. For outstanding recent examples of rational deterrence theory, see Betts, *Nuclear Blackmail;* Paul K. Huth, *Extended Deterrence and the Prevention of Nuclear War* (New Haven: Yale Unviversity Press, 1988); Robert Powell, *Nuclear Deterrence Theory: The Search for Credibility* (Cambridge: Cambridge University Press, 1990); Powell, "Crisis Bargaining, Escalation, and MAD," *American Political Science Review* 81, no. 3 (September 1987), pp. 719–35; R. Harrison Wagner, "Nuclear Deterrence, Counterforce Strategies, and the Incentive to Strike First," *American Political Science Review* 85, no. 3 (Sept. 1991), pp. 727–50; Paul Huth and Bruce Russett, "General Deterrence Between Enduring Rivals: Testing Three Competing Models," *American Political Science Review* 87, no. 1 (March 1993), pp. 61–73; Paul Huth, C. Gelpi, and D. S. Bennett, "The Escalation of Great Power Militarized Disputes: Testing Rational Deterrence Theory and Structural Realism," *American Political Science Review* 87, no. 3 (September 1993), pp. 609–23; Steven J. Cimballa, *Military Persuasion: Deterrence and Provocation in Crisis and War* (University Park: Pennsylvania State University Press, 1994); and Frank P. Harvey, "Deterrence Theory Revisited: A Progress Report," *Canadian Journal of Political Science* 28, no. 3 (September 1995), pp. 403–37.

4. Richard Ned Lebow, *Nuclear Crisis Management: A Dangerous Illusion* (Ithaca: Cornell University Press, 1987); Richard Ned Lebow and Janice Gross Stein, "Beyond Deterrence," *Journal of Social Issues* 43, no. 2 (Winter 1987), pp. 5–72; Lebow and Stein, "Rational Deterrence Theory: I Think, Therefore I Deter," *World Politics* 41, no. 2 (January 1989), pp. 220–24, "When Does Deterrence Succeed and How Do We Know?" (Toronto: Canadian Institute for International Peace and Security Occasional Paper no. 8, 1990), and "Deterrence and the Cold War," *Political Science Quarterly*, 110, no. 2 (Summer 1995), pp. 157–81.

5. Huth, *Extended Deterrence*, pp. 201–3.

6. Christopher H. Achen and Duncan Snidal, "Rational Deterrence Theory and Comparative Case Studies," *World Politics* 41, no. 2 (January 1989), pp. 160–67.

7. Lebow and Stein, *We All Lost the Cold War*, pp. 291–376.

8. Downs, pp. 225–37.

9. V. M. Sergeev, V. P. Aklimov, V. B. Lukov, and P. B. Barshin, "Interdependence in a Crisis Situation: A Cognitive Approach to Modeling the Caribbean Crisis," *Journal of Conflict Resolution* 34, no. 2 (June 1990), pp. 179–207.

10. George and Smoke, pp. 78–79.

11. Huth, p. 201; E. Herring, pp. 37–61; Lebow and Stein, "When Does Deterrence Succeed," pp. 64–75; and Ted Hopf, *Peripheral Visions: Deterrence and American Foreign Policy in the Third World, 1965–1990* (Ann Arbor: University of Michigan Press, 1994).

12. See Daniel Kahneman, Jack L. Knetsch, and Richard H. Thaler, "The Endowment Effect, Loss Aversion, and Status Quo Bias," *Journal of Economic Perspectives* 5, no. 2 (Winter 1991), pp. 193–206, and Robert Jervis, "Political Implications of Loss Aversion," *Political Psychology* 13, no. 3 (June 1992), pp. 187–204.

13. For contending perspectives on deterrence and reassurance in the Persian Gulf crisis, see Lawrence Freedman and Efraim Karsh, "How Kuwait Was Won: Strategy in the Gulf War," *International Security* 16, no. 2 (Fall 1991), pp. 5–41, and Janice Gross Stein, "Deterrence and Compellence in the Gulf, 1990–91: A Failed or Impossible Task?" *International Security* 17, no. 2 (Fall 1992), pp. 147–79.

14. Snyder and Diesing, pp. 189–90, 285–89.

15. See for example Alexander L. George, "U.S.-Soviet Efforts to Cooperate," pp. 581–600.

16. Lebow and Stein, *We All Lost the Cold War*, p. 196.

17. For more on the potential impact on deterrence of proliferation of weapons of mass destruction, see Quester, "The Future of Nuclear Deterrence"; A. Hashim, "The State, Society, and the Evolution of Warfare in the Middle East: The Rise of Strategic Deterrence," *Washington Quarterly* 18, no.4 (Fall 1995), pp. 53–72; C. T. Allan, "Extended Deterrence: In from the Cold and Out of the Nuclear Fire," *Washington Quarterly* 17, no.3 (Summer 1994), pp. 203–33, David Goldfischer and Thomas W. Graham, eds., *Nuclear Deterrence and Global Security in Transition* (Boulder: Westview, 1992); Aharon Klieman and Ariel Levite, eds., *Deterrence in the Middle East: Where Theory and Practice Converge* (Tel Aviv: Jaffee Center for Strategic Studies, 1993); Bradley S. Klein, *Strategic Studies and World Order* (Cambridge: Cambridge Studies in International Relations no. 34, 1994); John Arquilla, "Bound

to Fail: Regional Deterrence After the Cold War," *Comparative Strategy* 14, no. 2 (April-June 1995), pp. 123–36, Keith B. Payne, "Deterring the Use of Weapons of Mass Destruction: Lessons from History," *Comparative Strategy* 14, no. 4 (October–December 1995); pp. 347–60, and Gregory Pickell, "Strength in an Unsettled World: The Role of Nuclear Weapons in Nuclear Nonproliferation and Deterrence," *Comparative Strategy* 15, no. 1 (January–March 1996), pp. 81–91.

18. For an extensive discussions of reassurance, see Janice Gross Stein, "Deterrence and Reassurance," in Philip E. Tetlock et al., *Behavior, Society, and Nuclear War,* vol. 1 (New York: Oxford University Press, 1991), pp. 8–72. See also Cimbala, *Military Persuasion,* and Lebow and Stein, "Deterrence and the Cold War."

19. Kissinger, *White House Years,* p. 570.

20. See Sagan, *Nuclear Alerts,* pp. 99–139.

21. Daniel Kahneman and Amos Tversky discuss the certainty effect in their pioneering article, "Prospect Theory: An Analysis of Decision Under Risk," *Econometrica* 47, no. 3 (March 1979), pp. 263–91.

22. Most useful among the many works discussing the difficulties of collective response to aggression are Charles A. Kupchan and Clifford Kupchan, "Concerts, Collective Security, and the Future of Europe," *International Security* 16, no. 1 (Summer 1991), pp. 114–61; Ashton B. Carter, William J. Perry, and John D. Steinbrunner, *A New Concept of Cooperative Security* (Washington: Brookings, 1992); Kenneth N. Waltz, "The Emerging Structure of International Politics," *International Security* 18, no. 2 (Fall 1993), pp. 44–79; Janne E. Nolan, ed., *Global Engagement: Cooperation and Security in the 21st Century* (Washington: Brookings, 1994); John J. Mearsheimer, "The False Promise of International Institutions," *International Security* 19, no. 3 (Winter 1994, no. 95), pp. 5–49; Miller, *When Opponents Cooperate,* and Barry R. Posen and Andrew L. Ross, "Competing Visions for U.S. Grand Strategy," *International Security* 21, no. 3 (Winter 1996, no. 97), pp. 5–53.

23. Jack Snyder challenges cognitive theories to do this in "Rigor, Richness, and Relevance."

24. BBC Home Service broadcast, 1 October 1939.

25. For more on this point, see Jervis, *Perception and Misperception,* p. 142.

26. See Barry M. Blechman, Steven S. Kaplan, et al., *Force Without War: U.S. Armed Forces as a Political Instrument* (Washington: Brookings, 1978), and Alexander L. George and William E. Simons, eds., *The Limits of Coercive Diplomacy,* 2nd ed.(Boulder: Westview, 1994).

27. Snyder, "Rationality at the Brink," pp. 20–31, and *The Ideology of the Offensive, passim.*

28. The potential for conflict and crisis among Russia's southern neighbors is assessed in Shirin Akiner, *Central Asia: New Arc of Crisis?* (London: Royal United Services Institute, 1993); Rosemarie Forsythe, "The Politics of Oil in the Caucasus and Central Asia" (London: International Institute for Strategic Studies Adelphi Paper, no. 300, 1996); Rajan Menon, "In the Shadow of the Bear: Security in Post-Soviet Central Asia," *International Security* 20, no. 1 (Summer 1995), pp. 149–81; Vitaly V. Naumkin, *Central Asia and Transcaucasia: Ethnicity and Conflict* (Westport: Greenwood, 1994); William E. Odom and Robert Dujarric, *Commonwealth or*

Empire? Russia, Central Asia, and the Transcaucasus (Indianapolis: Hudson Institute, 1995); Martha Brill Olcott, *Central Asia's New States: Independence, Foreign Policy, and Regional Security* (Washington: United States Institute of Peace Press, 1996); Yaacov Ro'i, ed., *Muslim Eurasia: Conflicting Legacies* (London: Frank Cass, 1995); and Jed. C. Snyder, *After Empire: The Emerging Geopolitics of Central Asia* (Washington: National Defense University Press, 1993).

29. A definitive study of the conflict in Chechnya has yet to be written from any perspective, but useful works for understanding the conflict and its potential consequences include John Colarusso, "Chechnya: The War Without Winners," *Current History* 94, no. 594 (October 1995), pp. 329–36; Mark Feigin, "Vtoraia Kavkazskaia voina," *Noviy Mir* 12 (December 1995), pp. 159–72; Paul A. Goble, "Chechnya and its Consequences—A Preliminary Report," *Post-Soviet Affairs* 11, no. 1 (January–March 1995), pp. 23–27; Michael McFaul, "Russian Politics after Chechnya," *Foreign Policy* 99 (Summer 1995), pp. 149–65; Christopher Panico, "Conflicts in the Caucasus: Russia's War in Chechnya" (London: Research Institute for the Study of Conflict and Terrorism, 1995); M. Anthony Smith, "Background to Intervention: Russian Decision-Making in the Chechen Crisis" (Sandhurst: Conflict Studies Research Centre, June 1995); and Fred Wehling, ed., "Ethnic Conflict and Russian Intervention in the Caucasus" (San Diego: IGCC Policy Paper no. 16, August 1995).

30. Russia's strategic interests and security concerns are outlined authoritatively in the Russian Federation Foreign Ministry concept paper "Kontseptsiia vneshney politiki Rossiiskoi Federatsii" (Document 1615, no. IS, 25 January 1993). For strong analyses of Russian objectives and strategies in these regions, see D. A. Afinogenov, "Voyennye voprosy bezopasnosti Rossii," *Voyennaia Mysl'* 2 (February 1993), pp. 10–14; V. Y. Belokrenitsky, "Russia and Greater Central Asia," *Asian Survey* 34, no. 12 (December 1994), pp. 1093–08; Sherman W. Garnett, "The Integrationist Temptation," *Washington Quarterly* 18, no. 2 (Spring 1995), pp. 35–44; John Lepingwell, "The Russian Military and Security Policy in the 'Near Abroad'," *Survival* 36, no. 3 (Autumn 1994), pp. 70–92; Vitaly V. Naumkin, ed., "Sovremenniy Islam: kultura i politika" (Moscow: Institute for Oriental Studies, 1994); William E. Odom and Robert Dujarric, "Commonwealth or Empire? Russia, Central Asia, and the Transcaucasus"; Barnett R. Rubin, "The Fragmentation of Tajikistan," *Survival* 35, no. 4 (Winter 1993–94), pp. 71–91; Jessica Eve Stern, "Moscow Meltdown: Can Russia Survive?" *International Security* 18, no. 4 (Spring 1994), pp. 40–65; and Irina D. Zviagelskaia, "The Russian Policy Debate on Central Asia" (London: Royal Institute of International Affairs, 1995).

31. The sordid history of the Suez crisis is told in Erskine B. Childers, *The Road to Suez* (London: MacGibbon & Kee, 1962); Anthony Moncrieff, ed., *Suez: Ten Years After* (New York: Pantheon, 1967); Anthony Nutting, *No End of a Lesson* (New York: Potter, 1967); and William Roger Louis and Roger Owen, *Suez 1956: The Crisis and Its Consequences* (New York: Oxford University Press, 1989). For an application of prospect theory to British decision making during the crisis, see Louise Richardson, "Avoiding and Incurring Losses: Decision-Making in the Suez Crisis," in Janice Gross Stein and Louis W. Pauly, *Choosing to Cooperate: How States Avoid Loss* (Baltimore: Johns Hopkins University Press, 1993), pp. 170–201.

32. See for example Menon, 1995, pp. 156–74.

33. Good places to begin exploring the extensive literature on the "democratic peace" include Michael Doyle, "Liberalism and World Politics," *American Political Science Review* 80, no. 4 (March 1986), pp. 1151–69, Zeev Maoz and Bruce. M. Russett, "Normative and Structural Causes of Democratic Peace, 1946–86," *American Political Science Review* 87, no. 3 (September 1993), pp. 624–38; Henry S. Farber and Joanne Gowa, "Polities and Peace," *International Security* 20, no. 2 (Fall 1995), pp. 123–46; Bruce Russett, *Grasping the Democratic Peace: Principles for a Post–Cold War World* (Princeton: Princeton University Press, 1993); and Michael E. Brown, Sean M. Lynn-Jones, and Steven E. Miller, eds., *Debating the Democratic Peace* (Cambridge: MIT Press, 1996).

34. Some Russian international relations specialists have also come to this conclusion. Sergei Solodovnik, for example, argues that Russia possesses insufficient means to exercise hegemony over Central Asia in "Central Asia: A New Geopolitical Profile," *International Affairs* 10 (October 1993), pp. 56–65.

35. Outstanding analyses of the course of hegemony are presented in A. F. K. Organski, *World Politics,* 2nd ed. (New York: Knopf, 1968); George Modelski, *Long Cycles in World Politics* (Seattle: University of Washington Press, 1987); and Paul Kennedy, *The Rise and Fall of the Great Powers: Economic Change and Military Conflict from 1500 to 2000* (New York: Random House, 1987).

36. Niccolò Machiavelli, "Discourses on the First Ten Books of Titus Livius," trans. Christian E. Detmold, in *The Prince and The Discourses* (New York: Random House, 1950), p. 260.

Selected Bibliography

N.B.: All names are transliterated as they appear in the source listed.

Abelson, Robert P. "Whatever Became of Consistency Theory?" *Personality and Social Psychology Bulletin* 9, no. 1 (March 1983), pp. 37–54.

Achen, Christopher H., and Duncan Snidal. "Rational Deterrence Theory and Comparative Case Studies." *World Politics* 41, no. 2 (January 1989), pp. 143–69.

Adelman, Jonathan R. "The Soviet Use of Force: Four Cases of Soviet Crisis Decision Making." *Crossroads* 16 (Winter-Spring 1985), pp. 47–81.

Adomeit, Hannes. *Soviet Risk-Taking and Crisis Behavior: A Theoretical and Empirical Analysis*. London: Allen and Unwin, 1982.

———. "Soviet Crisis Prevention and Management: Why and When do the Soviet Leaders Take Risks?" Santa Monica: RAND / UCLA Center for the Study of Soviet International Behavior Occasional Paper OPS-008 (October 1986).

Afinogenov, D. A. "Voyennye voprosy bezopasnosti Rossii." *Voyennaia Mysl'* 2 (February 1993), pp. 10–14.

Akiner, Shirin. *Central Asia: New Arc of Crisis?* London: Royal United Services Institute, 1993.

Alexander, Arthur J. "Decision Making in Soviet Weapons Procurement." Adelphi Papers, nos. 147 & 148. London: International Institute for Strategic Studies, 1978.

Allison, Graham T. *Essence of Decision: Explaining the Cuban Missile Crisis*. Boston: Little, Brown, 1971.

Anderson, Richard D., Margaret G. Hermann, and Charles Hermann. "Explaining Self-Defeating Foreign Policy Decisions: Interpreting Soviet Arms for Egypt in 1973 Through Process or Domestic Bargaining Models." *American Political Science Review* 86, no. 3 (September 1992), pp. 759–66.

Arquilla, John. "Bound to Fail: Regional Deterrence After the Cold War." *Comparative Strategy* 14, no. 2 (April–June 1995), pp. 123–36.

Axelrod, Robert, ed. *Structure of Decision: The Cognitive Maps of Political Elites*. Princeton: Princeton University Press, 1976.

———. *The Evolution of Cooperation*. New York: Basic Books, 1984.

Banuazizi, Ali, and Myron Weiner, eds. *The New Geopolitics of Central Asia and its Borderlands*. Bloomington: Indiana University Press, 1994.

Bar-Siman-Tov, Yaacov. *The Israeli-Egyptian War of Attrition, 1969–1970: A Case Study of Limited Local War*. New York: Columbia University Press, 1980.

Baumeister, Roy F., and Diane M. Tice. "Roles of Self-Presentation and Choice in Cognitive Dissonance under Forced Compliance: Necessary or Sufficient Causes?" *Journal of Personality and Social Psychology* 46, no. 1 (January 1984), pp. 5–13.

Beliaev, Igor. "Aziatskii bumerang Vashingtona." *Mezhdunarodnaia zhizn'* 5 (May 1969), pp. 83–89.

———. "Blizhnovostochniy krizis i manevri Vashingtona." *Mezhdunarodnaia zhizn'* 3 (March 1970), pp. 28–35.

Beliaev, Igor, and Evgeniy Primakov. "Izrail'skaia agressiia i Arabskii mir." *Mezhdunarodnaia zhizn'* 3 (March 1968), pp. 56–65.

Belokrenitsky, V. Y. "Russia and Greater Central Asia." *Asian Survey* 34, no. 12 (December 1994), pp. 1093–108.

Ben-Zur, Hasida, and Shlomo J. Breznitz. "The Effect of Time Pressure on Risky Choice Behavior." *Acta Psychologica* 66, no. 4 (February 1981), pp. 89–104.

Betts, Richard K. *Nuclear Blackmail and Nuclear Balance.* Washington: Brookings, 1987.

Blight, James G., and David A. Welch. *On the Brink: Americans and Soviets Reexamine the Cuban Missile Crisis.* New York: Hill and Young, 1989.

Blight, James G., Bruce J. Allyn, and David A. Welch, *Cuba on the Brink: Castro, the Missile Crisis, and the Soviet Collapse.* New York: Pantheon, 1993.

Blum, Douglas W. "The Soviet Foreign Policy Belief System: Beliefs, Politics, and Foreign Policy Outcomes." *International Studies Quarterly* 37, no. 4 (1993), pp. 373–95.

Brecher, Michael. "Toward a Theory of International Crisis Behavior: A Preliminary Report." *International Studies Quarterly* 21, no. 1 (March 1977), pp. 39–74.

———, with Benjamin Geist. *Decisions in Crisis: Israel, 1967 and 1973.* Berkeley: University of California Press, 1980.

Brehm, Jack W., and Arthur R. Cohen. *Explorations in Cognitive Dissonance.* New York: John Wiley & Sons, 1962.

Breslauer, George W. "Soviet Policy in the Middle East 1967–1972: Unalterable Antagonism or Collaborative Competition?" in Alexander L. George et al., *Managing U.S.-Soviet Rivalry: Problems of Crisis Prevention* (Boulder: Westview, 1983), pp. 139–54.

———, ed. *Soviet Strategy in the Middle East.* Boston: Unwin Hyman, 1990.

Britton, Stuart. "Competition or Collaboration? The Soviet Union, Détente, and the October 1973 War." *Comparative Strategy,* 9, no. 3 (July 1990), 287–306.

Brown, Michael E., Sean M. Lynn-Jones, and Steven E. Miller, eds. *Debating the Democratic Peace.* Cambridge: MIT Press, 1996.

Burner, W. "Soviet New Thinking and the Middle East: Gorbachev's Arab-Israeli Options." *Comparative Strategy* 9, no. 4 (1990), pp. 385–401.

Bueno de Mesquita, Bruce. *The War Trap.* New Haven: Yale University Press, 1981.

Bueno de Mesquita, Bruce, and David Lalman. *War and Reason: Domestic and International Imperatives.* New Haven: Yale University Press, 1992.

Bull, Odd. *War and Peace in the Middle East: The Experiences and Views of a UN Observer.* London: Leo Cooper, 1978.

Canavan, G. H. "Traditional Notions of Deterrence: Stability in a Multipolar, Proliferated Environment." *Comparative Strategy* 13, no. 1 (January–March 1994), pp. 147–54.

Carlin, Peter. "The Soviet Union and the Middle East: Perestroika and the New Soviet Policy." London: Gulf Center for Strategic Studies, 1990.

Carter, Ashton B., William J. Perry, and John D. Steinbrunner. *A New Concept of Cooperative Security.* Washington: Brookings, 1992.

Childers, Erskine B. *The Road to Suez.* London: MacGibbon & Kee, 1962.

Cimballa, Steven J. *Military Persuasion: Deterrence and Provocation in Crisis and War.* University Park: Pennsylvania State University Press, 1994.

Colarusso, John. "Chechnya: The War Without Winners." *Current History* 94, no. 594 (October 1995), pp. 329–36.

Coombs, Clyde H. "The Structure of Conflict." *American Psychologist* 42, no. 4 (April 1987), pp. 355–63.

Crow, Suzanne. "Strategic Withdrawal Resumes." *RFE/RL Research Institute Report on the USSR* 3, no. 39 (27 September 1991), pp. 7–10.

———. "Restoration of Ties with Israel." *RFE/RL Research Institute Report on the USSR* 3, no. 44 (1 November 1991), pp. 1–4.

———. "Russia Asserts Its Strategic Agenda." *RFE/RL Research Institute Report on the USSR* 20, no. 50 (17 December 1993), pp. 1–5.

Dagan, Avigdor. *Moscow and Jerusalem: Twenty Years of Relations Between Israel and the Soviet Union.* New York: Abelard-Schuman, 1970.

Dannereuther, Roland. "Russia, Central Asia, and the Persian Gulf." *Survival* 35, no. 4 (Winter 1993), pp. 92–112.

———. "Creating New States in Central Asia: The Strategic Implications of the Collapse of Soviet Power in Central Asia." Adelphi Paper, no. 288. London: Brassey's / International Institute for Strategic Studies, 1994.

Dawisha, Adeed. "The Soviet Union in the Arab World: The Limits to Superpower Influence," in Adeed Dawisha and Karen Dawisha, eds., *The Soviet Union in the Middle East: Policies and Perspectives* (New York: Holmes and Meier, 1982), pp. 8–23.

Dawisha, Karen. *Soviet Foreign Policy Towards Egypt.* New York: St. Martins Press, 1979.

Dayan, Moshe. *The Story of My Life.* Jerusalem and Tel Aviv: Steimatzky's Agency, 1976.

Dimant-Kass, Ilana. "The Soviet Military and Soviet Policy in the Middle East 1970–1973." *Soviet Studies* 26, no. 4 (October 1974), pp. 502–21.

Dishon, Daniel et al., eds. *Middle East Record 1967.* Vol. 3. Jerusalem: Israel Universities Press, 1971.

———, ed. *Middle East Record,* Vol. 5, *1969–1970.* Jerusalem: Israel Universities Press, 1977.

Dmytryshyn, Basil, and Frederick Cox. *The Soviet Union and the Middle East 1917–1985.* Princeton: Kingston, 1987.

Dobrynin, Anatoliy. "The Caribbean Crisis: An Eyewitness Account." *International Affairs* (Moscow) 8 (August 1992).

Downs, George W. "The Rational Deterrence Debate." *World Politics* 41, no. 2 (January 1989), pp. 225–37.

Dowty, Alan. *Middle East Crisis: U.S. Decision-Making in 1958, 1970, and 1973.* Berkeley: University of California Press, 1984.

Doyle, Michael. *Empires.* Ithaca: Cornell University Press, 1986.

———. "Liberalism and World Politics." *American Political Science Review* 80, no. 4 (March 1986), pp. 1151–69.

Dupuy, Trevor N. *Elusive Victory: The Arab-Israeli Wars, 1947–1974.* New York: Harper & Row, 1978.

Duskell, James E., and Eduardo Salas. "Group Decision Making Under Stress." *Journal of Applied Psychology* 76, no. 3 (June 1991), pp. 473–78.

Dzirkals, Lilita, Thane Gustafson, and A. Ross Johnson. "The Media and Intra-Elite Communication in the USSR." Santa Monica: RAND Report R-2869, September 1982.

Eban, Abba. *Abba Eban: An Autobiography.* New York: Random House, 1977.

Eran, Oded. "Soviet Policy Between the 1967 and 1973 Wars," in Itamar Rabinovich and Haim Shaked, eds., *From June to October: The Middle East Between 1967 and 1973* (New Brunswick: Transaction, 1978), pp. 25–52.

Efrat, Moshe, and Jacob Bercovitch, eds. *Superpowers and Client States in the Middle East: The Imbalance of Influence.* London: Routledge, 1991.

Farber, Henry S., and Joanne Gowa. "Polities and Peace." *International Security* 20, no. 2 (Fall 1995), pp. 123–46.

Farid, Abd-al-Majid. "Abd-al-Nasir's Secret Papers." U.S. Joint Publications Research Service Translations on Near East and Africa, no. 1865. Arlington: Joint Publications Research Service, 14 November 1978.

Feigin, Mark. "Vtoraia Kavkazskaia voina." *Noviy Mir* 12 (December 1995), pp. 159–72.

Festinger, Leon. *A Theory of Cognitive Dissonance.* Stanford: Stanford University Press, 1957.

———, ed. *Conflict, Decision, and Dissonance.* Stanford, CA: Stanford University Press, 1964.

Fiske, Susan T., and Shelley E. Taylor. *Social Cognition.* 2nd ed. New York: McGraw-Hill, 1991.

Fleming, Paula. "Unstable Ground: The Rationality Critique of Deterrence Theory." Paper presented at the 87th Annual Meeting of the American Political Science Association, Washington, August 1991.

Forsythe, Rosemarie. "The Politics of Oil in the Caucasus and Central Asia." Adelphi Paper, no. 300. London: International Institute for Strategic Studies, 1996.

Foushee, H. C. "Dyads and Triads at 35,000 Feet: Factors Affecting Group Process and Aircrew Performance." *American Psychologist* 39 (1984), pp. 885–93.

Foushee, H. C., and R. L. Hemrech. "Group Interaction and Flight Crew Performance" In E. L. Warner and D. C. Nagel, eds., *Human Factors in Aviation* (San Diego: Academic Press, 1988.

Freedman, Robert O. "The Soviet Union and Sadat's Egypt," in Michael MccGwire et al., eds., *Soviet Naval Policy: Objectives and Constraints* (New York: Praeger, 1975), pp. 211–36.

———. "Détente and U.S.-Soviet Relations in the Middle East During the Nixon Years (1969–1974)," in Della W. Sheldon, ed., *Dimensions of Détente* (New York: Praeger, 1978), pp. 84–121.

———. *Soviet Policy Toward the Middle East Since 1970.* 3rd ed. New York: Praeger, 1982.

———. "Moscow and the Gulf War." *Problems of Communism* 40, no. 4 (July–August 1991), pp. 1–17.

———. *Soviet Policy Toward Israel under Gorbachev.* The Washington Papers, no. 150. New York: Praeger, 1991.

Fukuyama, Francis. "Soviet Threats to Intervene in the Middle East 1956–1973." Santa Monica: RAND Note N-1577-FF, June 1980.

Fuller, Graham E. "The Middle East in United States-Soviet Relations." *Middle East Journal* 44, no. 3 (Summer 1990), pp. 415–30.

Garnett, Sherman W. "The Integrationist Temptation." *Washington Quarterly* 18, no. 2 (Spring 1995), pp. 35–44.

Garthoff, Raymond L. *Deterrence and the Revolution in Soviet Military Doctrine.* Washington, DC: Brookings, 1990.

———. *Détente and Confrontation: American-Soviet Relations from Nixon to Reagan.* Rev. ed. Washington: Brookings, 1994.

Gelman, Harry. *The Brezhnev Politburo and the Decline of Détente.* Ithaca: Cornell University Press, 1984.

George, Alexander L. "The Operational Code: A Neglected Approach to the Study of Political Leaders and Decision-Making." *International Studies Quarterly* 13, no. 2 (June 1969), pp. 190–222.

———. "Case Studies and Theory Development: The Method of Structured, Focused Comparison," in Paul Gordon Lauren, ed., *Diplomacy: New Approaches in History, Theory, and Policy* (New York: Free Press, 1979), pp. 43–68.

———. *Presidential Decisionmaking in Foreign Policy: The Effective Use of Information and Advice.* Boulder: Westview, 1980.

———. "The Arab-Israeli War of October 1973: Origins and Impact," in George et al. (1983), pp. 139–54.

———. "Missed Opportunities for Crisis Prevention: The War of Attrition and Angola," in George et al. (1988), pp. 187–224.

———. "Crisis Management: The Interaction of Political and Military Considerations." *Survival* 26, no. 5 (September–October 1984), pp. 223–34.

———. "The Impact of Crisis-Induced Stress on Decision Making," in National Academy of Sciences, Institute of Medicine, *The Medical Implications of Nuclear War* (Washington: National Academy Press, 1986), pp. 529–52.

———. "U.S.-Soviet Efforts to Cooperate in Crisis Management and Crisis Avoidance," in George et al. (1988), pp. 581–600.

George, Alexander L., and Gordon Alexander Craig. *Force and Statecraft: Diplomatic Problems of Our Time.* 2nd ed. New York : Oxford University Press, 1990.

George, Alexander L., Philip J. Farley, and Alexander Dallin, eds., *U.S.-Soviet Security Cooperation: Achievements, Failures, Lessons.* New York: Oxford University Press, 1988.

George, Alexander L., and Richard Smoke. *Deterrence in American Foreign Policy: Theory and Practice.* New York: Columbia, 1974.

———. "Deterrence and Foreign Policy." *World Politics* 41, no. 2 (January 1989), pp. 170–82.

Glass, Arnold Lewis, and Keith James Holyoak. *Cognition.* 2nd ed. New York: Random House, 1986.

Glassman, Jon D. *Arms for the Arabs: The Soviet Union and War in the Middle East.* Baltimore: Johns Hopkins University Press, 1975.

Goble, Paul A. "Chechnya and its Consequences—A Preliminary Report." *Post-Soviet Affairs* 11, no. 1 (January–March 1995), pp. 23–27.

Golan, Galia. "The Soviet Union and the Arab-Israeli War of October 1973." Jerusalem Papers on Peace Problems, no. 7. Jerusalem: Hebrew University of Jerusalem, 1974.

———. *Yom Kippur and After: The Soviet Union and the Middle East Crisis.* Cambridge: Cambridge University Press, 1977.

———. "The Arab-Israeli Conflict in Soviet-U.S. Relations." In, *The Limits to Power: Soviet Policy in the Middle East,* edited by Yaacov Ro'i, 7–31. London: Croom Helm, 1979.

———. "Soviet Decisionmaking in the Yom Kippur War, 1973," in Valenta and Potter, eds. *Soviet Decisionmaking for National Security* (London: Allen & Unwin, 1984), pp. 185–217.

———. "The Soviet Union in the Middle East after Thirty Years," in Andrzej Korbonski and Francis Fukuyama, eds., *The Soviet Union and the Third World: The Last Three Decades* (Ithaca: Cornell University Press, 1987), pp. 178–207.

———. *The Soviet Union and National Liberation Movements in the Third World.* Boston: Unwin Hyman, 1988.

———. *Soviet Policies in the Middle East from World War II to Gorbachev.* Cambridge: Cambridge University Press, 1990.

———. "Superpower Cooperation in the Middle East," in Roger E. Kanet and Edward A. Kolodziej, eds., *The Cold War as Cooperation* (Baltimore: Johns Hopkins University Press, 1991), pp. 121–46.

Goldberg, David H., and Paul Marantz, eds. *The Decline of the Soviet Union and the Transformation of the Middle East.* Boulder: Westview, 1994.

Goldgeier, James Marc. *Leadership Style and Soviet Foreign Policy: Stalin, Khrushchev, Brezhnev, Gorbachev.* Baltimore: Johns Hopkins University Press, 1994.

Goodman, M. A., and Eckdahl, C. M. "Trends in Soviet Policy in the Middle East and the Gulf." *International Journal* 45, no. 3 (Summer 1990), pp. 603–30.

Hart, Douglas M. "Soviet Approaches to Crisis Management: The Military Dimension." *Survival* 26, no. 5 (September/October 1984), pp. 214–23.

Harvey, Frank P. "Deterrence Theory Revisited: A Progress Report." *Canadian Journal of Political Science* 28, no. 3 (September 1995), pp. 403–37.

Heikal, Mohamed H. *The Cairo Documents: The Inside Story of Nasser and His Friendship with World Leaders, Rebels, and Statesmen.* Garden City: Doubleday, 1973.

———. *The Road to Ramadan.* New York: Ballantine, 1975.

———. *The Sphinx and the Commissar: The Rise and Fall of Soviet Influence in the Arab World.* London: Collins, 1978.

Heller, Mark. *The Dynamics of Soviet Policy in the Middle East.* Boulder: Westview, 1992.

Henze, Paul. "Russia and the Caucasus" Santa Monica: RAND, 1996.

Herek, Gregory M., Irving L. Janis, and Paul Huth. "Decision Making During International Crises: Is Quality of Process Related to Outcome?" *Journal of Conflict Resolution* 31, no. 2 (June 1987), pp. 203–26.

Herring, Eric. *Danger and Opportunity: Explaining International Crisis Outcomes.* Manchester: Manchester University Press, 1995.

Herring, George C. *America's Longest War: The United States and Vietnam, 1950–1975.* New York: Wiley & Sons, 1979.

Herrmann, Richard K. *Perceptions and Behavior in Soviet Foreign Policy.* Pittsburgh: University of Pittsburgh Press, 1985.

Herzog, Chaim. *The War of Atonement: October, 1973.* Boston: Little, Brown, 1975.

———. *The Arab-Israeli Wars: War and Peace in the Middle East.* New York: Random House, 1982.

Hollis, Rosemary, ed. *The Soviets, Their Successors, and the Middle East: Turning Point.* New York: St. Martin's Press, 1993.

Holsti, Ole R. "The 1914 Case." *American Political Science Review* 59, no. 2 (June 1965), pp. 365–78.

———. *Crisis, Escalation, War.* Montreal: McGill-Queen's University Press, 1972.

———. "The 'Operational Code' as an Approach to the Analysis of Belief Systems." *Final Report to the National Science Foundation,* Grant No. SOC 75–15368. Duke University, 1977.

Hopf, Ted. *Peripheral Visions: Deterrence and American Foreign Policy in the Third World, 1965–1990.* Ann Arbor: University of Michigan Press, 1994.

Horelick, Arnold L. "Soviet Policy in the Middle East, Part I: Policy from 1955 to 1969," in Paul Y. Hammond and Sidney S. Alexander, *Political Dynamics in the Middle East* (New York: American Elsevier, 1972), pp. 553–604.

Horelick, Arnold L., A. Ross Johnson, and John D. Steinbruner, "The Study of Soviet Foreign Policy: A Review of Decision-Theory Related Approaches." Santa Monica: RAND Report R-1334, December 1973.

Horelick, Arnold L., and Myron Rush. *Strategic Power and Soviet Foreign Policy.* Chicago: University of Chicago Press, 1966.

Hosmer, Stephen T., and Thomas W. Wolfe. *Soviet Policy and Practice Toward Third World Conflicts.* Lexington, MA: Lexington Books, 1983.

Huth, Paul K. *Extended Deterrence and the Prevention of War.* New Haven: Yale University Press, 1988.

Huth, Paul K., and Bruce Russett, "Testing Deterrence Theory: Rigor Makes a Difference." *World Politics* 42, no. 4 (July 1990), pp. 466–501.

International Institute for Strategic Studies. *Strategic Survey 1970.* London: International Institute for Strategic Studies, 1971.

———. *Strategic Survey 1973.* London: International Institute for Strategic Studies, 1974.

Israelyan, Victor. *Inside the Kremlin During the Yom Kippur War.* University Park: Pennsylvania State University Press, 1995.

Jabber, Paul and Roman Kolkowicz. "The Arab-Israeli Wars of 1967 and 1973," in Stephen S. Kaplan et al., *The Diplomacy of Power* (Washington: Brookings, 1981), pp. 412–67.

Janis, Irving L. *Groupthink: Psychological Studies of Policy Decisions and Fiascoes.* 2nd ed. Boston: Houghton Mifflin, 1983.

Janis, Irving L., and Leon Mann. *Decision Making: A Psychological Analysis of Conflict, Choice, and Commitment.* New York: Free Press, 1977.

Jecker, Jon D. "Conflict and Dissonance: A Time of Decision," in Robert P. Abelson et al., eds., *Theories of Cognitive Consistency: A Sourcebook* (Chicago: Rand McNally, 1968), pp. 571–76.

Jervis, Robert. "Hypotheses on Misperception." *World Politics* 20, no. 3 (April 1968), pp. 454–79.

———. *Perception and Misperception in International Politics.* Princeton: Princeton University Press, 1976.

———. "Cooperation Under the Security Dilemma." *World Politics* 30, no. 2 (July 1978), pp. 168–214.

———. "Deterrence Theory Revisited." *World Politics* 31, no. 2 (July 1979), pp. 289–324.

———. "Why Nuclear Superiority Doesn't Matter." *Political Science Quarterly* 94, no. 4 (Winter 1979–80), pp. 617–33.

———. "Rational Deterrence: Theory and Evidence." *World Politics* 41, no. 2 (January 1989), pp. 183–207.

———. "Political Implications of Loss Aversion." *Political Psychology* 13, no. 3 (June 1992), pp. 187–204.

Jervis, Robert, Richard Ned Lebow, and Janice Gross Stein. *Psychology and Deterrence.* Baltimore: Johns Hopkins University Press, 1985.

Johnson, Lyndon Baines. *The Vantage Point: Perspectives of the Presidency, 1963–1969.* New York: Holt, Rinehart & Winston, 1971.

Jones, Ellen. "The Defense Council in Soviet Leadership Decisionmaking." Occasional Paper, no. 188. Washington: Kennan Institute for Advanced Russian Studies, 1984.

Jowitt, Kenneth. "Images of Détente and the Soviet Political Order." Policy Papers in International Affairs, no. 1. Berkeley: University of California Institute of International Studies, 1977.

Kahneman, Daniel, Jack L. Knetsch, and Richard H. Thaler. "The Endowment Effect, Loss Aversion, and Status Quo Bias." *Journal of Economic Perspectives* 5, no. 2 (Winter 1991), pp. 193–206.

Kahneman, Daniel, and Amos Tversky. "Prospect Theory: An Analysis of Decision Under Risk." *Econometrica* 47, no. 3 (March 1979), pp. 263–91.

Kalb, Bernard, and Marvin L. Kalb *Kissinger.* Boston: Little, Brown, 1974.

Kaplan, Stephen S. et al. *The Diplomacy of Power: Soviet Armed Forces as a Political Instrument.* Washington: Brookings, 1981.

Karsh, Efraim. *Soviet Policy Towards Syria Since 1970.* New York: St. Martin's Press, 1991.

Kass, Ilana. *Soviet Involvement in the Middle East: Policy Formulation, 1966–1973.* Boulder: Westview, 1978.

Katz, Mark N. *The Third World in Soviet Military Thought.* London: Croom Helm, 1982.

Kennedy, Paul. *The Rise and Fall of the Great Powers: Economic Change and Military Conflict from 1500 to 2000.* New York: Random House, 1987.

Kennedy, Robert F. *Thirteen Days: A Memoir of the Cuban Missile Crisis.* New York: Norton, 1969.

Kimche, David, and Dan Bawly. *The Sandstorm: The Arab-Israeli War of June 1967: Prelude and Aftermath.* New York: Stein and Day, 1968.

Kinder, Donald R. and Janet Weiss. "In Lieu of Rationality: Psychological Perspectives on Foreign Policy Decision Making." *Journal of Conflict Resolution* 22, no. 4 (December 1978), pp. 707–35.

Kissinger, Henry A. *White House Years.* Boston: Little, Brown, 1979.

———. *Years of Upheaval.* Boston: Little, Brown, 1982.

Klein, Bradley S. *Strategic Studies and World Order: The Global Politics of Deterrence.* Cambridge: Cambridge Studies in International Relations, no. 34, 1994.

Klieman, Aharon, and Ariel Levite, eds. *Deterrence in the Middle East: Where Theory and Practice Converge.* Tel Aviv: Jaffee Center for Strategic Studies, 1993.

Kohler, Foy D., Leon Goure, and Mose L. Harvey. "The Soviet Union and the October 1973 Middle East War: The Implications for Détente." Miami: Center for Advanced International Studies, 1974.

Korn, David A. *Stalemate: The War of Attrition and Great Power Diplomacy in the Middle East, 1967–1970.* Boulder: Westview, 1992.

Kostrikov, Sergei P. "Tret"yi mir: kontseptsiia i real'nost'." *MEMO* 11 (November 1990), pp. 21–32.

Kozyrev, Andrei V. "OON—demokratiia protiv totalitarizma." *MEMO* 12 (December 1990), pp. 5–15.

Kramer, Mark. "Archival Research in Moscow: Progress and Pitfalls." *Cold War International History Project Bulletin* 3 (Fall 1993), pp. 1, 18–39.

Kriesberg, Louis. *International Conflict Resolution: The U.S.-USSR and Middle East Cases.* New Haven: Yale University Press, 1992.

Kupchan, Charles A., and Clifford Kupchan. "Concerts, Collective Security, and the Future of Europe." *International Security* 16, no. 1 (Summer 1991), pp. 114–61.

Laird, Roy D. *The Politburo: Demographic Trends, Gorbachev, and the Future.* Boulder: Westview, 1986.

Laqueur, Walter. *The Soviet Union and the Middle East.* New York: Praeger, 1959.

———. *The Road to Jerusalem: The Origins of the Arab-Israeli Conflict 1967.* New York: Macmillan, 1968.

————. *The Struggle for the Middle East: The Soviet Union in the Mediterranean 1958–1968.* New York: Macmillan, 1969.

Larson, Deborah Welch. "Problems of Content Analysis in Foreign Policy Research: Notes from the Study of the Origins of Cold War Belief Systems." *International Studies Quarterly* 32, no. 2 (June 1988), pp. 241–55.

Lebow, Richard Ned. *Between Peace and War: The Nature of International Crisis.* Baltimore: Johns Hopkins University Press, 1981.

————. *Nuclear Crisis Management: A Dangerous Illusion.* Ithaca: Cornell University Press, 1987.

Lebow, Richard Ned and Janice Gross Stein. "Beyond Deterrence." *Journal of Social Issues* 43, no. 2 (Winter 1987), pp. 5–72.

————. "Rational Deterrence Theory: I Think, Therefore I Deter." *World Politics* 41, no. 2 (January 1989), pp. 208–24.

————. "When Does Deterrence Succeed and How Do We Know?" Canadian Institute for International Peace and Security Occasional Paper, no. 8. Toronto: Canadian Institute for International Peace and Security, 1990.

————. *We All Lost the Cold War.* Princeton: Princeton University Press, 1994.

Leites, Nathan. *The Operational Code of the Politburo.* New York: McGraw-Hill, 1951.

————. *A Study of Bolshevism.* Glencoe, IL: Free Press, 1953.

————. "Kremlin Moods." Santa Monica: RAND Memorandum RM-3535-ISA, January 1964.

Lepingwell, John. "The Russian Military and Security Policy in the 'Near Abroad'." *Survival* 36, no. 3 (Autumn 1994), pp. 70–92.

Levy, Jack S. "An Introduction to Prospect Theory." *Political Psychology,* 13, no. 2 (June 1992), pp. 171–86.

————. "Prospect Theory and International Relations: Theoretical Applications and Analytical Problems." *Political Psychology* 13, no. 2 (June 1992), pp. 283–310.

————. "Loss Aversion, Framing, and Bargaining: The Implications of Prospect Theory for International Conflict." *International Political Science Review* 17 (1996), pp. 177–93.

Louis, William Roger, and Roger Owen. *Suez 1956: The Crisis and its Consequences.* New York: Oxford University Press, 1989.

Makarov, D. "'Neizvestnaia voina na Vostoke," *Argumenty i Fakty* 34, (30 July 1990), p. 5.

Malashenko, Igor Y. "Interesy strany: mnimye i realnye." *Kommunist* 13, September 1989, pp. 114–23.

Mandelbaum, Michael, ed. *Central Asia and the World.* New York: Council on Foreign Relations, 1994.

Maoz, Zeev. *National Choices and International Processes.* Cambridge: Cambridge University Press, 1990.

Maoz, Zeev, and Bruce. M. Russett. "Normative and Structural Causes of Democratic Peace, 1946–86." *American Political Science Review* 87, no. 3 (September 1993), pp. 624–38.

McFaul, Michael. "Russian Politics after Chechnya." *Foreign Policy* 99 (Summer 1995), pp. 149–65.

McInerney, Audrey. "Prospect Theory and Soviet Policy Towards Syria, 1966–1967." *Political Psychology* 13, no. 2 (1992), pp. 265–82.

McLaurin, Ronald D. *The Middle East and Soviet Policy.* Lexington, MA: Lexington Books, 1975.

Mearsheimer, John J. "The False Promise of International Institutions." *International Security* 19, no. 3 (Winter 1994–95), pp. 5–49.

Menon, Rajan. "In the Shadow of the Bear: Security in Post-Soviet Central Asia." *International Security* 20, no. 1 (Summer 1995), pp. 149–81.

Meyer, Stephen. "Soviet National Security Decisionmaking: What Do We Know and What Do We Understand?" in Jiri Valenta and William C. Potter, eds., *Soviet Decisionmaking for National Security* (London: Allen and Unwin, 1984), pp. 255–98.

———. "Soviet Perspectives on the Paths to Nuclear War," in Graham Allison, Albert Carnesale, and Joseph S. Nye, eds., *Hawks, Doves, and Owls: An Agenda for Avoiding Nuclear War* (New York: Norton, 1985), pp. 167–205.

———. "Soviet Nuclear Operations," in Ashton B. Carter, John D. Steinbruner, and Charles A. Zraket, eds., *Managing Nuclear Operations* (Washington: Brookings, 1987), pp. 470–534.

Milburn, Thomas W. "The Management of Crises." In Charles F. Hermann, ed., *International Crises: Insights from Behavioral Research* (New York: Free Press, 1972), pp. 259–81.

Miller, Benjamin. *When Opponents Cooperate: Great Power Conflict and Collaboration in World Politics.* Ann Arbor: University of Michigan Press, 1995.

Mirskii, Georgii. "Ob"edinenaia Arabskaia Respublika v god tiazhelykh ispytanii," *Mezhdunarodniy Ezhegodnik 1968* (Moscow: Politicheskaia Literatura, 1968), pp. 219–24.

———. "Vnutrenniy front v OAR," *Novoe vremia* 50 (13 December 1968), pp. 8–11.

Modelski, George. *Long Cycles in World Politics.* Seattle: University of Washington Press, 1987.

Moncrieff, Anthony, ed. *Suez: Ten Years After.* New York: Pantheon, 1967.

Moore, Barrington. *Soviet Politics: The Dilemma of Power.* New York: Harper & Row, 1965.

Morgan, Patrick M. *Deterrence: A Conceptual Analysis.* Beverly Hills: Sage, 1983.

Morgan, T. Clifton. *Untying the Knot of War: A Bargaining Theory of International Crises.* Ann Arbor: University of Michigan Press, 1994.

Naumkin, Vitaly V. *Central Asia and Transcaucasia: Ethnicity and Conflict.* Westport: Greenwood, 1994.

———, ed. "Sovremenniy Islam: kultura i politika." Moscow: Institute for Oriental Studies, 1994.

Newhouse, John. *Cold Dawn: The Story of SALT.* New York: Holt, Rinehart & Winston, 1973.

Nixon, Richard Milhous. *RN: The Memoirs of Richard Nixon.* New York: Grosset & Dunlap, 1978.

Nolan, Janne E., ed. *Global Engagement: Cooperation and Security in the 21st Century.* Washington: Brookings, 1994.

Nutting, Anthony. *No End of a Lesson.* New York: Potter, 1967.

O'Ballance, Edgar. *The Third Arab-Israeli War.* London: Faber & Faber, 1972.

———. *The Electronic War in the Middle East, 1968–1970.* London: Faber & Faber, 1974.

———. *No Victor, No Vanquished: The Yom Kippur War.* San Rafael: Presidio, 1978.

Odom, William E., and Robert Dujarric. *Commonwealth or Empire? Russia, Central Asia, and the Transcaucasus.* Indianapolis: Hudson Institute, 1995.

Olcott, Martha Brill. *Central Asia's New States: Independence, Foreign Policy, and Regional Security.* Washington: United States Institute of Peace Press, 1996.

Organski, A. F. K. *World Politics.* 2nd ed. New York: Knopf, 1968.

Panico, Christopher. "Conflicts in the Caucasus: Russia's War in Chechnya." London: Research Institute for the Study of Conflict and Terrorism, 1995.

Parker, Richard B. *The Politics of Miscalculation in the Middle East.* Bloomington: Indiana University Press, 1993.

Payne, Keith B. "Deterring the Use of Weapons of Mass Destruction: Lessons from History." *Comparative Strategy* 14, no. 4 (October–December 1995), pp. 347–60.

Peterson, Walter J. "Deterrence and Compellence: a Critical Assessment of Conventional Wisdom." *International Studies Quarterly* 30, no. 3 (September 1986), 269–94.

Pickell, Gregory. "Strength in an Unsettled World: The Role of Nuclear Weapons in Nuclear Nonproliferation and Deterrence." *Comparative Strategy* 15, no. 1 (January–March 1996), pp. 81–91.

Posen, Barry R., and Andrew L. Ross, "Competing Visions for U.S. Grand Strategy." *International Security* 21, no. 3 (Winter 1996–97), pp. 5–53.

Potter, William C. "The Study of Soviet Decisionmaking for National Security: What is To Be Done?" In *Soviet Decisionmaking for National Security,* edited Valenta and Potter, 299–307. London: Allen and Unwin, 1984.

———. "The Soviet Union and Nuclear Proliferation." *Slavic Review* 44, no. 3 (Fall 1985), pp. 468–88.

Powell, Robert. "Crisis Bargaining, Escalation, and MAD." *American Political Science Review* 81, no. 3 (September 1987), pp. 719–35.

———. *Nuclear Deterrence Theory: The Search for Credibility.* Cambridge: Cambridge University Press, 1990.

Quandt, William B. "Soviet Policy in the October 1973 War." Santa Monica: RAND Report R-1864-ISA, May 1976.

———. *Decade of Decisions: American Policy Toward the Arab-Israeli Conflict, 1967–1976.* Berkeley: University of California Press, 1977.

———. *Camp David: Peacemaking and Politics.* Washington: Brookings, 1986.

———. *U.S.-Soviet Rivalry in the Middle East.* Washington: Brookings, 1996.

———. *Peace Process: American Diplomacy and the Arab-Israeli Conflict Since 1967.* Washington and Berkeley: Brookings/University of California Press, 1993.

Quester, George H. "The Future of Nuclear Deterrence." *Survival* 34, no. 1 (Spring 1992), pp. 75–88.

Ra'anan, Uri. "Soviet Decision Making in the Middle East, 1969–1973," in Michael MccGwire, Ken Booth, and John McDonnell, eds., *Soviet Naval Policy: Objectives and Constraints* (New York: Praeger, 1975), pp. 182–210.

Ramet, Sabrina P. "Soviet Policy Toward Syria, 1976–1986: Factionalism and the Limits of Influence." Washington: Kennan Institute for Advanced Russian Studies Occasional Paper, 212, 1986.

Reisch, Alfred. "Agreements Signed with Ukraine to Upgrade Bilateral Relations." *RFE/RL Research Report on the USSR* 25 (21 June 1991), pp. 14–17.

Rice, Condoleezza. "The Party, The Military, and Decision Authority in the Soviet Union." *World Politics* 40, no. 1 (October 1987), pp. 55–81.

Richardson, James L. *Crisis Diplomacy: The Great Powers Since the Mid-Nineteenth Century.* Cambridge: Cambridge University Press, 1994.

Richardson, Louise. "Avoiding and Incurring Losses: Decision-Making in the Suez Crisis." In Janice Gross Stein and Louis W. Pauly, *Choosing to Cooperate: How States Avoid Loss* (Baltimore: Johns Hopkins University Press, 1993,) pp. 170–201.

Richter, James G. *Khrushchev's Double Bind: International Pressures and Domestic Coalition Politics.* Baltimore: Johns Hopkins University Press, 1994.

Ro'i, Yaacov, ed. *From Encroachment to Involvement: A Documentary Study of Soviet Policy in the Middle East, 1945–1973.* New York: John Wiley & Sons, 1974.

———, ed. *Muslim Eurasia: Conflicting Legacies.* London: Frank Cass, 1995.

Rosenfeld, Paul, John G. Kennedy, and Robert A. Giacalone. "Decision Making: A Demonstration of the Postdecision Dissonance Effect." *Journal of Social Psychology* 126, no. 5 (October 1986), pp. 663–65.

Rubin, Barnett R. "The Fragmentation of Tajikistan." *Survival* 35, no. 4 (Winter 1993–94), pp. 71–91.

Rubinstein, Alvin Z. "The Soviet-Egyptian Influence Relationship Since the June 1967 War," in MccGwire et al. (1975), pp. 153–81.

———. *Red Star on the Nile: The Soviet-Egyptian Influence Relationship since the June War.* Princeton: Princeton University Press, 1977.

———. *Moscow's Third World Strategy.* Princeton: Princeton University Press, 1990.

Russett, Bruce. *Grasping the Democratic Peace: Principles for a Post–Cold War World.* Princeton: Princeton University Press, 1993.

Russian Federation Ministry of Foreign Affairs. "Kontseptsiia vneshney politiki Rossiiskoi Federatsii." Document 1615/IS (25 January 1993).

el-Sadat, Anwar. *In Search of Identity: An Autobiography.* New York: Harper & Row, 1977.

Safran, Nadav. *From War to War: The Arab-Israeli Confrontation, 1948–1967.* New York: Pegasus, 1969.

Sagan, Scott D. "Nuclear Alerts and Crisis Management." *International Security* 9, no. 4 (Spring 1985), pp. 99–139.

———. "The Perils of Proliferation: Organization Theory, Deterrence Theory, and the Spread of Nuclear Weapons." *International Security* 18, no. 4 (Spring 1994), pp. 66–107.

Saunders, Harold H. "Regulating Soviet-U.S. Competition in the Arab-Israeli Arena, 1967–86." In Alexander L. George, Philip J. Farley, and Alexander Dallin, eds., *U.S.-Soviet Security Cooperation: Achievements, Failures, Lessons* (New York: Oxford University Press, 1988), pp. 540–80.

Schelling, Thomas C. *The Strategy of Conflict.* Cambridge, MA: Harvard University Press, 1960.

———. *Arms and Influence.* New Haven: Yale University Press, 1966.

Sergeev, V. M., V. P. Aklimov, V. B. Lukov, and P. B. Barshin. "Interdependence in a Crisis Situation: A Cognitive Approach to Modeling the Caribbean Crisis." *Journal of Conflict Resolution* 34, no. 2 (June 1990), pp. 179–207.

el Shazly, Saad. *The Crossing of the Suez.* San Francisco: American Mideast Research, 1980.

Shenfeld, Stephen. "Crisis Management: The Soviet Approach." In Carl G. Jacobsen, ed., *Strategic Power USA / USSR* (London: Macmillan, 1990), pp. 198–205.

Skilling, H. Gordon. "Groups in Soviet Politics: Some Hypotheses." In *Interest Groups in Soviet Politics,* edited by H. Gordon Skilling and Franklyn Griffifths, pp. 19–46. (Princeton: Princeton University Press, 1971).

Slusser, Robert M. *The Berlin Crisis of 1961.* Baltimore: Johns Hopkins University Press, 1973.

Smith, M. Anthony. "Background to Intervention: Russian Decision-Making in the Chechen Crisis." Sandhurst: Conflict Studies Research Centre, June 1995.

Smolansky, Oles M., with Bettie M. Smolansky. *The USSR and Iraq: The Soviet Quest for Influence.* Durham: Duke University Press, 1991.

Snyder, Glenn H. "'Prisoner's Dilemma' and 'chicken' Models in International Politics." *International Studies Quarterly* 15, no. 1 (March 1971), pp. 66–103.

Snyder, Glenn H., and Paul Diesing. *Conflict Among Nations: Bargaining, Decision Making, and System Structure in International Crises.* Princeton: Princeton University Press, 1977.

Snyder, Jack. "Rationality at the Brink: The Role of Cognitive Processes in Failures of Deterrence." Santa Monica: RAND Paper P-5740 (October 1976).

———. *The Ideology of the Offensive: Military Decision Making and the Disasters of 1914.* Ithaca: Cornell University Press, 1984.

———. "Rigor, Richness and Relevance in the Study of Soviet Foreign Policy." *International Security* 9, no. 3 (Winter 1985), pp. 89–109.

———. *Myths of Empire: Domestic Politics and International Ambition.* Ithaca: Cornell University Press, 1991.

Snyder, Jed C., ed. *After Empire: The Emerging Geopolitics of Central Asia.* Washington: National Defense University Press, 1995.

Solodovnik, Sergei. "Central Asia: A New Geopolitical Profile." *International Affairs* 10 (October 1993), pp. 56–65.

Spechler, Dina Rome. *Domestic Influences on Soviet Foreign Policy.* Washington: University Press of America, 1978.

———. "The USSR and Third-World Conflicts: Domestic Debate and Soviet Policy in the Middle East, 1967–1973." *World Politics* 38, no. 3 (April 1986), pp. 435–61.

Stein, Arthur A. "When Misperceptions Matter." *World Politics* 34, no. 4 (July 1982), pp. 525–26.

Stein, Janice, and Louis W. Pauly, eds. *Choosing to Cooperate: How States Avoid Loss.* Baltimore: Johns Hopkins University Press, 1993.

Steinbruner, John D. *The Cybernetic Theory of Decision: New Dimensions of Political Analysis.* Princeton: Princeton University Press, 1974.

———. "Beyond Rational Deterrence: The Struggle for New Conceptions." *World Politics* 28, no. 2 (January 1976), pp. 223–45.

Stern, Jessica Eve. "Moscow Meltdown: Can Russia Survive?" *International Security* 18, no. 4 (Spring 1994), pp. 40–65.

Stewart, Philip D., Margaret G. Hermann, and Charles F. Hermann, "Modeling the 1973 Decision to Support Egypt." *American Political Science Review* 83, no. 1 (March 1989), pp. 35–60.

Stevenson, Richard W. *The Rise and Fall of Détente: Relaxations of Tension in U.S.-Soviet Relations.* New York: Macmillan, 1985.

Svenson, Ola, and Anne Edland. "Changes of Preferences Under Time Pressure: Choices and Judgments." In Henry Montgomery and Ola Svenson, eds., *Process and Structure in Human Decision Making* (Chicester, UK: John Wiley & Sons, 1989), pp. 225–38.

Svenson, Ola, Anne Edland, and Paul Slovic. "Choices and Judgments of Incompletely Described Decision Alternatives under Time Pressure." *Acta Psychologica* 75, no. 2 (November 1990), pp. 153–69.

Trachtenberg, Marc, ed. "White House Tapes and Minutes of the Cuban Missile Crisis." *International Security* 10, no. 1 (Summer 1985), pp. 164–203.

Troitskii, Yevgeniy. "'Russkaia ideia' i sud'by otechestvo." *Armiia* 23 (December 1991), pp. 3–10.

Troyanovski, Oleg. "The Cuban Crisis: A Viewpoint from the Kremlin." *International Affairs* (Moscow) 4–5, April–May 1992.

Tsebelis, George. *Nested Games: Rational Choice in Comparative Politics.* Berkeley: University of California Press, 1990.

Tversky, Amos, and Daniel Kahneman. "The Framing of Decisions and the Psychology of Choice." *Science* 2, no. 11 (1981), pp. 453–58.

———. "Rational Choice and the Framing of Decisions." *Journal of Business* 59, no. 4 (1986), pp. 251–78.

———. "Advances in Prospect Theory: Cumulative Representation of Uncertainty." *Journal of Risk and Uncertainty* 5 (1992), pp. 297–323.

Ulam, Adam B. *Dangerous Relations: The Soviet Union in World Politics, 1970–1982.* New York: Oxford University Press, 1983.

U.S. Central Intelligence Agency. "Probable Soviet Objectives in Rearming Arab States." Special National Intelligence Estimate 11–13–67, 20 July 1967.

———."Soviet Interests and Activities in Arab States." Special National Intelligence Estimate 11–9–68, 18 January 1968.

———. "Soviet Policies in the Middle East and Mediterranean Area." National Intelligence Estimate 11–6–70, 5 March 1970.

———. "The USSR and the Egyptian-Israeli Confrontation." Special National Intelligence Estimate 30–70, 14 May 1970.

———. "Soviet Military Posture and Policies in the Third World." 2 vols. National Intelligence Estimate 11–10–73, 2 August 1973.

Valenta, Jiri. *Soviet Intervention in Czechoslovakia, 1968: Anatomy of a Decision.* Baltimore: Johns Hopkins University Press, 1979.

———. "Soviet Decisionmaking on Afghanistan, 1979." In Valenta & Potter (1984), pp. 218–36.

Valenta, Jiri and William C. Potter, eds., *Soviet Decisionmaking for National Security.* London: Allen and Unwin, 1984.

Van Evera, Stephen. "The Cult of the Offensive and the Origins of the First World War." *International Security* 9, no. 1 (Summer 1984), pp. 58–107.

Vassiliev, Alexei. *Russian Policy in the Middle East: From Messianism to Pragmatism.* Reading, UK: Ithaca Press, 1993.

Wagner, R. Harrison. "Nuclear Deterrence, Counterforce Strategies, and the Incentive to Strike First." *American Political Science Review* 85, no. 3 (September 1991), pp. 727–50.

Walker, Steven G. "The Motivational Foundations of Political Belief Systems: A Re-Analysis of the Operational Code Construct." *International Studies Quarterly* 27, no. 2 (June 1983), pp. 179–221.

Wallander, Celeste A. "International Institutions and Modern Security Strategies." *Problems of Communism* 41, no. 1–2 (1992), pp. 44–63.

Waltz, Kenneth N. "The Emerging Structure of International Politics." *International Security* 18, no. 2 (Fall 1993), pp. 44–79.

Wehling, Fred L. "The Dilemma of Superpower: Soviet Decision Making in the Six-Day War, 1967." In Steven L. Spiegel, ed., *Conflict Management in the Middle East* (Boulder: Westview, 1992), pp. 175–216.

———. "Three Scenarios for Russia's Middle East Policy." *Communist and Post-Communist Studies* 26, no. 2 (June 1993), pp. 182–204.

———. "Prospects for US-Russian Cooperation in the Middle East." In Sharyl Cross and Marina A. Oborotova, eds., *The New Chapter in United States-Russian Relations: Opportunities and Challenges* (Westport: Praeger, 1994), pp. 169–92.

———,ed. "Ethnic Conflict and Russian Intervention in the Caucasus." San Diego: Institute on Global Conflict and Cooperation Policy Paper, no. 16, August 1995.

———. "Pitfalls on the Silk Road: Moscow's Dilemmas in Central Asia and the Caucasus" *Orient* (Moscow) 6 (November–December 1996).

Weinland, Robert G. "Superpower Naval Diplomacy in the October 1973 Arab-Israeli War." Alexandria, VA: Center for Naval Analyses, 1978.

Whetten, Lawrence L. *The Canal War: Four-Power Conflict in the Middle East.* Cambridge: MIT Press, 1974.

Wicklund, Robert A., and Jack W. Brehm. *Perspectives on Cognitive Dissonance.* New York: John Wiley & Sons, 1976.

Wohlforth William C. *The Elusive Balance: Power and Perceptions During the Cold War.* Ithaca: Cornell University Press, 1993.

Wright, Peter. "The Harassed Decision Maker: Time Pressure, Distractions, and the Use of Evidence." *Journal of Applied Psychology* 59, no. 5 (October 1974), pp. 555–61.

Yaha, Ali M. *Egypt and the Soviet Union, 1972–1955.* Washington: Harbinger, 1989.

Yost, Charles W. "The Arab-Israeli War: How It Began." *Foreign Affairs* 46, no. 3 (Winter 1968), pp. 304–20.

Zakay, Dan, and Stuart Wooler. "Time Pressure, Training, and Decision Effectiveness." *Ergonomics* 27, no. 3 (March 1984), pp. 273–84.

Zlenko, Anatolli. "The Ukraine, the UN, and World Policy." *International Affairs* (Moscow) 12 (December 1990), pp. 3–14.

Zviagelskaia, Irina D. "The Russian Policy Debate on Central Asia." London: Royal Institute of International Affairs, 1995.

Index